COMING-OF-AGE CINEMA IN NEW ZEALAND

Traditions in World Cinema

General Editors
Linda Badley (Middle Tennessee State University)
R. Barton Palmer (Clemson University)

Founding Editor
Steven Jay Schneider (New York University)

Titles in the series include:

Traditions in World Cinema
Linda Badley, R. Barton Palmer, and Steven Jay Schneider (eds)

Japanese Horror Cinema
Jay McRoy (ed.)

New Punk Cinema
Nicholas Rombes (ed.)

African Filmmaking
Roy Armes

Palestinian Cinema
Nurith Gertz and George Khleifi

Czech and Slovak Cinema
Peter Hames

The New Neapolitan Cinema
Alex Marlow-Mann

American Smart Cinema
Claire Perkins

The International Film Musical
Corey Creekmur and Linda Mokdad (eds)

Italian Neorealist Cinema
Torunn Haaland

Magic Realist Cinema in East Central Europe
Aga Skrodzka

Italian Post-Neorealist Cinema
Luca Barattoni

Spanish Horror Film
Antonio Lázaro-Reboll

Post-beur Cinema
Will Higbee

New Taiwanese Cinema in Focus
Flannery Wilson

International Noir
Homer B. Pettey and R. Barton Palmer (eds)

Films on Ice
Scott MacKenzie and Anna Westerståhl Stenport (eds)

Nordic Genre Film
Tommy Gustafsson and Pietari Kääpä (eds)

Contemporary Japanese Cinema Since Hana-Bi
Adam Bingham

Chinese Martial Arts Cinema (2nd edition)
Stephen Teo

Slow Cinema
Tiago de Luca and Nuno Barradas Jorge

Expressionism in Cinema
Olaf Brill and Gary D. Rhodes (eds)

French Language Road Cinema: Borders, Diasporas, Migration and 'New Europe'
Michael Gott

Transnational Film Remakes
Iain Robert Smith and Constantine Verevis

Coming-of-age Cinema in New Zealand
Alistair Fox

www.euppublishing.com/series/tiwc

COMING-OF-AGE CINEMA IN NEW ZEALAND

Genre, Gender, and Adaptation

Alistair Fox

EDINBURGH
University Press

For Jeremy

Edinburgh University Press is one of the leading university presses in the UK. We publish academic books and journals in our selected subject areas across the humanities and social sciences, combining cutting-edge scholarship with high editorial and production values to produce academic works of lasting importance. For more information visit our website: edinburghuniversitypress.com

© Alistair Fox, 2017

Edinburgh University Press Ltd
The Tun – Holyrood Road
12 (2f) Jackson's Entry
Edinburgh EH8 8PJ

Typeset in 10/12.5 pt Sabon by
Servis Filmsetting Ltd, Stockport, Cheshire

A CIP record for this book is available from the British Library

ISBN 978 1 4744 2944 3 (hardback)
ISBN 978 1 4744 2946 7 (webready PDF)
ISBN 978 1 4744 2947 4 (epub)

The right of Alistair Fox to be identified as author of this work has been asserted in accordance with the Copyright, Designs and Patents Act 1988 and the Copyright and Related Rights Regulations 2003 (SI No. 2498).

CONTENTS

List of Illustrations   vii
Preface   ix
Traditions in World Cinema   xi

PART 1   THE COMING-OF-AGE GENRE AND NATIONAL CINEMA

1. The Coming-of-age Film as a Genre: Attributes, Evolution, and Functions   3
2. New Zealand Coming-of-age Films: Distinctive Characteristics and Thematic Preoccupations   16

PART 2   THE NEW ZEALAND NEW WAVE: 1976–89

3. The Formation of a Budding Man Alone: *The God Boy* (Murray Reece, 1976)   31
4. An Angry Young Man Seeks to Justify Himself: *Sleeping Dogs* (Ian Donaldson, 1977)   42
5. An Immigrant Filmmaker Substitutes an Alternative Vision of Adolescence: *The Scarecrow* (Sam Pillsbury, 1982)   55
6. Art-cinema, Cultural Dislocation, and the Entry into Puberty: *Vigil* (Vincent Ward, 1984)   68

7. A Māori Girl Watches, Listens, and Learns – Coming of Age from an Indigenous Viewpoint: *Mauri* (Merata Mita, 1988)   80

PART 3   THE SECOND WAVE OF THE 1990s

8. Creativity as a Haven: *An Angel at My Table* (Jane Campion, 1990)   95
9. Desperation Turned Outwards: *Heavenly Creatures* (Peter Jackson, 1994)   108
10. Confronting Domestic Violence and Familial Abuse: *Once Were Warriors* (Lee Tamahori, 1994)   121

PART 4   PREOCCUPATIONS OF THE NEW MILLENNIUM

11. An Adolescent Girl Experiments with Sexuality: *Rain* (Christine Jeffs, 2001)   137
12. Asserting Feminist Claims within Māori Culture: *Whale Rider* (Nicki Caro, 2002)   148
13. Family Secrets and their Destructive Consequences: *In My Father's Den* (Brad McGann, 2004)   161
14. A Gay Boy Comes to Terms with his Sexuality: *50 Ways of Saying Fabulous* (Stewart Main, 2005)   175

PART 5   PERSPECTIVES ON MĀORI CULTURE SINCE 2010

15. Parental Abandonment and the Trauma of Loss: *Boy* (Taika Waititi, 2010)   189
16. A Māori Boy Contests the Old Patriarchal Order: *Mahana* (Lee Tamahori, 2016)   203
17. Delinquency and Bicultural Relations: *Hunt for the Wilderpeople* (Taika Waititi, 2016)   216

Conclusion   231

Bibliography   235
Index   240

ILLUSTRATIONS

3.1	Jimmy listens through the wall to his parents fighting, in *The God Boy*	34
3.2	Jimmy about to be strapped by a nun, in *The God Boy*	38
3.3	Jimmy on the Cross, in *The God Boy*	39
4.1	A youthful Roger Donaldson on location during the filming of *Sleeping Dogs*	46
4.2	Smithy and Gloria ride on a bike, recalling *Butch Cassidy and the Sundance Kid*, in *Sleeping Dogs*	49
4.3	A Skyhawk firing rockets, in *Sleeping Dogs*	52
5.1	Hubert Salter, the 'scarecrow,' in *The Scarecrow*	60
5.2	Ned begins to see through Salter, in *The Scarecrow*	63
5.3	Les and Ned receive their first kiss, in *The Scarecrow*	65
6.1	The Father's hand, in *Vigil*	72
6.2	Mangled trees – an autobiographical memory, in *Vigil*	73
6.3	Toss with Ethan in her ballet tutu and gumboots, in *Vigil*	77
7.1	Awatea observes the adult world, in *Mauri*	85
7.2	Awatea learns how to make a flax *kete* from her grandmother Kara, in *Mauri*	87
7.3	Awatea waves farewell to the departing spirit of her grandmother, in *Mauri*	90
8.1	Janet in a psychiatric hospital, in *An Angel at My Table*	102
8.2	Janet experiments with her sensuality, in *An Angel at My Table*	103
8.3	Young Janet shamed in class, in *An Angel at My Table*	103

9.1	Pauline, bored and resentful, in *Heavenly Creatures*	116
9.2	Juliet suffers grief at the thought of separation, in *Heavenly Creatures*	117
9.3	The fantasy world of Borovnia, in *Heavenly Creatures*	118
10.1	Terrified children listen to their parents fighting, in *Once Were Warriors*	125
10.2	Grace and Toot, in *Once Were Warriors*	129
10.3	Boogie exercises newfound pride in his culture, in *Once Were Warriors*	132
11.1	Janey imitates her mother's glitzy ostentation, in *Rain*	143
11.2	Little Jim, in *Rain*	144
11.3	Janey puts on her mother's makeup, in *Rain*	145
12.1	Paikea reproaches Hemi for smoking, in *Whale Rider*	155
12.2	Paikea fixes her grandfather's outboard motor, in *Whale Rider*	155
12.3	Paikea breaches *tapu* by sitting on the *paepae*, reserved for men, at a *pōwhiri*, in *Whale Rider*	157
13.1	Celia imagines the excitement of traveling overseas, in *In My Father's Den*	166
13.2	Symbolic use of landscape, in *In My Father's Den*	169
13.3	Jonathan, in his own version of a den, in *In My Father's Den*	170
14.1	Billy fantasizes about wearing his cow's tail, in *50 Ways of Saying Fabulous*	182
14.2	Lou and Billy in a fantasy sequence, in *50 Ways of Saying Fabulous*	183
14.3	Lou tries to disguise her burgeoning female body, in *50 Ways of Saying Fabulous*	184
15.1	Boy imitating his father, in *Boy*	196
15.2	Rocky, like E.T., tries to heal his father Alamein, in *Boy*	198
15.3	Alamein finally joins his sons in facing up to his grief, in *Boy*	200
16.1	Simeon and Poppy decide to go on a date together, in *Mahana*	209
16.2	Disruption during a screening at the cinema, in *Mahana*	210
16.3	Simeon stands up to Tamihana, his grandfather, while his father Joshua stands by, in *Mahana*	212
17.1	Barry Crump carrying a pig on his back, in the television documentary *Crump*	219
17.2	Hec carrying a pig on his back, in *Hunt for the Wilderpeople*	220
17.3	Ricky saves Hec from the hunters, in *Hunt for the Wilderpeople*	225

PREFACE

At the outset of this book, I feel a need to explain why I wrote it. New Zealand cinema as a coherent creative industry with a regular output is a fairly recent phenomenon, and New Zealanders tend to underestimate its achievement and significance (possibly as a result of vestigial, post-colonial 'cultural cringe'). I want to counter this habitual reaction by pointing to the insights that New Zealand cinema can provide as to the forces that have influenced the formation of our national character(s). I am also aware of a growing interest in World Cinema, and of the cinema of small nations and post-colonial societies in particular. This book is intended to place New Zealand cinema in the mix of national cinemas available for viewing and for study, both for students and scholars, and for the general public. Finally, after an academic career spanning forty years, I have realized, in retrospect, that I have lived through some of the critically formative moments in the development of New Zealand's cultural identity/identities since the Second World War, and that the coming-of-age films I analyze in this book reflect the nature of those changes.

In many respects, this book is a companion work to my earlier *Ship of Dreams* (2008), which traced the consequences of New Zealand's value systems and cultural practices in the emotional lives of adult men. While this earlier book often touched, given its focus on masculinity, on the coming-of-age experiences of boys, it largely bypassed the experience of girls and women, and did not cover the full spectrum of the formative influence on children of the local cultural environments. This book fills in that gap, especially given that New Zealand coming-of-age films engage with, and are virtually inseparable from, many of the most iconic works of New Zealand literature. For this reason, my discussion of each major film includes an analysis of the novel upon which it is based where this occurs, which is in all cases except four films that are based on original scripts.

I should also add that this corpus of coming-of-age films provides an invaluable source of evidence of cultural changes in New Zealand that historians tend to overlook. Accordingly, in approaching each of the films discussed in this volume, I have tried to point to the historical significance of the representations they imaginatively depict.

There are a number of persons I would like especially to acknowledge who have contributed, sometimes without their knowledge, to the evolution of this project. As always, my primary debt is to Hilary Radner, my wife and intellectual partner, who often sees the implications of what I am doing before I do, and who offers me unfailing encouragement in pursuing them: it was she who suggested that I write this book in the first place. My thanks go also to my friend and colleague Frédéric Dichtel, a cinephile who takes as much delight as I do in exploring the interpretive and aesthetic intricacies of films, and Raphaël Richter-Gravier, who is equally '*fou de cinéma.*' Another cinephile who, apart from fostering interest in high-quality films in our city, has offered encouragement for this project is Vicki Evans, the President of the Dunedin Film Society – a film-lover who has a deep conviction of the importance of New Zealand cinema.

Finally, I should acknowledge the work of the filmmakers and writers themselves, with some of whom I am acquainted, in offering to New Zealand and the world these imaginative representations of growing up in this country, often by being prepared to draw upon, and reveal, their own experience. Along with them, I acknowledge the scholars and critics who have pioneered the study of New Zealand film, Brian MacDonnell and Nicholas Reid especially, among others.

This work is dedicated affectionately to my son Jeremy, who sadly departed this world long before his time.

Alistair Fox
Dunedin
29 December 2016

TRADITIONS IN WORLD CINEMA

General editors: **Linda Badley and R. Barton Palmer**
Founding editor: **Steven Jay Schneider**

Traditions in World Cinema is a series of textbooks and monographs devoted to the analysis of currently popular and previously underexamined or undervalued film movements from around the globe. Also intended for general interest readers, the textbooks in this series offer undergraduate- and graduate-level film students accessible and comprehensive introductions to diverse traditions in world cinema. The monographs open up for advanced academic study more specialised groups of films, including those that require theoretically oriented approaches. Both textbooks and monographs provide thorough examinations of the industrial, cultural, and socio-historical conditions of production and reception.

The flagship textbook for the series includes chapters by noted scholars on traditions of acknowledged importance (the French New Wave, German Expressionism), recent and emergent traditions (New Iranian, post-Cinema Novo), and those whose rightful claim to recognition has yet to be established (the Israeli persecution film, global found footage cinema). Other volumes concentrate on individual national, regional, or global cinema traditions. As the introductory chapter to each volume makes clear, the films under discussion form a coherent group on the basis of substantive and relatively transparent, if not always obvious, commonalities. These commonalities may be formal, stylistic, or thematic, and the groupings may, although they need not, be popularly identified as genres, cycles, or movements (Japanese horror, Chinese martial arts cinema, Italian Neorealism). Indeed, in cases in which a group of films is not already commonly identified as a tradition, one purpose of the volume is to establish its claim to importance and make it visible (East Central European Magical Realist cinema, Palestinian cinema).

Textbooks and monographs include:

- An introduction that clarifies the rationale for the grouping of films under examination
- A concise history of the regional, national, or transnational cinema in question
- A summary of previous published work on the tradition
- Contextual analysis of industrial, cultural, and socio-historical conditions of production and reception
- Textual analysis of specific and notable films, with clear and judicious application of relevant film theoretical approaches
- Bibliograph(ies)/filmograph(ies)

Monographs may additionally include:

- Discussion of the dynamics of cross-cultural exchange in light of current research and thinking about cultural imperialism and globalisation, as well as issues of regional/national cinema or political/aesthetic movements (such as new waves, postmodernism, or identity politics)
- Interview(s) with key filmmakers working within the tradition.

PART I

THE COMING-OF-AGE GENRE AND NATIONAL CINEMA

1. THE COMING-OF-AGE FILM AS A GENRE: ATTRIBUTES, EVOLUTION, AND FUNCTIONS

Ever since François Truffaut stunned the cinematic world with his autobiographical film *The 400 Blows* in 1959, a work that portrayed the emotional life of an adolescent with unprecedented insight and realism, national cinemas around the world have seen a proliferating output of coming-of-age films in cinemas beyond that of Hollywood. The reason for this efflorescence is that Truffaut's film heralded a new kind of low-cost, auteur cinema (along with the arrival of the French New Wave) that suited both the purpose and the budgets of filmmakers in countries with more limited financial means than those of Hollywood.

New Zealand has not been exempt from this trend, and there are several compelling reasons for devoting a book to this subject. First, if one looks at the New Zealand-made films on New Zealand stories that have either achieved the greatest success at the national box office, and/or have been selected for prestigious international film festivals and acclaimed by critics, it is striking how many of them are coming-of-age films. Second, these films reveal more about the evolution of cultural identity in this country than any other source of evidence, not only because they depict characters in the process of discovering who they are, or want to become (or want to escape from being), but also because they invite spectators to experience what it feels like, emotionally and imaginatively, to be in that condition. Finally, even though coming-of-age movies constitute one of the most frequent genres of film made in New Zealand, there has, as yet, been no extended study of this genre as a national phenomenon outside of Hollywood. Indeed, there have been few studies anywhere of the coming-of-age film as an important genre in its own right, as distinct from the American 'teen film,' which has been studied extensively, but which is not coterminous in any way with the national films that will be studied in this volume.[1]

My aim in writing this book is to suggest that an investigation of the New Zealand coming-of-age film, treated both as a subject in its own right and also as a case study, will not only shed light on this nation's cultural history, but will deepen understanding of the coming-of-age genre as an international phenomenon generally, especially with regard to the important place it occupies in virtually all national cinemas. It will be shown that rather than being a standardized genre that maintains 'a remarkable consistency' in the image of adolescent experience it presents – the conclusion reached by those who have focused on the American teen film[2] – New Zealand coming-of-age films reveal an engagement with the factors influencing this formative stage in human development that is distinctive because of the degree to which it is informed by the presence of local (that is, national) concerns. Moreover, an exploration of the New Zealand coming-of-age film provides a striking example of the symbiotic relationship that exists between a national cinema and the country's national literature, given that the adaptation of a national story, most often a work that originates from an earlier generation, enables a triangulation to take place that in turn promotes an updating and redefinition of cultural identity, both at the level of the individual and also of the nation as a whole.

Before looking at the specific ways in which these processes are manifest in New Zealand cinema, mostly through its relationship with iconic New Zealand literary works, it is useful to identify the most basic characteristics of the coming-of-age film as a genre.

The Coming-of-age Film: Generic Attributes

I have chosen to use the term 'coming-of-age film' rather than 'teen film' because the former term is far less restrictive and prescriptive, and less tied to American cinema, especially that of the 1950s, which supported the formulation of the latter term. 'Coming-of-age' as a generic descriptor encompasses a much broader spectrum of adolescent experiences than those attributed to the American teen film, which Catherine Driscoll summarizes as 'youth as a social problem, the institutionalization of the teenager, and youth as a celebration of present pleasure and future potential.'[3] In contrast, New Zealand coming-of-age films do not show youth as a social problem, but rather social values and practices as a problem for youth; and while a number of films, especially those made more recently, celebrate the prospect of future potential that remains to be realized, none of them presents youth as a celebration of present pleasure – to the contrary: the present is most often shown to be a time that produces anxiety and distress, prompting the protagonist to seek a better future in which present problems are ameliorated.

The defining attributes of the coming-of-age film have been well described by the screenwriter Julie Selbo. Films in this genre revolve around a character who is on a journey of self-discovery: 'Through one or more moments of revelation in the film story, the main character is able to move forward in his or her life and mature into a "new age" – a more developed sense of self.'[4] Coming-of-age films have their forerunner in literature in the *Bildungsroman*, which was created in the second half of the eighteenth century in response to the educational ideals of the German Enlightenment.[5] *Bildungsromane* show, in the words of Mikhail Bakhtin, 'the image of *man in the process of becoming*' – a preoccupation that distinguishes this form, the 'novel of emergence,' from the majority of other kinds of novels that 'know only the image of the *ready-made* hero.'[6] The same is true of coming-of-age films, and in this respect many of them differ from the American teen films as described by critics adopting a sociological approach.

Coming-of-age stories can be told with characters of any age, but no matter what the age of the character, they all explore a *growth* into some form of mature awareness. As Selbo puts it, 'even if the characters *are* adult, there may still be traits of childhood or adolescence (insecurities, residual anger, neuroses that block forward progress, and more).'[7] Characteristically, however, coming-of-age films fall into three categories: (1) the *pre-teen*, involving a protagonist who is twelve years of age or younger; (2) the *teen/adolescent*, with a protagonist who is between thirteen and nineteen years of age; and (3) the *post-adolescence*, in which the protagonist is twenty years and over.[8] In rare cases, as in Jane Campion's *An Angel at My Table* (1990), a coming-of-age film will explore all three stages.

In filmic versions of these 'stories of emergence,' the process of change is often precipitated by an experience of loss, an encounter with a difficult or threatening situation, the impact of life-changing events, and/or a desire to find meaning in life, or the answers to life's questions. Typical situations that give rise to coming-of-age films are a fear of being unloved by one's parents, as in Truffaut's *The 400 Blows*; emotional or physical suffering caused by family dysfunction, as in *Once Were Warriors* (Lee Tamahori, 1994); the awakening of sexuality or the entry into puberty, as in *Vigil* (Vincent Ward, 1984), or *Rain* (Christine Jeffs, 2001); the encounter with repressive cultural codes and values, as in *The God Boy* (Murray Reece, 1976), or *Heavenly Creatures* (Peter Jackson, 1994); the experience of marginalization on account of one's personality, as in *An Angel at My Table*, or sexual orientation, as in *50 Ways of Saying Fabulous* (Stewart Main, 2005); the experience of growing up within an indigenous culture, as in *Mauri* (Merata Mita, 1988), or *Mahana* (Lee Tamahori, 2016); a clash with tyrannical authority figures or institutions, as in

Sleeping Dogs (Roger Donaldson, 1977); or the impact of the loss of a loved one, as in *Boy* (Taika Waititi, 2010), or *The Hunt for the Wilderpeople* (Taika Waititi, 2016).

Often, the coming-of-age film involves an exploration of trial scenarios, values, and modes of behavior. A classic instance, to take an example from a different national cinema, is *The Dreamers* (Bernardo Bertolucci, 2003), which shows three young adults experimenting with different facets of sexuality. Such films can be structured around a rites-of-passage challenge that requires bravery and involves overcoming fears: for example, *Whale Rider* (Niki Caro, 2002), and *The Life of Pi* (Ang Lee, 2012). In many cases, the problems or issues faced initially by the protagonist are resolved by the end of the film, but, in other instances, there is a failure of resolution, leading to a tragic outcome, as in *Rebel Without a Cause* (Nicholas Ray, 1955), or *Sleeping Dogs* (to take a New Zealand example).

As far as their form is concerned, coming-of-age movies, like most film narratives, are film-genre hybrids: that is, they blend coming-of-age preoccupations and tropes with elements of other genres. To take some examples from New Zealand cinema, in his two immensely successful films *Boy* and *The Hunt for the Wilderpeople*, Taika Waititi blends typical coming-of-age narratives with comedy; in *50 Ways of Saying Fabulous*, Stewart Main incorporates elements from the fantasy and science fiction genres into his story of a boy who discovers he is gay; and in *Braindead* (1992), Peter Jackson even embeds a classic coming-of-age Oedipal drama within a horror film that exploits elements from the splatstick and zombie genres. Most commonly, however, the coming-of-age narrative is combined with elements typical of the family melodrama, which often involves a character's struggle to attain individuality and escape from the domination of overbearing parents or other forms of oppressive authority. A film like Roger Donaldson's *Sleeping Dogs* displays a particularly rich blend of different genres, combining elements of the action film, the adventure film, the buddy film, the thriller, the romance, and the war film with a classic New Zealand Man Alone story involving a rite-of-passage ordeal that ends in the protagonist's tragic death.

The Influence of the French New Wave

Coming-of-age films were a comparatively late development in the evolution of cinema. As David Considine, in his overview of the depiction of adolescents on film, recounts, juveniles began to have a major impact on Hollywood during the 1930s, a time when filmmakers sought to articulate the family values of small-town, middle-class America, as in the sixteen movies featuring the Andy Hardy character played by Mickey Rooney, for example, *Love Finds Andy Hardy* (George B. Seitz, 1938).[9] In Considine's account, the depiction of young people between 1930 and 1980 was 'generalized and highly stereotyped,' fluctuating back and forth 'between the cute, lovable Andy Hardy-type character and the crazy, mixed-up kid of the juvenile delinquency genre,' as represented by *The Wild One* (László Benedek, 1953), *East of Eden* (Elia Kazan, 1954), or *Rebel without a Cause* (Nicholas Ray, 1955).[10] Characteristic themes of these American coming-of-age movies were the fractured family that was unable to fulfil the needs of its children – especially their need for love – juvenile delinquency, and teenage sexuality.[11]

The popularity and number of these American movies focusing on adolescents increased after the Second World War with the advent of the 'Pearl Harbor babies,' and the recognition by Hollywood that it needed to pay attention to an emerging new market. In Considine's words, 'The baby boom served to strengthen the position of the youth market. Aided by peace and prosperity, young people assumed an economic independence that did not go unnoticed in Hollywood.'[12]

The advent of this new youth market also coincided with the emergence of a new type of film from Europe: the auteur film, strongly shaped by autobiographical material and made with a small budget, was thrust to the forefront of international attention, as already mentioned, by the phenomenal success of François Truffaut's film about his own childhood, *The 400 Blows* (1959). This film, which inaugurated the French New Wave, was to have a profound effect on other cinemas around the world, given that they did not depend upon the resources of a studio, and did not require as large a budget as the films characteristically made in Hollywood.

French New Wave films introduced many elements that would crucially influence the making of subsequent coming-of-age films, especially those produced in national cinemas, like that of New Zealand. First, the movies they made were low-budget films, shot with light equipment that enabled these movies to be filmed on location, which, apart from making the film more financially practicable, invested them with a different kind of verisimilitude. Second, they were stylistically unconventional and ambitious, not hesitating to transgress against the rules of the classical continuity system (for example, by using intentional jump cuts and long takes, thus breaching requirements for the invisibility of the edit and the elimination of extraneous time through elliptical edits). Third, and most importantly, they were concerned to make *personal* films.

The personal nature of this new kind of auteur film is well expressed by François Truffaut, writing in 1957:

> The film of tomorrow appears to me as even more personal than an individual and autobiographical novel, like a confession or a diary. The young filmmakers will express themselves in the first person and will

relate what has happened to them: it may be the story of their first love or their most recent; of their political awakening [. . .] it will be enjoyable because it will be true.[13]

Being more personal, New Wave films treated their subjects with a greater intensity of subjective emotion (because of their autobiographical origins), which affected other aspects of the film's production. New Wave filmmakers, and those subsequently influenced by them, tended to write their own original screenplays, as Truffaut did, for example, with *The 400 Blows*, Jean-Luc Godard with *A Woman Is a Woman* (1961), Éric Rohmer with *Suzanne's Career* (1963), and Jean Eustache with *My Little Loves* (1974). Even when they chose to adapt a literary source, as in Truffaut's *Jules and Jim* (1962), based on a novel by Henri-Pierre Roché, or Godard's *Contempt* (1963), based on a novel by Alberto Moravia, the chosen source was selected mainly for its potential to serve as a vehicle for personal projection on the part of the filmmaker.[14] This tendency to adapt a literary source in such a way as to turn it into a vehicle for personal self-projection is very marked in the case of New Zealand coming-of-age cinema.

Generally, in terms of shooting style, the New Wave filmmakers and their followers privileged techniques that allow the spectator to enter into the very intimate, personal space of a character – particularly through the use of medium close-up and close-up shots that reveal emotions and reactions through facial expressions.[15] Such shooting choices served to intensify the expression of emotion and promote strong audience identification with the character concerned. The influence of this technique on subsequent filmmakers is apparent, for example, in André Téchiné's widely esteemed coming-of-age film, *Wild Reeds* (1993), in which the density of medium close-up and close-up shots of the characters' faces is remarkable. In New Zealand cinema, Peter Jackson's *Heavenly Creatures*, among many others, makes extensive use of this strategy. As far as film style is concerned, the influence of the New Wave on coming-of-age films continues to the present day, in New Zealand as elsewhere, as evidenced by Taika Waititi's admission that the first five minutes of his smash-hit *Boy* is modeled on the opening of Truffaut's *Jules and Jim*, which he saw as feeding the spectator a lot of information and layers of visual and aural stimulation, while at the same time giving the impression of simplicity.[16]

A complementary device in this new form of personal cinema is the use of evocative, or 'subjective' objects. As the psychoanalyst Christopher Bollas explains, certain objects act like 'psychic "keys",' in that they open doors to unconscious self-experience and release our subjective 'idiom.'[17] Such objects can be anything that the mind selects – a physical object, a landscape, a piece of music – and the self-expression they enable is 'a potent means not only of representing unconscious phantasies but of conjuring dense psychic textures that constitute a form of thinking by experiencing.'[18] Evocative objects abound in auteur cinema, and they are usually identifiable by their recurrence as an insistent motif with metaphoric suggestiveness.[19] In Truffaut's films, for example, books are a recurrent symbol – those of Balzac in particular – because they associate to the way Truffaut as a child sought to escape from the feeling of being unloved by his indifferent mother by entering the alternative imaginary world they provided. Similarly, Jane Campion's often feature toy horses, which associate to a collection owned by her sister, and cats, which associate to her mother's passion for her pets. Such objects embody associations that activate emotional feelings that are then transmitted to the spectator through a process of intersubjective transfer.[20] Whether or not an image constitutes an evocative object is revealed chiefly through the means of enunciation that the filmmaker chooses: if he or she opts for a close-up of an object, and the camera lingers on it for a significant length of time, accompanied by a movement (or lack of it) that draws attention to the object, then the spectator derives a sense that the image is over-determined – that is, that it contains a latent signification that is greater than its literal content would suggest. This type of technique is crucial to the achievement of the kind of emotional impact, and hence audience identification, for which most coming-of-age films strive.

Once the French New Wave filmmakers had shown what could be done with these new preoccupations and highly subjective style on a low budget, this new mode of film rapidly spread to other parts of the world, including the USA – encouraged by the demise of the studio system after the Paramount Decree of 1948 – where it fostered the American New Wave, which spanned the mid-1960s through to the mid-1970s.[21] Among the films of the 'New Hollywood' was a raft of coming-of-age films, including *The Graduate* (Mike Nichols, 1967), *Summer of '42* (Robert Mulligan, 1971), *American Graffiti* (George Lucas, 1973), and *Breaking Away* (Peter Yates, 1979). Both directly and indirectly via the New Hollywood films, the new modes of auteur cinema fostered other New Waves in various national cinemas, including New Zealand, and it was out of this movement that the New Zealand coming-of-age film was born, signaled by the appearance of Roger Donaldson's surprise hit *Sleeping Dogs* in 1977.

European Art Cinema and its Influence on the Style of Coming-of-age Films

Because coming-of-age films, for the most part, are concerned to convey the subjective feelings of personal experience, filmmakers who attempt this genre have found it particularly useful to draw on the expressive strategies and devices of European art cinema. Art cinema arose from a desire to exploit the artistic potential of cinema by drawing on the techniques of various modernist movements in the fine arts, theater, and literature.[22] Chief among them were German expressionism, which sought to depict an inner emotional reality by introducing distortions in the scenery and lighting to deepen the mood of a film, and French impressionism, which aimed to convey mental states and processes as a visual reality. To these two movements can be added surrealism, futurism, dadaism, and cubism, all of which furnished practices that could be imported into cinema.

French 'impressionist' cinema, which used such devices as unusual camera movements and angles, superimposed images, rhythmic editing, and magical optical effects to destabilize objective ways of seeing, was perhaps the most important of all these influences because of its synthetic nature. While remaining fundamentally narrative-based, in terms of its representational strategies, it could apply extra-cinematic effects as found in German expressionism; the manipulation of movement and articulation of time (or 'rhythm') as favored in 'pure cinema'; and unusual associations of images as presented by surrealism. Instead of the realist, linear, continuous, chronological narration that characterized classical American cinema until Orson Welles and film noir films introduced expressionist techniques into Hollywood in the 1940s, impressionist cinema, as found in the films of Abel Gance (for example, *Napoléon*, 1927), Jean Epstein (for example, *Coeur fidèle*, 1923), and Jean Renoir (for example, *Nana*, 1926), favored a visual rhythm that followed the poetic logic of the work, in order to convey the sense of 'a psychic reality in which external and internal sensual stimuli tended to replace physical events.'[23] Such an approach relied upon severe ellipses in the narrative, separating narrative construction from dramatic motivation by eschewing preparatory aspects of scene construction and by withholding verbal explanation. In contrast to the realism of classical cinema, impressionist cinema was also heavily symbolic, especially in its use of landscapes and expressive objects.

As far as style was concerned, this new preoccupation with subjectivity and a non-realistic mode of representation tended to incline art cinema towards minimalism – that is, 'a reduction of redundancy as well as eliminating random diversity.'[24] Minimalism can manifest itself in a variety of forms, and an art-cinema auteur wanting to make a coming-of-age film has an array of minimalist styles to choose between, or combine. One of the most influential is that of Robert Bresson, who achieves an extreme reduction of narrative redundancy by frequently using medium close-up shots to focus on the most important visual element in an image, and by placing that element in the middle of the frame, thus eliminating the extraneous details usually found in the background of the long shots and medium long shots commonly favored in classical cinema. Rather than altering the shot length or moving the camera, Bresson uses cuts instead, which enables him to achieve a striking visual austerity. This is the style that Jane Campion would use in *An Angel at My Table* (1990), and later in *Bright Star* (2009).

Ingmar Bergman provided another model for achieving an expressive minimalism. His minimalist style consisted of combining symbolic landscapes with expressionist lighting effects, and a consistent use of close-up shots to register emotions in the faces of characters who are placed in the context of these psychic mindscapes, as in *Persona* (1966), or *The Passion of Anna* (1969).

All of these devices and strategies are available to the director who is making a coming-of-age film, and are ideally suited to that purpose. As I shall demonstrate in later chapters, New Zealand filmmakers who have attempted this genre have drawn heavily on all of these resources, most notably the two with art-school backgrounds, Vincent Ward and Jane Campion.

The Functions of Coming-of-age Films

Coming-of-age narratives are ubiquitous in all cinemas, as in all national literatures, because they offer people a symbolic figuration that makes it possible for them to understand who they are, and how they have come to be the way they recognize themselves as being. Adolescence is a crucial time during which the formation of one's adult personality and the structure of one's psychic mechanism is consolidated, but in order to be able even to register consciously what it is one feels and thinks, one needs to retrieve, or invent, an image that associates to the experience that provokes the feeling; otherwise, the effects of that experience remain locked in one's implicit memory, which is unconscious, even though it retains the power to influence one's thoughts, emotions, and actions in later, adult life.[25]

The reason why coming-of-age narratives are so frequently produced in literature and cinema is because they provide a means for both the author/filmmaker and reader/spectator to realize what it is they themselves are thinking and feeling, or have thought and felt in the past, about their own experience, and this, in turn, is an essential precondition for the ongoing evolution of one's personality, and for personal growth.

It is not insignificant that when a filmmaker makes a coming-of-age film by adapting a literary source, he or she invariably updates the setting of the story to the time period of his or her own youth. This reflects the filmmaker's desire to make the story serve the functions I have intimated above: that is, to facilitate a self-interpretation, self-experience, and self-understanding that is then offered to the audience for the sake of corroborating validation and confirmation.

The Role of Coming-of-age Films in the Output of National Cinemas

One consequence of the international dominance of Hollywood cinema has been the emergence of national cinemas that aim to provide representations of the local cultural experience as an alternative to American globalized culture. Accordingly, the films that constitute a national cinema embody a distinctive local specificity.[26] Lacking the financial resources to make movies on the scale of Hollywood blockbusters, national cinemas tend to favor the auteur art film as a vehicle for presenting images and values that are set against those of a hegemonic American cinema that threatens to overwhelm them.[27] Art cinema, in addition, has the advantage of employing narrative resources that facilitate the representation of the 'uncanny' sensation frequently experienced by those who descend from settlers who have colonized a country from elsewhere. This experience of the 'uncanny,' which is so often expressed in coming-of-age films that are made in a post-colonial society, derives from an experience of feeling strange or dislocated in an environment that should – because it is 'home' – feel knowable and comforting.[28]

The attributes that make these films 'national' comprise specific content and subject matter, specific narrative discourses and themes, and local narrative traditions and source material that have become embedded in what is locally construed to be the national heritage – in other words, those aspects of historical and cultural experience that have become registered in the nation's collective memory. As Maurice Halbwachs has postulated, memory is framed in the present as much as in the past, given that remembering is a matter not merely of retrieval, but of recombination and creation, owing to the fact that memories are repetitions that are 'successively engaged in very different systems of notions at different periods of our lives.'[29] The promotion of such a process of memorialization is one of the main functions of the films that constitute a national cinema, and they do so through the reactivated, recreated memories of the filmmakers who create auteur coming-of-age films, which recall their childhood and the discursive frameworks and social conditions that were formative in their own development.

In this regard, the subjective style of auteurist coming-of-age films is very important because it allows the filmmaker to represent the specific sensibilities, and structures of feeling that pertained in the environment in which he or she grew up. Such representations tell us more about the specificities of a national culture at an emotional level than any other form of historical evidence, and when they are shared with spectators who see their own experience reflected in them, or else identify empathically with them, a collective feeling eventuates that consolidates a feeling of national identity.

In addition to the style, the nature of the formal systems of these films and the ways in which they construct space and stage actions is equally revealing of the specificities of a local culture,[30] and in the case of New Zealand coming-of-age films this is strikingly apparent in how filmmakers exploit landscape as a means of symbolically figuring internal states of feeling. Such a procedure allows social conditions and the way they affect individuals not merely to be known abstractly, but to be experienced feelingly and emotionally.

More than any other genre, therefore, the coming-of-age film performs a vital role in the evolution and transmission of a national culture. Furthermore, in its own narrative structure and trajectory, it often mirrors the movement that is taking place in the nation at large. In a post-colonial society like that of New Zealand, for example, which was only systematically colonized after 1840 and did not truly begin to separate from the mother country until Britain joined the European Union in 1973, the process of becoming an individual that informs the coming-of-age film provided a parallel to the process of becoming as a nation that was necessary after Britain unilaterally loosened the bonds that had provided the colony with its economic and cultural security as a far-flung province of England. While there had been a steady, if intermittent, production of *Bildungsromane* in New Zealand during the first half of the twentieth century, they had not been the dominant literary form, given that didactic works of social realism, romances, and melodramas were more frequently the genres of choice for writers.[31] In contrast, coming-of-age narratives occupy a much more prominent place in the domain of New Zealand cinema, highlighting the possibility that it is not coincidental that coming-of-age films begin to appear in New Zealand cinema very shortly after the forced cutting of the apron strings from the mother country following Britain's entry into the European Union, nor that they often deal with the issue of cruel or indifferent parents, and the effects of separation, suggesting that the symbolic figuration implicit in stories relating to individuals may, in fact, have a larger, perhaps unconscious, significance.

To summarize, then, coming-of-age films as a genre are central to the imaginative experience of human beings both at a personal and a national level. Many of the cultural influences they depict are local and specific, but many of them are also universal – such as the inevitable struggle to define oneself in the face of dominant social values with which one does not agree, or the wishes of parents who do not share the same aspirations of oneself. The important thing is, such narratives will always need to be made, and consumed.

Notes

1. For studies of the American teen film, see David M. Considine, *The Cinema of Adolescence* (Jefferson, NC: McFarland, 1985); Thomas Doherty, *Teenagers and Teenpics: The Juvenilization of American Movies in the 1950s*, 2nd edn (Philadelphia: Temple University Press, 2002); Catherine Driscoll, *Teen Film: A Critical Introduction* (Oxford: Berg, 2011); and Jon Lewis, *The Road to Romance & Ruin: Teen Films and Youth Culture* (New York: Routledge, 1992). For one of the few scholarly works to look beyond American films, see Timothy Shary and Alexandra Seibel (eds), *Youth Culture in Global Cinema* (Austin: University of Texas Press, 2007).
2. See Driscoll, 4–5.

3. Driscoll, 29.
4. Julie Selbo, *Film Genre for the Screenwriter* (New York and London: Routledge, 2015), 290.
5. Thomas L. Jeffers, *Apprenticeships* (London: Palgrave, 2005), 2.
6. M. M. Bakhtin, 'The *Bildungsroman* and Its Significance in the History of Realism (Toward a Historical Typology of the Novel),' in M. M. Bakhtin, *Speech Genres and Other Late Essays*, trans. Vern W. McGee, ed. Caryl Emerson and Michael Holquist (Austin: University of Texas Press, 1981), 19–20.
7. Selbo, 56, 290.
8. Ibid., 292.
9. See David M. Considine, 'The Cinema of Adolescence,' *Journal of Popular Film & Television* 9:3 (Fall 1981), 123–37, esp. 124.
10. Ibid.
11. For a full account, see David M. Considine, *The Cinema of Adolescence* (Jefferson, NC: McFarland, 1985).
12. Considine, 'The Cinema of Adolescence,' 131.
13. François Truffaut, *The Films in My Life* (New York: Da Capo Press, 1994), 19.
14. For a detailed discussion of how Truffaut converted the source of *Jules and Jim* into a vehicle for personal projection, see Alistair Fox, *Speaking Pictures: Neuropsychoanalysis and Authorship in Film and Literature* (Bloomington and Indianapolis: Indiana University Press, 2016), 174–92.
15. For a useful account of the effect of these techniques, see Mick Hurbris-Cherrier, *Voice & Vision: A Creative Approach to Narrative Film and DVD*, 2nd edn (New York and London: Focal Press, 2013), 53–4.
16. *Boy*, Presskit (Paladin and Unison Films in association with Radius Films, 2010), http://boythefilm.com/wp-content/uploads/boy-final-presskit.pdf, accessed 4 January 2017.
17. Christopher Bollas, *Being a Character: Psychoanalysis and Self Experience* (London and New York, 1992), 17.
18. Ibid., 30.
19. For a theoretical exposition of the purpose of these reiterated motifs, see Charles Mauron, *Des métaphores obédantes au mythe personnel: Introduction à la psychocritique* (Paris: J. Conti, 1963), discussed in my book *Speaking Pictures: Neuropsychoanalysis and Authorship in Film and Literature* (Bloomington and Indianapolis: Indiana University Press, 2017), 215–17.
20. For an account of the neurobiological processes involved in this process, see Fox, *Speaking Pictures*, 158–65.
21. See David A. Cook, 'Auteur Cinema and the "Film Generation" in 1970s Hollywood,' in Jon Lewis (ed.), *The New American Cinema* (Durham and London: Duke University Press, 1998), 12–37.
22. See András Bálint Kovács, *Screening Modernism: European Art Cinema, 1950–1980* (Chicago and London: University of Chicago Press, 2007), 7–25, which my account of art cinema in this section echoes.
23. Kovács, *Screening Modernism*, 19.
24. Ibid., 140.
25. For a detailed exploration of why human beings need fictive representations, see Alistair Fox, *Speaking Pictures: Neuropsychoanalysis and Authorship in Film and Literature* (Bloomington and Indianapolis: Indiana University Press, 2016).
26. See Andrew Higson, 'The Concept of National Cinema,' *Screen* 30:4 (1989), 36–47.
27. Higson, 41.
28. For pertinent comments, see Stephanie Rains, 'Making Strange: Journeys through

the Unfamiliar Films of Vincent Ward,' in Ian Conrich and Stuart Murray (eds), *New Zealand Filmmakers* (Detroit, MI: Wayne State University Press, 2007), 273–88.
29. See Maurice Halbwachs, *On Collective Memory*, ed. and trans. Lewis A. Coser (Chicago: University of Chicago Press, 1992), 45.
30. See Higson, 43.
31. See Lawrence Jones, 'The Novel,' in Terry Sturm (ed.), *The Oxford History of New Zealand Literature in English*, 2nd edn (Auckland: Oxford University Press, 1998), 119–244.

2. NEW ZEALAND COMING-OF-AGE FILMS: DISTINCTIVE CHARACTERISTICS AND THEMATIC PREOCCUPATIONS

Vincent Ward, speaking of his coming-of-age film *Vigil* (1984), observed that 'Childhood is a common theme in New Zealand writing.' He ascribed the omnipresence of this theme – rightly, in my opinion – to the youth of the country itself, which was only systematically colonized from Europe after 1840, and did not gain full independence until the adoption of the Statute of Winchester in 1947: 'Perhaps this is due to the relative newness of the national identity, and "rites of passage" stories reflect this coming of age.'[1] Given the importance of the coming-of-age theme in New Zealand literature and its critical role in registering an emerging cultural identity as the country sought to define itself, it is not surprising to find that coming-of-age films occupy an equally prominent place in the rapidly growing canon of New Zealand feature films, nor that their preoccupations reflect issues of concern in each subsequent decade as the emerging identity of the nation has evolved. It is almost as if creative minds in the country, aware of momentous changes taking place in the nation's sense of its own emerging identity, chose the cinematic coming-of-age genre as a vehicle through which to work through the complex emotional reactions that were elicited by this phenomenon. In the rest of this book, I will trace the shifts that have occurred in these preoccupations, relating them to the social, cultural, and political contexts that motivated them.

The Advent of the Coming-of-age Film

Even though fiction films began to be made in New Zealand as early as 1913, with three romances on Māori subjects directed by Gaston Méliès – *Loved by a Maori Chieftess, Hinemoa*, and *How Chief Te Ponga Won His Bride* – coming-of-age films did not begin to be made until the mid-1970s, with the possible exception of *Runaway* (John O'Shea, 1964), which can be regarded as a post-adolescence exercise in the genre. The first true coming-of-age film was *The God Boy* (Murray Reece, 1976), a television-feature made for the newly created national broadcasting channel, Television One.[2] Shortly afterwards, there occurred a remarkable flowering of New Zealand feature-filmmaking following the commercial success of the next coming-of-age film, Roger Donaldson's *Sleeping Dogs* (1977) – a flourishing that occurred partly as a result of a tax loophole that aspiring filmmakers suddenly realized they could exploit.[3] Even after this loophole was closed by the right-wing prime minister Robert Muldoon in the mid-1980s, the impetus created by this stimulus to feature-filmmaking continued into the 1990s and beyond, particularly after the formation of the New Zealand Film Commission in 1978, which was created once the success of *Sleeping Dogs* had demonstrated that New Zealand-made cinema could attract a large local audience.

Other coming-of-age films soon followed in this sudden flowering of local feature films, now referred to as the 'New Zealand New Wave.'[4] Perhaps unexpectedly, one of the first of them was *Sons for the Return Home* (Paul Maunder, 1979), based on a novel by the Samoan-New Zealand author Albert Wendt, which dealt with the effects on a young Pacific Islander of his emigration to New Zealand and his encounter with racial prejudice and cultural deracination in a country that still regarded itself as 'British.'[5] Upon reflection, the fact that this should be an early exercise in the coming-of-age genre is not surprising: Samoan immigrants, sooner than Pākehā, British-descended New Zealanders, had experienced what it was like to be people who were separated by distance and cultural difference from the emotional prospect of returning 'home.'

These two early coming-of-age films were soon followed by *The Scarecrow* (Sam Pillsbury, 1982), *Braindead* (Peter Jackson, 1982), *Among the Cinders* (Rolf Hädrich, 1983), and *Vigil* (Vincent Ward, 1984). Since then, there has been a steady stream of films focusing on young people, who are often shown as undergoing a rite of passage, or else confronting psychological pressures or social forces that they either succeed in overcoming, or fail to resolve.

Following the closing of the tax shelter that was introduced in the late 1970s/early 1980s, as New Zealand filmmaking slowly recovered, coming-of-age films continued to be one of the most prominently represented genres. Merata Mita created the first feature film by an indigenous woman with *Mauri*

(1988), and that was followed by a raft of films made by filmmakers from the next generation: Jane Campion's *An Angel at My Table* (1990), Lee Tamahori's *Once Were Warriors* (1994), Peter Jackson's *Heavenly Creatures* (1994), Werner Meyer's *Flight of the Albatross* (1995), and Robert Sarkies' *Scarfies* (1999).

In the new millennium, this trend continued with *Rain* (Christine Jeffs, 2001), *Whale Rider* (Nicki Caro, 2003), *In My Father's Den* (Brad McGann, 2004), *50 Ways of Saying Fabulous* (Stewart Main, 2005), *The Strength of Water* (Armagan Ballantyne, 2009), *Under the Mountain* (Jonathan King, 2009), and *Boy* (Taika Waititi, 2010). In the second decade of the twenty-first century, it shows no sign of diminishing, judging by the popularity of recent coming-of-age movies such as *Born to Dance* (Tammy Davis, 2015), *Mahana* (Lee Tamahori, 2016), and *Hunt for the Wilderpeople* (Taika Waititi, 2016).

One of the most striking aspects of this corpus is that it comprises almost all of the New Zealand-made films that have either achieved high critical acclaim internationally, especially as a result of having been chosen for prestigious film festivals, or else success at the national box office, and sometimes both together, as in the case of *Once Were Warriors* and *Hunt for the Wilderpeople*. The extraordinary popularity of the most successful of these coming-of-age films shows that they appeal to a far broader audience in New Zealand than to the predominantly youth audience associated with the American teen film, which furnishes a further reason why the former should be considered as distinct from the latter, which arise out of a different cultural context and have a different purpose.

The Dialogue with the Nation's Literature

With very few exceptions, most of the coming-of-age films made in New Zealand are adaptations from literature: of the fifteen movies examined in this study, all but four (*Vigil*, *Mauri*, *Heavenly Creatures*, and *Boy*) are based on literary sources, and, of these four, *Heavenly Creatures* is drawn largely from the diary kept by Pauline Parker, one of the two girls at the center of the tragic real-life event that the film dramatizes. This relationship with the nation's literature is very significant because it points to the most important functions that the coming-of-age genre serves in the context of a national cinema, and hence of a nation's collective sense of identity.

Among these adaptations, there are three distinct categories. The first comprises films that maintain a fidelity to the literary source in terms of the plot events, the characters portrayed, the narrative perspective, and the thematic vision of the original work, as in *The God Boy*, which remains extremely close to the famous novel by Ian Cross. In this film, the director, Murray Reece, acts exclusively as a *metteur-en-scène*, making no significant changes other than shifting the time frame from the 1930s to the 1950s.

A second type consists of films that transform the original work by integrating into the source story new material imported from foreign genres, especially those of American cinema. Usually, the effect of this importation is to 'rewrite' the source so as to turn it into a vehicle for personal self-expression, as in Roger Donaldson's *Sleeping Dogs* (1977), which contains a large number of tropes derived from the New Hollywood films of the 1970s – tropes that were absent from the source novel by Karl Stead, and which transform the story utterly. Lee Tamahori's *Mahana* (2016) displays a similar infusion of alien generic elements in its heavy use of tropes drawn from the American western.

The third type of adaptation involves a substantial reshaping of the source literary work so as to move it in a different direction altogether, largely through the suppression of key elements in the original, so as to alter the thematic complexion of the story. Such omissions can have the effect of transforming the mythos, or vision, that informs the original work, which is what occurs in Sam Pillsbury's adaptation of Ronald Hugh Morrieson's novel *The Scarecrow*. This adaptation strips the novel of many of the morally ambiguous elements that Morrieson had depicted in his adolescent narrator – ambiguities that had made his novel a distinctively New Zealand one, in that it reflected the combination of a desire to rebel against oppressive puritan values and guilt arising from the transgressions entailed in that rebellion. In part, this transformation may have come from the fact that the film's director, Sam Pillsbury, was not born and raised in New Zealand, but it also reflects a desire to produce a film that is sufficiently universalized to appeal to an international audience.

One very striking characteristic of all these adaptations is that the time period during which a film is set is routinely updated to correspond to that of the filmmaker's own childhood, so that the film becomes set in the formative years of his or her youth. This updating opens the way for the fable being adapted to be invested with personal projections, whether simply through details included in the mise-en-scène, and/or through a more complicated transformation of the source material so as to turn it into an instrument for a variety of possible psychological operations relating to the filmmaker's individual personality and autobiography.

The effect of such updating is to give the films a 'bifocal' perspective: on one hand, the spectator is put in touch with the forces that induced the author of the literary original to create the fiction in the first place; on the other, the ways in which the cinematic auteur transforms the source invites the spectator to enter into the perceptions of formative experience that are important to the filmmaker's understanding of himself or herself. There is thus a simultaneous registration of formative influences from the nation's cultural past with significant changes in historical experience and cultural value that have informed the life of the filmmaker. At the same time, these are presented to the contemporary audience of the film as material designed to waken the awareness of its members to issues of ongoing relevance to their personal lives, and, consequently, to the life of the nation as a whole as it moves into the future. Accordingly, a process of triangulation takes place that assists in the location of identity, both on the part of the filmmaker, and of spectators who are familiar with the national literary stories that are being adapted.

Coming-of-age Films as Personal Cinema

A further characteristic of New Zealand coming-of-age films is that they are almost without exception autobiographical, to a greater or lesser extent, and with varying degrees of displacement, in the manner encouraged by Truffaut and other young filmmakers of the French New Wave. Films based on an original script are always set in the period of the filmmaker's own childhood, and even those derived from literary sources are updated so that they reflect the world in which he or she spent their youth. Thus, *The Scarecrow* is shifted from the 1930s setting of Ronald Hugh Morrieson's novel to the 1950s, the time of the early adolescence of Sam Pillsbury (born in 1946). Similarly, the timeframe of *In My Father's Den* (2004) is shifted from the 1960s of Maurice Gee's novel to the 1980s of Brad McGann's own post-adolescence, with the location being changed from Henderson in the North Island to Central Otago in the South Island, a place with which he had strong associations, having been a student at the University of Otago in Dunedin.

Sometimes, a source novel is chosen because it represents the circumstances in which the filmmaker grew up. Taika Waititi, for example, in adapting Barry Crump's novel *Wild Pork and Watercress* as *The Hunt for the Wilderpeople* (2016), chose a novel that was published in 1986 – the time at which he himself would have been eleven, the exact age of the Maori boy protagonist. In addition, Waititi chose a story that locates the action of the film in the mountainous region of the East Coast of the North Island, where he grew up. Even when the protagonist is depicted in an era that is not that of the filmmaker, as in Jane Campion's *An Angel at My Table*, this dimension of personal identification is apparent in other ways. As Campion herself has let it be known, her treatment of *An Angel at My Table* is closely related to her awareness of her own mother's depression, as well as her personal identification with the sense of being an outsider that Janet Frame, like her, felt.[6]

All the films examined in this volume, in fact, reflect personal investments on the part of the filmmaker. In making *Vigil*, Vincent Ward drew upon his own memories of his mother's unhappiness at being a displaced immigrant, as well as his own feelings of loneliness as a child; Peter Jackson and Fran Walsh, in creating *Heavenly Creatures*, based on the account of a shocking matricide that took place in Christchurch during the 1950s, used it as a vehicle for expressing the memory of their own resentments at the oppressive restrictions that pertained at the time; Lee Tamahori's first film, *Once Were Warriors*, reflected certain aspects of his own experience as a youth living in an urban environment (drinking, fights) and then made a radically contrasting film, *Mahana*, that was set in the homeland of the Māori side of his family. And so on.

This personal dimension in coming-of-age films attests to the importance of their function as an instrument of self-experience, self-interpretation, and self-expression that is offered to a national audience for the purpose of providing an opportunity for its members to see a reflection of themselves in the representation, thus according it a degree of validation, both for the filmmakers and themselves.

A Rural Genre

To a striking extent, New Zealand coming-of-age films are staged in rural settings. In *Sleeping Dogs*, Smithy, the protagonist, takes refuge in the bush of the Coromandel uplands, and *The Hunt for the Wilderpeople* is set in the rugged high country of the Urewera on the East Coast of the North Island (but actually filmed in the Coromandel); *Vigil* is set in a remote Taranaki valley surrounded by bush-clad hills; *Mauri* is set in the rural farmlands of the Bay of Plenty, as is *Boy*; *An Angel at My Table* opens with a shot of Janet as a child on a lonely country road bordered by paddocks, and later shows Janet on a farm wearing gumboots; *Rain* is set on a remote inlet on the Coromandel Peninsula; *Whale Rider* is set in a rural town on the East Coast of the North Island; *In My Father's Den* and *50 Ways of Saying Fabulous* are located in the arid landscapes of Central Otago; *Mahana*, too, is set on an East Coast farm. Of the films discussed in this volume, only *Once Were Warriors* is set in an urban location. The pattern is too insistent to ignore, inviting a question as to why a rural setting is so important.

There are three reasons for this preference of location. First, the rural setting reflects the experience of many New Zealanders in a new, relatively raw country – the last major landmass, in fact, to be settled by humans, with the exception of Antarctica. Second, the rural setting allows the crucial issues addressed by the filmmaker to be isolated, and hence to be brought under the microscope of the exploratory and investigative fictive imagination. Third, the rural settings serve, as if constituting the kind of pathetic fallacy found in the poetry of earlier eras, as a metaphor for the emotional experience that the protagonist is undergoing in the course of the movie.[7] The parched, bare, arid landscape of Central Otago provides a symbolic correlative for the sense of alienation that grips Paul Prior in *In My Father's Den*, and for the 'scorching' incomprehension of the rural society in *50 Ways of Saying Fabulous*, in which

Billy has to find a place as a gay boy. The surrounding bush and mountainous terrain serve as an emblem of Nature's indifference, and even hostility, towards puny human beings and their endeavors in *Vigil*, while in *Sleeping Dogs* and *Hunt for the Wilderpeople* it offers a protective place of refuge and the opportunity for escape from the oppressive social or political forces that threaten the protagonist in the outer world. The big, cloudless sky and wide-open spaces in *An Angel at My Table* serve as a correlative for a sense of liberation from class and social expectations (for example, in the scene where Janet returns from Europe), while the beaches that characters often frequent serve variously as a site of play (as in *The God Boy* and *Boy*), of a transformative rite of passage (as in *Whale Rider*), of erotic or illicit encounter (as in *Nights in the Gardens of Spain* [Katie Wolfe, 2010]), or as the site of tragic events that underline a sense of guilt in the protagonist (as in *Rain*).

The only exception, Lee Tamahori's *Once Were Warriors*, based on Alan Duff's powerful and provocative novel (published in 1990), is set in the socio-economically depressed suburbs of Auckland, depicting negative consequences of the migration of Māori in large numbers from their rural homelands to the urban centers following the Second World War. But, until recently, such urban-based movies have been unusual in the canon of New Zealand coming-of-age films. One suspects that the rural setting of most coming-of-age films is both specific to the particular history of this country as the most recently colonized landmass in the history of mankind, and also as the outward register of an 'uncanny' emotional awareness on the part of Pākehā (New Zealanders of European descent) of being displaced arrivals who are separated by vast geographical distance from their cultures of origin.

Thematic Preoccupations

New Zealand coming-of-age films invariably deal with effects of cultural value systems that are felt to be oppressive or unduly restrictive, whether those informing Pākehā culture, or those that dominate Māori traditional culture. For Pākehā, the source of this oppression derives mainly from the legacy of the specific form of puritanism that was implanted in New Zealand by settlers who brought with them a blend of Victorian stoicism combined with a religious conviction of the intrinsic sinfulness of human nature.[8] Many films engage with the consequences of this value system, whether in its religious expression, as in *The God Boy*, or its secular form, manifest as a concern to maintain outward social propriety and respectability, as in *Heavenly Creatures* (1994) or *In My Father's Den* (2004).

The puritanical values of Pākehā society are shown as producing dysfunction within the family, as in *The God Boy*, with its depiction of parents trapped in a loveless marriage, in which each partner blames the other for their unhappiness; a father who takes refuge in drinking and womanizing; and a joyless mother who finds compensation for her discontent in assuming a role as the enforcer of a restrictive puritan morality. Alternatively, or concomitantly, coming-of-age films show tyrannical social codes and cultural values generating pressures or expectations that inhibit the youthful protagonist's ability to become the self he or she would like to be. Frequently, the frustration or distress caused by these pressures propels the young person to 'act out,' whether mildly in the form of delinquency and transgressions (such as thieving and vandalism, as in *The God Boy* or *Hunt for the Wilderpeople*), or extremely (to the extent of committing violence, and even murder, as in *Heavenly Creatures*).

These twin themes – of family dysfunction on one hand, and oppressive belief systems and restrictive social codes on the other – recur in many of the films to follow. Marital infidelity, indifference, and discontent on the part of the parents precipitate a tragedy in *Rain* (2001), when the thirteen-year-old heroine Janey discovers her sexuality by seducing her mother's lover in a form of Oedipal competition. Tragedy similarly eventuates in *In My Father's Den* as the result of marital transgression, this time because of family secrets that a code of respectability will not allow to be spoken. This belief in the need to maintain the appearance of respectability – a secularized form of New Zealand puritanism – also provokes the horrific matricide in Peter Jackson's *Heavenly Creatures*, and is relentlessly satirized and demolished in the extreme violence of the same filmmaker's *Braindead* (1992).

Often, a preoccupation with sexuality – not as something to celebrate, but rather as the outcome of emotional disturbance, or a source of guilt or disillusionment – lies at the heart of these movies, as in the case of *Rain*, in which an Electra complex[9] in the teenage heroine, Janey, manifest in her determination to seduce her mother's lover, produces a tragedy when the young brother she was supposed to watch over drowns, leaving her with an intense mixture of grief and guilt. Similarly, in Vincent Ward's *Vigil* (1984), which also has a teenage protagonist who experiences a version of an Electra complex, the entry into puberty of the thirteen-year-old heroine, Toss, is associated with violence through the link between the sight of her menstrual blood on her fingers and the blood that spatters her face when Ethan, the stranger who takes her father's place, docks the tails of the lambs on the farm. Thus, even when religion is not explicitly present, there is often an association of sex with something sinful and illicit, through images of violence, in the national imaginary.

With Māori coming-of-age films and films on Māori subjects, the sources of perturbation are shown to be different. The sexism and patriarchal authoritarianism of traditional Māori culture provoke rebellion in the case of Paikea in *Whale Rider* and Simeon in *Mahana*, and parental abandonment or neglect is presented as a source of grief in *Boy* and *Hunt for the Wilderpeople*. In *Once Were Warriors*, this neglect eventuates in actual sexual abuse, when a family member rapes a teenage girl, which causes her to hang herself.

Although not foregrounded as a major theme, the legacy of colonial dispossession is shown to exert an influence on young Māori, producing an urban environment of poverty and abjection in *Once Were Warriors* from which young people seek to escape in various ways, and promoting a desire to embrace the culture of the Pākehā world as in *Boy*, or its learning as well as its culture in *Mahana*. Providing a counterpoint to these aspirations, certain values of traditional Māori culture (*aroha*, pride, a concern for the collectivity) are presented as offering a sustaining source of security and comfort in a world that otherwise would be experienced as having the potential to be destructive – seen, for example, in *Mauri* and *Once Were Warriors*.

Taken as a whole, the coming-of-age films made in New Zealand to date overwhelmingly emphasize the vulnerability of children to the unresolved issues of parents; to dysfunction within families; and to the effects of more general environmental factors such as oppressive social codes and cultural value systems, socio-economic deprivation, marginalization, and cultural dispossession. In response to such circumstances, adolescents are shown variously as acting out (in the form of various transgressive acts such as stealing, violence, or sex); turning inwards as a form of psychic retreat; taking refuge in a fantasy world; or simply seeking escape from emotional suffering by opting for suicide. Conversely, these films present young adults as flourishing when attachment relationships are restored, ameliorated, or replaced; when marginalization is countered by an affirmation of one's true identity; and when pride in one's culture and appreciation of its positive values acts as an antidote to social abjection, even if in certain respects it needs to be reformed.

It is the concentration on these recurrent themes that makes it a mistake to assume that the coming-of-age films in New Zealand's national cinema simply represent the importation of a standardized generic model derived from the American teen film, or that they are even primarily dealing with the same concerns. To the contrary, the concerns that these films address are local and specific, even though they may be embedded within a general process of human development that is timeless and universal.

Trends in the Evolution of the New Zealand Coming-of-age Film

As the first wave of New Zealand filmmakers in the late 1970s and the 1980s passed into the second wave of the 1990s, the emphasis of coming-of-age films shifted from the oppressiveness of the dominant culture into a new focus on individuals and groups (Māori, in particular) who perceived themselves as being marginalized because of their inability to conform to, or accept, its hegemonic norms.

In 1990, New Zealand celebrated the 150th anniversary of its founding as a colony, formalized in the Treaty of Waitangi, which was signed with the

Māori tribes in 1840. As this sesquicentennial approached, indigenous Māori New Zealanders began to reassert their own claims, and one can see signs of this emergent Māori nationalism in demands for an indigenous cinema, the principles of which the pioneering Māori filmmaker Barry Barclay delineated in his description of a 'Fourth Cinema.'[10] Barclay believed that every culture has a right and responsibility to present its own culture to its own people in ways that answer to its own values and needs, meaning that a Māori film needs to be 'made by Māori,' using Māori actors, and resisting 'Pākehā plots,' given that the latter inevitably reflect a different value system.[11] His theory was exemplified in Barclay's own *Ngati* (1987), the first feature film to be made by an indigenous filmmaker, which contains coming-of-age elements, and Merata Mita's *Mauri*, which depicts the entry into, and maturation within, the values of the indigenous culture in the experience of three generations of Māori women.

Another Māori director, Lee Tamahori, painted a less benign picture of Māori life in the second half of the twentieth century in *Once Were Warriors* by showing the harmful effects on three children of the realities of urban life – a dysfunctional family caught in the poverty trap; a violent, abusive father; a drunken, negligent mother; sexual abuse perpetrated by relatives – generating circumstances that propel the children variously into delinquency, gang membership, drug abuse, and suicide. *Once Were Warriors* is a Māori equivalent of *The God Boy*, except that the misery suffered by its young protagonists is more extreme owing to the physical violence that attends it.

On the Pākehā side, as the dominance of the normative Anglo-Celtic monoculture that had prevailed in New Zealand until the 1970s began to weaken, filmmakers started to use coming-of-age films as a vehicle for exploring marginalized characters, with the aim of liberating a new space for a greater diversity of gendered, sexual, and ethnic identities. *An Angel at My Table* (Jane Campion, 1990), adapted from Janet Frame's famous *Autobiography* (written between 1982 and 1984), presents a character passing through three stages of personal maturation whose hyper-shyness and sensitivity is so badly misconstrued that she is nearly subjected to a leucotomy (a surgical cutting of nerve fibers to alter the functioning of the brain). In the domain of sexual identity, Stewart Main's *50 Ways of Saying Fabulous* (2005), based on the novel by Graeme Aitken, is the first feature film to depict the trials of a boy in the process of discovering that he is gay.

After the turn of the new millennium, the focus shifted again, this time moving on to an updating and rewriting of the traditional cultural systems themselves, not only for Pākehā, but also for Māori. This trend is most clearly seen in the films that have been based on the novels of Witi Ihimaera: *Whale Rider*, which seeks to claim the right of a girl to leadership in the tribe that is normally reserved for males in traditional Māori culture; *Mahana*, which asserts the right of a teenage boy to resist the patriarchal bullying and cultural expectations of his grandfather, in order to be free to follow his own inclinations and interests; and *Nights in the Gardens of Spain*, a post-adolescence coming-out film in which Kawariki decides to accept, and be open about, his homosexuality, despite its prohibition in traditional Māori culture.

A significant development apparent in the evolution of the New Zealand coming-of-age film is a marked movement towards stories that adopt a bicultural perspective, or else explore the effects of growing up as a member of an ethnic group in what is becoming an increasingly multicultural society. In the first category, Taika Waititi's two coming-of-age films, *Boy* and *The Hunt for the Wilderpeople*, are the outstanding examples, with the latter providing a symbolic figuration that virtually encapsulates the history of race relations between Māori and Pākehā generally. Other films attest to the emergence of other ethnic groups; for example, *My Wedding and Other Secrets* (Roseanne Liang, 2011), which presents the Romeo-and-Juliet-type experience of a Chinese New Zealand girl who tries to negotiate the difficulties attending her determination to marry her Pākehā boyfriend against the wishes of her disapproving Chinese parents, and *Apron Strings* (Sima Urale, 2008), which deals with the experience of an Indian Muslim family.

In general, one might say that the spectrum of New Zealand coming-of-age movies, approached chronologically, and viewed as a whole, reflects the historical evolution of the nation's sense of the identities that compose it, and hence of the country as a society at large. The configuration of the diverse elements to be found in these films, together with the ways in which they are combined, establishes a distinctive local specificity, even though the themes with which they deal are in certain respects universal. Their stories manifest an equally distinctive sensibility that is, by turns, quirky, often dark, irreverent, and frequently leavened with humor, whether comic or sardonic. Above all, these films are almost invariably informed by the extraordinarily powerful emotional impact of the New Zealand landscape itself – to which almost all writers and filmmakers attest – which is invoked as a mirror for the representation of the intense interior experiences that their protagonists undergo.

In the chapters that follow, my aim will be to analyze how the New Zealand coming-of-age films under consideration exemplify the characteristics and explore the preoccupations identified above. This will involve looking at how generic elements are handled, particularly how genres, including elements of Hollywood genres, are mixed in the cinematic treatment of local stories, and what that mixing implies in terms of the vision of each film. It will also mean looking at the personal dimension that informs each representation, and how these personal investments contribute to the creation of a distinctively Kiwi flavor in these films. In analyzing each film, I will pay close attention to the cinematic style, and how it is used as a vector for the expression of distinctive masculine and feminine subjectivities – especially through its choice of shots and camera movements, as well as the ways in which landscape is exploited for purposes of symbolic figuration.

Because most New Zealand coming-of-age films are adaptations, this book will investigate the relationship between the source novel and the film that is based on it, identifying any changes that have occurred in the process of adaptation. The reason for this investigation is to make it possible to speculate on the significance of such changes in terms of the cinematic auteur's vision relative to that of the original author, and the relevance of the adaptation to the circumstances in the contemporary world in which it is produced. Such analyses will show that where an adaptation remains close to its literary source, the closeness of the relationship reflects a desire on the part of the auteur to propagate the myth embedded in the original (as, for example, in Reece's adaptation of Cross' *The God Boy*). In contrast, it will be shown that where there are significant changes to the source (as in McGann's adaptation of Gee's *In My Father's Den*), these changes reflect a desire to update or modify the myth in the source novel.

Although the list of films discussed in this volume is fairly comprehensive, it is still necessarily selective because of the constraints of space. In making the selection, I have chosen films that have either been chosen for inclusion in international film festivals; or because they have achieved notable success at the New Zealand box office; or because they are historically important in the evolution of the genre in New Zealand. Viewed as a collectivity, these films constitute a local 'geography' of cultural identities as they have evolved during the course of this nation's history since the 1970s. In particular, they show how gendered identities have been constructed in response to specific local discourses and cultural pressures, and how the subjective self-sense and self-experience of young New Zealand males and females has been generated in response to local circumstances. Finally, for those who are interested in world cinema, this book, by exploring and elucidating such issues, will furnish a case study that illuminates the role and dynamics of coming-of-age movies in the context of any national cinema at large.

Notes

1. Vincent Ward, *Edge of the Earth: Stories and Images from the Antipodes* (Auckland: Heinemann Reed, 1990), 70.
2. See Helen Martin and Sam Edwards, *New Zealand Film 1912–1996* (Auckland: Oxford University Press, 1997), 60.
3. See Bruce Babington, 'Boom Times: The Early 1980s,' in Diane Pivac (ed.) with Frank Stark and Lawrence McDonald, *New Zealand Film: An Illustrated History* (Wellington: Te Papa Press, 2011), 181–2.
4. See Ian Conrich and Stuart Murray (eds), *New Zealand Filmmakers* (Detroit: Wayne State University Press, 2007), 135–7.
5. For a description of this film, see Martin and Edwards, 70.

6. See Alistair Fox, *Jane Campion: Authorship and Personal Cinema* (Bloomington and Indianapolis: Indiana University Press, 2011), 88–93.
7. The actor Sam Neill makes this point in his documentary on New Zealand film, *Cinema of Unease: A Personal Journey of Sam Neill* (Sam Neill and Judy Rymer, 1995).
8. For a more detailed exposition of New Zealand puritanism, see Alistair Fox, *The Ship of Dreams: Masculinity in Contemporary New Zealand Fiction* (Dunedin: Otago University Press, 2008), 15–18.
9. The Electra complex was a concept identified by C. G. Jung to refer to 'the phenomenon of the little girl's attraction to her father and hostility towards her mother, whom she now sees as her rival.' See Jill Scott, *Electra after Freud: Myth and Culture* (Ithaca, NY: Cornell University Press, 2005), 8–9.
10. Barry Barclay, *Our Own Image: A Story of a Māori Filmmaker* (Minneapolis and London: University of Minnesota Press, 2015; originally published Auckland: Longman Paul, 1990).
11. Ibid., 20, 48.

PART 2

THE NEW ZEALAND NEW WAVE: 1976–89

3. THE FORMATION OF A BUDDING MAN ALONE: *THE GOD BOY* (MURRAY REECE, 1976)

Murray Reece's adaptation of Ian Cross' critically acclaimed novel *The God Boy* (1957) appeared on New Zealand screens in 1976, and is the first genuine coming-of-age film made in this country. Even though it did not achieve a theatrical release – it was the first television feature of the newly formed national network Television One, and is now no longer readily accessible other than online at the internet site, *NZ On Screen*[1] – it is historically important for a number of reasons. First, it showed a new generation of New Zealanders that their own stories could not only be entertaining when dramatized on the screen, but also that they were capable of bringing to light, and addressing, the most complex and challenging aspects of their existence in a distinctive, evolving culture. Second, *The God Boy* exemplifies the ongoing legacy of some of the major themes that had dominated New Zealand literary fiction since the 1930s.

These themes have been meticulously detailed by the literary scholar Lawrence Jones, and by social historians, such as Jock Phillips:[2] the dominance of 'puritan' moral values, whether religiously imposed or imposed in a displaced secular form;[3] a form of Stoicism manifest in a valorization of the necessity for steadfastness, self-reliance, and self-improvement (which were reinforced by the need to settle a new country); and an inculcated fear of worldly temptations, such as sex and other expressions of the senses or emotions that could make a man 'soft' or a 'sissy' – and hence unworthy of assuming the status of an effective provider or protector in the circumstances of the infant nation, separated from its mother country by the greatest geographical (but not cultural) distance it was possible to imagine.

In the literature of the inter-war period and the first two decades of the post-Second World War period, issues of this sort were reflected in a preoccupation with the family as the locus of the discontent and destructive psychological consequences that they generated. Numerous novels depicted the experience of children growing up in dysfunctional families: with fathers who had abdicated their responsibilities, partly because of the effects of the Great Depression, which had deprived many of them of their earning power or jobs, and hence their status within the family; and mothers who had, of necessity, turned into – in Lawrence Jones' words – 'terrible puritan mums,' owing to their need to keep a tight rein on the family's expenditure, and act as an upholder and enforcer of standards (moral and practical) in the face of the father's dereliction of any immediate responsibility, and his tendency to seek refuge in alcohol and homosocial male bonding at the local pub on his way home from work (if he were indeed employed).[4]

By 1976, when Murray Reece, an Englishman who had immigrated to New Zealand when he was fourteen years of age, was given the resources to make the first television drama in New Zealand's history, this ethos was still very much present in the national imaginary. John Mulgan had given expression in his novel *Man Alone* (1939) to a feeling of alienation and psychological isolation experienced by many men as a result of the puritanical oppressiveness of New Zealand society, and this figure of the alienated outsider was to recur so frequently in New Zealand literature that it would become regarded almost as an archetype.[5] Other novelists, like Frank Sargeson in *I Saw in My Dream* (1949), or Maurice Gee in *In My Father's Den* (1972), had explored the destructive effects of puritan repression and guilt. The most powerful depiction of all, however, had been Ian Cross' novel, *The God Boy*, published in 1957, which presented a harrowing image of the consequences of puritanism combined with the effects of family dysfunction in the emotional suffering of a pre-teen boy.

Ian Cross, born in Masterton in the Wairarapa district of the North Island in 1925, had spent his early adult years as a reporter for *The Dominion* (1943–56), the main newspaper of Wellington, the capital city in New Zealand. During this time, he had reported on a Wellington Supreme Court murder trial in 1944 involving a thirteen-year-old boy from a farm in the Wairarapa who had walked back from the cowshed one day, pointed a rifle through the kitchen window, and killed his mother, wounding his sister during the same assault.[6] This episode provided the germ of the novel that Reece adapted as the film under discussion.

A Dysfunctional Family

The story Cross presents in *The God Boy* concerns the experience of an eleven-year-old boy, Jimmy Sullivan, over a three-day period during which tensions between his parents reach breaking point, ending in the murder of his father by his mother. What leads to this catastrophic event is the mutual hatred that has developed between the couple, each of whom displays the attributes of stereotypical mothers and fathers depicted in New Zealand novels from the 1930s onward. Their relationship is summed up in the words of the father as he is walking home from work, with his son, near the beginning of the movie: 'Home we go to our loving wife and mother and one more round in the heavyweight championship of the world.'[7] The pair in this couple are presented as always nagging away at each other, each accusing the other of having ruined their lives. He repeatedly tells his son that he was a wealthy man until the Depression came, and that Jimmy's mother has 'given me rotten luck and smashed me down.' To find solace, he has turned to drink, prophesying to Jimmy that 'when you grow up, you'll probably find that all the decency in life you can find is in a bar, drinking with a few friends, real friends.'[8] There are also hints that he is conducting an affair, being frequently absent from the home. She, on the other hand, constantly shames her husband as a 'drunken pig,' jeering at his lack of success in the world, and complaining to her son behind his father's back that her husband does not earn enough money. Her discontent with her life causes her to retreat into depression and a joyless puritanism, which is reflected, for example, in her obsessive concern with her son's cleanliness, her disapproval of her daughter Molly's use of lipstick, and her condemnation of the fashionable floral dress the latter wears during a visit. The negative state of mind into which the mother has sunk is shown, in flashback, to have prompted her to procure an illegal abortion for which the father has never forgiven her, leaving the marital relationship in a state of damage that is beyond repair.

The effect on the boy of the fighting and mutual recrimination between his parents is emotionally traumatic. As he confides to Bloody Jack, a loner he recurrently meets on the wharf when the old man is fishing, the discord in the home makes Jimmy 'feel terrible,' prompting Jack to observe that 'you're always wandering around like a lost lamb.'[9] At school, Jimmy cannot concentrate, and gets into fights with other boys in the playground. When the situation at home deteriorates after the father spends money on a new bike for Jimmy, incurring the disapproval of his wife, and Jimmy receives no help from the priest to whom he confesses, he erupts into a spree of vandalism, throwing stones and hurling abuse at an old woman pensioner, smashing the window of a fruiterer's shop, and attacking Bloody Jack with stones, screaming 'I'm going to bash you to pieces.'[10] In short, the film shows how the misery Jimmy feels at his perception that his parents 'hate each other' builds up a pressure of emotional tension that has nowhere to escape except through acting out expressed in transgression.

For Jimmy, these tensions deriving from family dysfunction are compounded

Figure 3.1 Jimmy (Jamie Higgens) listens through the wall to his parents fighting in *The God Boy* (dir. Murray Reece, 1976).

by another source of psychic pressure: the harsh, religious beliefs that are pitilessly drilled into him by the nuns who teach at the Catholic school he attends. Their doctrine is summed up in the homily with which Sister Angela berates him when she upbraids him for being inattentive in class:

> There is a God in Heaven and a Devil in Hell and there is a constant battle going on for the possession of our immortal souls. The Devil fights to get the souls of little boys, too, you know, so that he can take them down to Hell and keep them there forever and forever.
> [. . .]
> Sometimes the Devil peers out of your eyes for other people to see, Jimmy. Sometimes the Devil takes possession of a person and makes that person neglect his work and get into mischief. The Devil makes you commit little sins until you have no conscience left to call on God. The Devil hates a clever little boy doing well at school, and he tries to make him neglect his lessons. The Devil hates to see a little boy doing well at school, he tries to make him neglect his lessons, and the Devil hates to see a good child of God not getting into mischief, so he tries to make him a bad boy of his own, who gets into all kinds of mischief.
> [. . .]

> Yes, Jimmy. [. . .] You are not the nice little boy that came to this school when you were six years old. Each year you have drifted a little further away from God.[11]

This relentless erosion of the boy's sense of self-worth by his religious instructors, whose egregious lack of insight into the real causes of his behavior means that they are unable to help him, leaves him in a perpetual state of anxiety accompanied by a profound sense of guilt that somehow he is responsible for his parents' unhappiness. We see this after Jimmy's mother has turned herself in to the police following the murder of her husband; when Jimmy is allowed to see her one last time before she is taken away to prison, he says: 'It's all because of me, isn't it? It's my fault, isn't it?'[12]

In an attempt to avoid being overwhelmed by such feelings, Jimmy tries to suppress them by having recourse to several 'prevention tricks': washing his hands under scalding hot water, and singing 'Jingle Bells,' or his father's wartime song, 'It's a Long Way to Tipperary.' After the catastrophe has occurred, and Jimmy has been placed in an orphanage, he takes refuge in a psychic retreat consisting of simple disavowal, as we see exemplified in the ending of the movie in his denial of his true feelings.

Some early critics of the novel asserted that 'the religious and clinical-psychological aspects of the novel are not convincingly blended,'[13] but in the light of more recent psychoanalytic insights into the effects on individual subjects of authoritarian religious doctrines – especially those based on a conviction of the corrupting power of Satan – both the novel and the cinematic adaptation of it seem very plausible in presenting the way familial dysfunction and oppressive religious beliefs intersect to wreak the havoc in the boy's mental equilibrium that this story presents. Indeed, this destructive nexus continued to be shown time and again by the New Zealand novelists who came after Cross, most notably by Maurice Gee in *In My Father's Den* and *The Plumb Trilogy*, which expose how New Zealand Presbyterianism could be equally destructive of the mental wellbeing of children whose parents were determined to enforce their notion of 'godliness' and the morality that sprang from it.[14]

The Style and Enunciation of Reece's Adaptation

One of the most striking aspects of the film version of *The God Boy* is how closely it adheres to the vision of the original source. Much of the dialogue, for instance, is lifted directly from Ian Cross' novel, with only a small amount of cutting and tightening on the part of the director, Murray Reece, and the scriptwriter, the actor Ian Mune (who would feature prominently, both as actor and director, in a number of the New Zealand New Wave films to come). Apart from this minor tinkering, the only other significant changes to the source were a simplification of the elaborate narrative structure of Cross' novel, which had involved multiple flashbacks, and an alteration of Jimmy's condition of awareness concerning his mother's violent act. Instead of replicating Cross' narrative, which constantly oscillates between Jimmy's perspective as a thirteen-year-old and episodes that present his subjective experience of the events that had taken place two years earlier when he was eleven, Reece and Mune, who collaborated in drafting the script,[15] presented the action as a single sequential narrative taking place in the present, with only a brief indication at the beginning of the film that the story is, in fact, an extended flashback, a brief flashback showing Jimmy's memory of encountering a fat woman coming down the stairs after she had performed an abortion on his mother, and two montage sequences containing disturbing images from Jimmy's memories of incidents that have occurred in the recent past. The only substantive change to the content is that whereas in the novel we learn that Jimmy knows his mother killed his father, in the film he remains ignorant of the real reason for his father's disappearance, which intensifies his sense of abandonment, and hence deepens the pathos of the film's ending.

We are thus presented with a cinematic adaptation that, rather than engaging in a substantive reauthoring of the source to transform it into a vehicle for new preoccupations, shows the filmmaker acting simply as a *metteur-en-scène*, rather than as the kind of auteur one associates with personal cinema. But what a superb mise-en-scène it is! In 1973, Reece had gone to Europe to study film, television, and theater on a Queen Elizabeth II Arts Council grant,[16] and it was undoubtedly at this time, if not earlier, that he was exposed to the films of the French New Wave. Certainly, *The God Boy* displays the lasting influence of the *ur*-coming-of-age film, Truffaut's *The 400 Blows*, in several respects. Reece exploits the Truffauldian device of the freeze frame, made famous by the final shot of *The 400 Blows*, on two occasions, both showing the anguished boy being restrained by representatives of the church following episodes in which he has been acting out to evacuate his psychic perturbation – the first near the beginning of the film, where two nuns restrain him from fighting other boys in the playground, and the second near the end of the film when Father Gilligan restrains him after Jimmy learns that something has gone wrong at home. Such freeze frames are designed to focus attention on the boy's inner state of mind.

Also reminiscent of *The 400 Blows* are the scenes set in the classroom, in which Jimmy is shown being punished for inattention, and is regularly detained after all the other children have gone out, just as Antoine Doinel is. Reece even replicates Truffaut's use of a long tracking shot to place us within Jimmy's sensibility, when he is shown cycling furiously after discovering that his father's gift of a bicycle has precipitated a new intensity of marital discord between his parents – a shot that recalls the long sequence shot that accompanies Antoine Doinel as he runs towards the sea, trying to escape the juvenile correction center in which he has been detained.

In other respects, Reece's shooting style reflects a very imaginative and skilled attempt to reproduce the subjective point of view that was so powerfully rendered in Ian Cross' first-person literary narrative. Rather than maintaining a level eye-line, as in classical shooting style, Reece includes many low-angle shots, and a number of high-angle shots, that induce a feeling in the spectator that he or she is not seeing from within an ordinary perspective. One striking example occurs early in the film when – to express his distress after his father stalks away to spend the night elsewhere (presumably with a mistress) after having learnt his wife has been bad-mouthing him to his son – Jimmy hurls his satchel skyward at God, crying 'You dirty bastard!'

An even more strikingly contrived low-angle shot occurs in the classroom when Sister Angela decides to strap Jimmy for his inattention. In this shot, the low angle, combined with a deep-focus lens, generates a metaphorical relationship between the three elements within the frame:[17] Jimmy's hand, vulnerably extended to receive pain; the punitive agent of religion, with her arm upraised to thrash him with a strap; and a portrait of Christ in the background, pointing to his bleeding heart. This image thus symbolically captures the way that an oppressive religious code intervenes to impede Jimmy's access to the compassion displayed by Jesus – with whose suffering on the cross Jimmy will come to identify – at the same time as it inflicts a painful punishment on him for a distraction that owes its origin to a situation for which he is not responsible. In combination with point-of-view sequences (consisting of a looking shot, a POV shot, and then a reaction shot), the shooting style thus places us very close to Jimmy, making us see things as he sees them.

A number of additional shooting devices take us still further into the reality of Jimmy's emotional experience. On several occasions, a close-up shot of Jimmy's contorted face becomes superimposed upon a picture of Jesus with his sacred heart through the use of a dissolve. Similarly, a slow zoom in to a close-up on Jimmy's face as he listens to his father's drunken ramblings on the night of the murder invites the spectator to recognize Jimmy's feeling of hopelessness as he registers the broken state of the man who should be his model and protector. Finally, Reece uses an expressionistic style with surrealistic effects (achieved through a phantasmagorical montage that recalls Ingmar Bergman, and the use of extreme wide-angle lenses)[18] to suggest the emotional disturbance that expresses itself in Jimmy's nightmares.

Apart from the shooting style, Reece exploits a number of figurative strategies to convey the boy's inner emotions – recurring motifs, actions, and episodes that punctuate the narrative at regular intervals, usually following an incident that causes Jimmy distress. We are repeatedly shown images of Jimmy washing his hands under hot water; close-up portraits of Jesus and his sacred heart; and images of Jimmy receding down the hallway in the family home, with his arms outspread as if extended on the Cross.

Figure 3.2 Jimmy (Jamie Higgens) about to be strapped by a nun (Judie Douglass) in *The God Boy* (dir. Murray Reece, 1976).

Near the end of the film, once Jimmy has become aware that something serious has happened between his parents, these suggested images of a crucifixion reach their apotheosis in a fantasmatic image in which Jimmy imagines himself actually nailed to the Cross. Both in its style and mode of enunciation, therefore, Reece's film of *The God Boy* achieves a fidelity to Cross' original vision of the suffering caused to the boy by his experience of dysfunction within the family that is nothing short of remarkable.

The Outcome of Jimmy's Coming of Age

All coming-of-age films deal with formative events that invite the protagonist to engage in, or precipitate, a growth towards maturity. A distinctive feature of New Zealand coming-of-age films is how often they show a coming-of-age outcome that leaves the protagonist in a condition that is problematic or undesirable. This failure to attain a kind of maturity that promotes a feeling of wellbeing can be observed at the conclusion of *The God Boy*. When his sister Molly comes to visit him in the orphanage in which he has been placed, one of the nuns tells Molly that he is a good boy – a model child, always top of his class, which, in its extreme contrast with what Sister Angela had said to him in the classroom several years earlier, suggests that, in the eyes of the

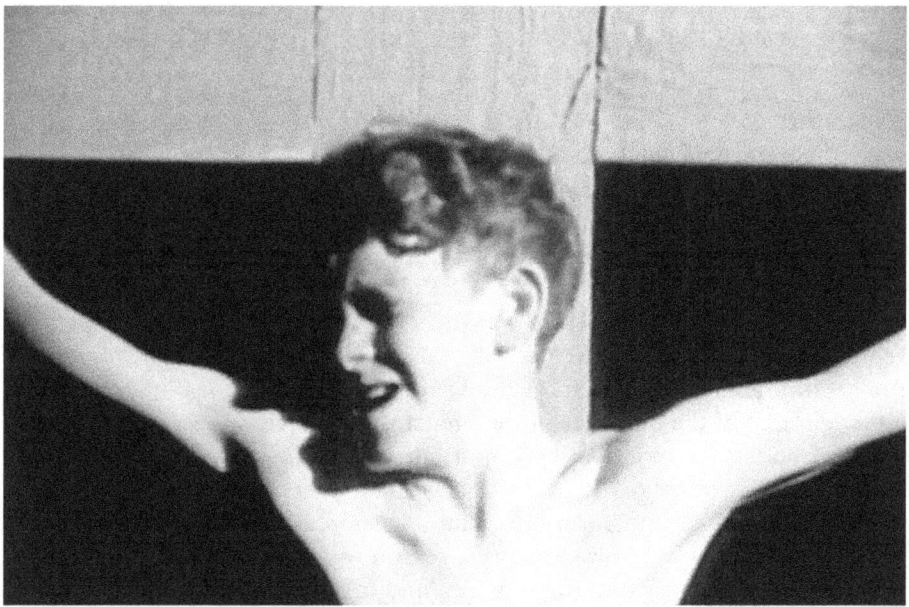

Figure 3.3 Jimmy (Jamie Higgens) on the Cross in *The God Boy* (dir. Murray Reece, 1976).

Church, he has been successfully 'reformed.' The reality, however, is very different, as we learn when the film suddenly cuts to a shot of Jimmy praying in a chapel, when he silently says to himself: 'Our Father who art in Heaven, . . . I think you're a pain in the neck!' What this contrast between outward appearances and the inner reality shows is that Jimmy's rectitude is the result of a constructed persona through which he presents himself stoically to the world. Jimmy, we see, has simply turned inward as yet another 'prevention trick' to deny the reality of what he actually thinks and feels, even to himself. This split within his own self-sense is reflected in the very last words he utters, addressed to the nun as the film ends: 'I'm all right Sister, you don't have to worry about me. I'm strong.' In this final view of Jimmy, one catches a glimpse of the typically stoical, self-contained, inward, New Zealand Man Alone – alienated from the reality of his own suppressed emotional life – that he is inevitably destined to become. Jimmy, as a Boy Alone, like other Man Alone characters who recur in New Zealand fictive representations, is trapped within a 'false self,' to use the terminology of the child psychiatrist D. W. Winnicott.[19] As such, he exemplifies a syndrome that would characterize the emotional life of many New Zealand males, younger and older, through much of the twentieth century.[20]

The God Boy as a Point of Reference for Subsequent Coming-of-age Films

As indicated at the beginning of this chapter, *The God Boy* is a very useful way of commencing this investigation into the coming-of-age genre in New Zealand cinema because it provides a convenient reference point against which subsequent films can be measured, both in terms of style and content. As far as content is concerned, it foreshadows a recurrent concern with the effects of dysfunctional families on the psychic life of a pubescent child, along with the social conditions and discourses that promote those dysfunctions – especially repressive value systems, whether religiously derived, or inherited from traditional cultural attitudes. As far as film style is concerned, the film also reveals a first glimpse of the influence of the French New Wave.

Nevertheless, in several very important respects, *The God Boy* diverges from what was to follow. Conspicuously missing is any attempt on the part of the filmmaker to transform or update the source so as to transform it into a vehicle for personal expression. One reason for this may have been that by the time Reece immigrated to New Zealand in 1957, at the age of fourteen, his own perspectives on the world had already been formed elsewhere, and in response to different social circumstances and a different cultural ethos compared with those depicted in Cross' novel. Reece himself confessed as much when he admitted that 'he found it an advantage to have been living outside New Zealand at Jimmy's age because it meant he could look at that period [that is, 1949, the year in which the film is set] with an outsider's point of view.'[21] Not having experienced at first hand the culture in which Cross' Jimmy grew up, Reece felt free to realize it disinterestedly, exploiting the potential of cinematic narrative language to create an empathic identification with Jimmy, without feeling any need to invest his personal experience overtly in the character through changes to the source. A similar degree of disinterestedness is apparent in *The Scarecrow* (1982) directed by Sam Pillsbury, another filmmaker who immigrated to New Zealand in his teens. (This film will be discussed in Chapter 5.) In the case of coming-of-age films made by native-born-and-raised New Zealand filmmakers, the source novel, if there is one, which is almost always, is routinely relocated to the period of their own childhood. Commensurately, substantive changes to the source invariably show the filmmaker transforming it through the inclusion of material derived from their personal biographical experience. This is what makes the coming-of-age film such a valuable source of evidence regarding a nation's culture: their shifting preoccupations, when traced chronologically, attest to the evolution of the society as a whole.

Notes

1. *The God Boy* can be viewed at https://www.nzonscreen.com/title/the-god-boy-1976, accessed 27 May 2016.
2. See Lawrence Jones, *Barbed Wire & Mirrors: Essays on New Zealand Prose* (Dunedin: Otago University Press, 1987), and Jock Phillips, *A Man's Country?: The Image of the Pakeha Male – A History* (Auckland: Penguin, 1987).
3. See Alistair Fox, *The Ship of Dreams: Masculinity in Contemporary New Zealand Fiction* (Dunedin: Otago University Press, 2008), 15–16.
4. See R. W. Chapman, 'Fiction and the Social Pattern; Some Implications of Recent Writing,' *Landfall* 7:1 (1953), 26–58.
5. See Robert Chapman, 'Fiction and the Social Pattern: Some Implications of Recent N. Z. Writing,' *Landfall* 7:1 (1953), 26–58; and Lawrence Jones, 'Man Alone,' in Roger Robinson and Nelson Wattie (eds), *The Oxford Companion to New Zealand Literature* (Melbourne: Oxford University Press, 1998), 331–2.
6. These details are recounted by Brian McDonnell, '*The God Boy*: Adaptation from Novel to TV Film. Part 1: Ian Cross's Novel,' *New Zealand Journal of Media Studies* 6:1 (1999), 61–9.
7. Ian Cross, *The God Boy* (Christchurch: Whitcombe & Tombs, 1972 [1957]), 15.
8. Ibid., 17.
9. Ibid., 48.
10. Ibid., 116.
11. Ibid., 98–9.
12. Ibid., 157.
13. See Joan Stevens, 'Introduction,' in Ian Cross, *The God Boy* (Christchurch: Whitcombe & Tombs, 1972), 10.
14. See Fox, *Ship of Dreams*, Chapters 2, 3.
15. See Brian McDonnell, '*The God Boy*: Adaptation from Novel to TV Film. Part 1: Ian Cross's Novel,' *New Zealand Journal of Media Studies* 6:1 (1999), 61–9.
16. 'Murray Reece, Director,' *NZ On Screen*, https://www.nzonscreen.com/person/murray-reece/biography, accessed 30 May 2016.
17. See McDonnell, '*The God Boy*: Adaptation from Novel to TV Film. Part 2,' 13.
18. See McDonnell, '*The God Boy*: Adaptation from Novel to TV Film. Part 2,' 13.
19. See D. W. Winnicott, 'Ego Distortion in Terms of True and False Self,' in D. W. Winnicott, *The Maturational Process and the Facilitating Environment: Studies in the Theory of Emotional Development* (New York: International Universities Press, 1965), 140–57.
20. See Fox, 'The Inward Man,' in *The Ship of Dreams*, Chapter 4, 71–84.
21. McDonnell, '*The God Boy*: Adaptation from Novel to TV Film. Part 2,' 6.

4. AN ANGRY YOUNG MAN SEEKS TO JUSTIFY HIMSELF: *SLEEPING DOGS* (ROGER DONALDSON, 1977)[1]

One year after *The God Boy* was screened on New Zealand television, the next major movie to be locally produced, *Sleeping Dogs* (Roger Donaldson, 1977), was launched in cinemas around the country and instantly became a box office hit. As Jonathan Dowling, a New Zealand producer, has observed, the film 'almost single-handedly created a climate of acceptance within the country for a Kiwi film industry.'[2] Even in the USA, where the film was released in 1982, it was critically acclaimed. The reviewer for the weekly American entertainment trade magazine *Variety*, for example, wrote: '*Sleeping Dogs* has sharp directional flair evident, particularly in the action segments, taut performances by the large cast and a handsome technical gloss in all departments.'[3] New Zealand feature-filmmaking had thus arrived, and *Sleeping Dogs* – the success of which encouraged the formation of the New Zealand Film Commission in 1978, which has provided funding for most of the local films made since – can justifiably be regarded as inaugurating the New Zealand New Wave.

More importantly for the purposes of this study, it announces the advent of a new mode of filmmaking – one that would characterize many of the coming-of-age films that would be made in the years to come. First, it exemplifies a new approach to the adaptation of a literary source. Rather than functioning simply as a *metteur-en-scène*, as Murray Reece had done with *The God Boy*, Roger Donaldson seized upon his literary source, C. K. Stead's novel *Smith's Dream* (1971, revised 1973), for its potential to be rewrought in ways that transformed it into a vehicle for personal expression, self-discovery, and even self-justification. He thus approaches the material from the perspective of an auteur who has selected it because of its latent capacity to be converted into a vehicle for personal cinema. Second, it displays the incursion of a globalized American youth culture into the experience of young Antipodeans, along with the influence of the American New Wave that flourished briefly between the mid-1960s and the mid-1970s.[4] Thus, whereas Reece's *The God Boy* shows the influence of the French New Wave and European directors like François Truffaut and Ingmar Bergman directly, *Sleeping Dogs* exemplifies that influence as refracted through the New Hollywood, especially in the forms in which it was hybridized with American genres. The effect of these new influences is to create a film that is very different in its style and complexion from *The God Boy*, and one that sets up a rival tradition for the New Zealand coming-of-age movie – one that would spectacularly find an ongoing life in Taika Waititi's reworking of Barry Crump's novel *Wild Pork and Watercress* as *Hunt for the Wilderpeople* (2016).

For the rest of this chapter, I will delineate the process of transformation and the generic features that make Donaldson's *Sleeping Dogs* an exercise in the making of a post-adolescent coming-of-age film, as well as turning it into the prototype for an alternative route for filmmaking in the coming-of-age genre as realized in the context of New Zealand's national cinema.

Sleeping Dogs: A Coming-of-age Film?

Even though the protagonist of *Sleeping Dogs* is a young married man, the film is, in fact, a coming-of-age film, but in a somewhat less obvious way than in films with younger protagonists. In outward appearance, *Sleeping Dogs* is a political thriller set in a dystopian state that is hybridized with several other American cinematic genres: the action film, the adventure film, and the buddy film. Within this hybrid mix, however, there is embedded a strong coming-of-age element that was entirely absent from the literary source.

In her analysis of the coming-of-age genre from a screenwriter's perspective, Julie Selbo emphasizes how personal maturation can take place in it at any age. All coming-of-age tales, she says, explore the idea that despite impediments to change, change is possible. Invariably, such tales examine character-changes that are precipitated by life-changing events.[5] In the case of *Sleeping Dogs*, Roger Donaldson transforms the original story into a coming-of-age fiction by investing it with elements drawn from his own life story. In the process, he completely reverses the intention and vision of Stead's novel, reshaping it into a film that expresses the prevailing sense among the members of his generation of a need to resist the preceding social order. As such, the film gives voice to the perspective of young people born in the aftermath of the Second World War – the so-called 'baby boomers' – in order to point towards the possibility of a different kind of future. At the same time as the protagonist of Donaldson's film comes of age in terms of perception and emotional self-realization, he points towards a future possibility in terms of social conditions that Smithy (the protagonist) can only dream of in the diegetic circumstances in which the film is set – which approximate to those of the New Zealand and the Australia (where Donaldson was born) of the filmmaker.

The Film's Relation to *Smith's Dream*, the Source Novel

Donaldson and his scriptwriters, Ian Mune and Arthur Baysting, based *Sleeping Dogs* on *Smith's Dream*, a novel by Karl Stead first published in 1971, and then reissued with a revised, more tragic ending in 1973. This work was brought to Donaldson's attention by a friend, Bob Harvey, who picked up a copy in Wellington Airport.[6] Stead's novel tells the story of a conventional New Zealander, named 'Smith,' who seeks to 'escape political and social responsibility by getting away and being a 'Man Alone' in the bush.'[7] Smith, whose very name, in its commonness, signifies his function as an Everyman, had lived a fairly complacent and untroubled life prior to the events that precipitate the action of the novel:

> He had married young, but not before a quarter acre section had been bought. And within a year of the wedding (church and family, group portraits, breakfast and honeymoon) he had raised the usual mortgage and built the standard suburban bungalow. Perhaps what surprised him most was the belated recognition that, observing the customs and rituals outwardly, without conviction, he had nevertheless achieved an inward tranquillity, remaining in one job and faithful to his wife throughout the eight years of his marriage.[8]

Smith's complacency is rocked, however, when his wife informs him that she is in love with another man, who turns out to be his friend Bullen, a teacher, subsequently running off with him, together with Smith's and her two children. Suddenly, finding himself alone as a result of his domestic crisis, Smith decides to opt out of his job at the library, sell his house, and leave Auckland to 'follow his dream,' which is to live an 'idyllic' life on a remote island in the Coromandel, in an attempt to achieve a 'rest from thought, from regret, from himself.'[9]

Apart from adopting flight as a response to the breakdown of his marriage, Smith is also seeking to evade having to think about the national crisis that is escalating in the wider world, where a larger breakdown is occurring at national level because of a creeping totalitarianism made possible by a perception being fostered by the Government that New Zealand was being 'threatened economically and even, it seemed, militarily,' owing to the relentless advance of communism through South-East Asia, 'its slant eyes fixed on fertile acres we no longer knew what to do with or how to defend.'[10] Despite his repeated attempts simply to opt out of involvement in these political issues, Smith discovers, to his dismay, that they continue to catch up with him: first, when he is arrested as a suspected member of the resistance on his island retreat; then when he becomes involuntarily embroiled in the guerrillas' plan to massacre American Special Forces billeted at Buck's Motel, which shatters the comfortable new identity he had forged for himself as 'Buck,' the manager of the motel; and, finally and most ironically, at the moment at the end of the novel when he is feeling most 'hopeful, confident,' having abandoned the other members of the resistance, only to be shot dead by a former classmate when he emerges from the hut in which he has sought refuge.[11]

As will be clear from this outline, Stead's purpose in the novel was not only to warn against the dangers to democracy of right-wing political tendencies manifest in the support of the New Zealand National Government of the day for the American war in Vietnam, but also to denounce the irresponsibility of those, like Smith, who foolishly believed they could afford to ignore the threat posed by these tendencies. Stead's Smith is in no way a hero; to the contrary, he is presented as an anti-hero whose attitudes and responses are to be viewed critically, not emulated.

In adapting *Smith's Dream* from the page to the screen, even though they followed the basic outline of the story, Donaldson and his scriptwriters altered Stead's work almost beyond recognition. Describing his response to the novel, Donaldson acknowledges the excitement it aroused in him: 'It was about everything I was interested in – it was about relationships; it was about politics; it potentially had action.'[12] From this statement, one can see that what engaged Donaldson's interest was the potential of the story to be overwritten by the concerns of a member of the baby-boomer generation, imbued with the values and the counter-culture of the 1960s and 1970s (Donaldson was born in 1945), rather than adhering to the perspectives of the previous generation, which had been expressed in the novel (Stead was born in 1932). Donaldson, in effect, had seen the opportunity to replace Stead's original intent with a new one that answered to the impulses of his own different generation, as well as addressing personal issues of his own. In the process, he turned the character of the protagonist inside out.

The Generic Rewriting of the Story

The most obvious changes Donaldson made to the novel were to add a set of new episodes embodying tropes drawn from American cinema, and to transform the main character, Smith, from being a nondescript, unimpressive anti-hero into an alienated, angry young man who is searching for his soul

Figure 4.1 A youthful Roger Donaldson on location during the filming of *Sleeping Dogs* (dir. Roger Donaldson, 1977).

and self. Consequently, instead of being a victim of the self-delusion that had led to the death of Stead's protagonist, Donaldson's reconceived young protagonist emerges as a tragic hero who is determined to assert his independent identity, even though this may be at the cost of his own life. To distinguish Donaldson's hero from Stead's anti-hero, I shall henceforth refer to the former by the diminutive 'Smithy,' which is the name by which he is addressed by his friends in the film.

As many critics have noted, the film incorporates many elements from 'American New Wave' movies of the late 1960s and early 1970s that reflect the values of the counter-culture at that time. It is Smithy who walks away from his marriage when he discovers his wife's affair with his friend – not his wife, as is the case in Stead's novel. In doing so, Smithy 'drops out' like any number of disaffected heroes who take to the road in films like *Easy Rider* (Dennis Hopper, 1969), or *Five Easy Pieces* (Bob Rafelson, 1970). Donaldson also incorporated tropes drawn from a range of genres, including the action thriller, the war film, the buddy film, the manhunt film, and the dropout film. Violent episodes are introduced, such as the scene where masked snipers fire on Government troops at the instigation of the Special Forces, or the scene showing the bloody bodies of members of the resistance after an ambush of their Kombi van by the Specials, which makes the Government-as-enemy more sinister and dangerous. New action sequences are introduced that are more heightened and sensational than anything in the novel, such as Smithy's escape by vomiting over the officer guarding him, and running through Queen Street pursued by soldiers in a chase scene, whereas in the novel he simply walks away from the Prime Minister's office through a side door while the latter is momentarily absent.

Smithy is also given a romantic interest in the form of Mary, an employee at Buck's Motel, where he seeks to go under cover, which allows Donaldson to introduce sex scenes – a first for New Zealand cinema – along with a wider range of emotions associated with heterosexual relationships (sexual jealousy, in particular), and the more tender capacities of men that contravene the expectations of the hypermasculine stereotype. Moreover, in contrast to the novel, Smithy and his arch-rival Bullen, the man who has stolen his wife, become rebonded as buddies in a heroic effort to flee the Special Forces pursuing them. The effect is to turn Smithy from a pathetic Man Alone anti-hero, whom the reader views from a critical distance, into a sympathetic hero, with whom the spectator is invited to identify as the result of a focalisation that consistently places us close to his point of view.

In short, the inclusion of these new generic elements converts the work from being a satirical prose fiction dystopia in the manner of George Orwell's *1984* into a heroic cinematic melodrama-cum-action-film, with the central protagonist transformed into a different kind of character altogether. This fundamental change is reflected in the very title of the movie. Donaldson explains that he wanted a title that carried a sense of 'unspecified menace,' and that he meant the change of the title from *Smith's Dream* to *Sleeping Dogs* to signal an important aspect of the New Zealand character:

> If someone stirred up New Zealanders, he would find them more difficult to control than he might expect. In this sense, the film (while it is pessimistic in the end) is defiant, heroic even. It's optimistic in terms of the New Zealand character because you'd have to shoot every last one of them before you'd get them to say 'yes.'[13]

In the film, Smithy comes to embody this heroic defiance, which means that Stead's original characterization of him is turned inside out, and neatly reversed. Smithy (Sam Neill) is thus transformed into an iconic representation of the angry young counter-cultural men of Donaldson's generation who, disenchanted with the values of their parents' generation, felt moved to resist the traditional modes of authority by which it sought to enforce its imperatives.

The Conversion of the Source into a Vehicle for Personal Expression

Apart from his concern to make a movie that would have box office appeal, Donaldson also had another compelling reason for altering the genre of the work. His subsequent interviews allow one to infer that most of the changes to the source were motivated by his desire to turn the adaptation into a displaced symbolic representation of a personal psychodrama that had been taking place within his consciousness prior to, and during, the making of *Sleeping Dogs*.

In a fascinating documentary filmed in 2005 to accompany the DVD release of *Sleeping Dogs* and *Smash Palace*, 'The Roger Donaldson Collection' produced by Magna Pacific, the scriptwriters Mune and Baysting reveal that the treatment they concocted from Stead's novel served little purpose other than to provide the pretext for gaining finance to make the film. Beyond that, they say, the scenario they had prepared was altered beyond recognition by the interventions of Donaldson himself. All the key members of the production team attest to his formative input. According to Mune (who also acted the part of Bullen in the film), the script 'evolved': it was 'cobbled together' as a way of 'giving form to the vision that Roger [Donaldson] had.' Arthur Baysting, the co-writer of the original script, adds that once Donaldson was on location, 'it was in his head,' meaning that the actual script became semi-redundant. Geoff Murphy, the special effects man for the production, and later a distinguished director in his own right, recalls that, even though *Sleeping Dogs* had been written by Mune and Baysting in theory, 'everyone was chipping in in practice – Roger was having a go.' The result, according to Murphy, was that 'we didn't know what the hell Roger was up to, but we knew he was up to something.'[14]

What Donaldson was 'up to' can be inferred both from what Donaldson suppressed from the script and what he included. The original screenplay as drafted by Mune and Baysting outlined a concluding sequence that was omitted from the final film. After Smith dies, according to the synopsis, there is a dramatic intervention by the Māori elder, Taupiri, from whom Smith had gained permission to live on Gut Island, in which the old man assaults Jesperson, Smithy's school friend, who has betrayed him:

> ... the old man flys [sic] into a violent fit of hatred. He half runs up behind Jesperson and smashes his walking stick down on his head. Jesperson falls to the ground his skull smashed by the violent blow. The old man performs a chant over the body of his victim.[15]

Clearly, apart from any bathos such a scene might generate in the eyes of an audience not imbued with political correctness, Donaldson must have felt that this episode was extraneous to his overriding concern, which was to focus the audience's attention on Smithy for the sake of eliciting sympathy.

All the symbolic tropes and intertextual allusions drawn from films of the American New Wave, in fact, serve this purpose. One thinks, in particular, of the allusions to *Butch Cassidy and the Sundance Kid* (George Roy Hill, 1969) that appear in the bike-riding scene shared by Smithy and Gloria (Nevan Rowe), which provides an idyllic interlude before the final catastrophe, so as to heighten the pathos of the tragic events that follow. Another instance is the similarity between Smithy and Bullen (Ian Mune) preparing to face the guns of Jesperson (Clyde Scott) and the Special Forces, and Butch Cassidy and the Kid 'preparing to finally freeze-frame under Bolivian gunfire' in the same film.[16] Even without any specific prompts, the attentive spectator can feel how these intertextual evocations are shaping the representation to function as a protest against, and a defiance of, the oppressive effects of a persecuting authority. In Donaldson's case, however, what is implicitly apparent is made even more explicit by his own revelations about the concerns and impulses that motivated him.

The American New Wave film that provides the real subtext for *Sleeping Dogs* is not *Butch Cassidy and the Sundance Kid*, or any of the other movies about rebels who defy the expectations of normative society, or flout the authority that seeks to enforce it (for example, Arthur Penn's 1967 film *Bonnie and Clyde*, and *Easy Rider*), but *Five Easy Pieces*, which Donaldson in 1986 revealed to be his favourite film.[17]

The similarities between *Sleeping Dogs* and *Five Easy Pieces* are instantly apparent. Both have as their main character a young man who feels alienated from the norms and expectations that govern their social backgrounds, and who, in the words of Bobby in *Five Easy Pieces*, 'move[s] around a lot' to avoid things getting bad if he stays. Both feel oppressed by the existing system,

Figure 4.2 Smithy (Sam Neill) and Gloria (Nevan Rowe) ride on a bike, recalling *Butch Cassidy and the Sundance Kid*, in *Sleeping Dogs* (dir. Roger Donaldson, 1977).

and want to escape from it. Significantly, Donaldson wanted Jack Nicholson, who acted Bobby in *Five Easy Pieces*, to play the role of Willoughby, the commander of the Special Forces, in *Sleeping Dogs*; Nicholson's agent, however, rejected the $5,000 fee that Donaldson was able to offer, which resulted in Sam Neill being cast in the lead part, in what would become his breakthrough role.[18]

A Comparison between *Five Easy Pieces* and *Sleeping Dogs*

A comparison between the way Rafelson presented Nicholson as Bobby and Donaldson presented Neill as Smithy shows just how powerful an influence the earlier film exerted on Donaldson's mind as he made his own movie. Neill's Smithy is made similar to Nicholson's Bobby in visual appearance. Neill's Smithy is made to engage in a casual sexual affair, just as Bobby habitually does, and at the climactic moment in each movie, each of the heroes weeps in response to his inability to master the situation in which he finds himself in a way that will answer to the imperatives of what prevailing social codes expect of him as a man. In Bobby's case, his weeping springs from his inability to meet the expectations of his upper middle-class father; in Smithy's case, it arises from his inability to light a sodden match in order to kindle a fire in the bush, as a good Kiwi bloke should be able to do, according to the popular myth. Both films show the hero refusing to submit himself to a requirement that he will conform to the expectations of the system from which he had previously sought to escape: a suffocating family system in the case of Bobby, and an oppressive political system, as well as a dysfunctional marital relationship, in the case of Smithy. The outcome for both protagonists is tragic. Concerning Bobby, we are told (in the slogan accompanying the release of the movie) that, 'He rode the fast lane on the road to nowhere.' In the case of Smithy, he is shot dead in the back after having given the finger to the authority that seeks to contain him.

The Autobiographical Motivations of *Sleeping Dogs*

What motivated Donaldson to reconceive Stead's conventional, unimpressive, ordinary anti-hero Smith as a defiant young man who resembled Rafelson's Bobby, to the bemusement of his scriptwriters and other members of his team who didn't know what he was doing, or why? The answer can be found in comments Donaldson let slip nearly thirty years later in the documentary on the making of *Sleeping Dogs*. After commenting on how he, with the help of another member of the team, managed to persuade the Wing Commander of the New Zealand Air Force to allow its new Skyhawk fighter jets to be used for a sequence in the film, and acknowledging the favourable reception of the film, Donaldson utters a startling personal revelation:

When I left Australia, I left estranged from my dad, who had been in the Australian Air Force during the War, and I was a draft dodger, and I came to New Zealand and became, really, a refugee here. I remember my dad outside the movie theatre, after he had seen the film, literally stopping people in the street, saying, 'Hey, you should see this movie – it's a good movie – my son made this movie.'[19]

In Stead's novel, there are no Skyhawks; the Government's Special Forces fire rockets at the rebels from helicopters, in accordance with images of the Vietnam War that were prevalent at the time.[20] Similarly, in the first draft of the screenplay there are no Skyhawks. Instead, there are several sequences in which two helicopters first spray the camp of the guerrillas with fire and drop grenades on it (scenes 103, 104), and then another helicopter returns with Jesperson and Taupiri, the old Māori, to fly over the campsite (scene 108). Subsequently, a further set of sequences alternates between exterior shots of the helicopters and interior views from the helicopters as they hunt Smithy, Bullen, and the guerrillas, involving exchanges of fire in which one of the choppers is eventually shot down (scene 113).[21] Donaldson's decision to replace this original conception involving helicopters with the introduction of the jet planes is highly significant: not only is it more cinematically spectacular – which would be sufficient reason in itself – but the foregrounding of the Skyhawk jets also strengthens an association with the idea of the Air Force, and hence with the father from whom Donaldson was at that time estranged, meaning that the Skyhawks in their relationship with Smithy and the guerrillas serve symbolically as a metonym for that relationship.

When this associative link is understood, the whole motive behind the conversion of the source text through the incorporation of images from the New American Cinema, with its emphasis on a disaffected, youthful counter-culture, becomes clear. For Donaldson, his film, *Sleeping Dogs*, functions (perhaps unconsciously) like the *apologia* that Bobby delivers to his father in *Five Easy Pieces*. At the climactic moment when Bobby is alone with his father, who is in a wheelchair, having been rendered mute by a stroke, Bobby opens his attempt at a dialogue – which necessarily takes the form of a monologue – by saying:

> I don't know if you'd be particularly interested in hearing anything about me. My life – most of it – doesn't add up to much I could relate as a way of life that you'd approve of . . .
>
> I'm trying to imagine your half of this conversation . . . If we could talk, you wouldn't be talking. That's pretty much the way it got to be before I left . . . I don't know what to say [weeps] . . . We were never that comfortable with one another to begin with. The best that I can do is apologise . . . I'm sorry it didn't work out.

Figure 4.3 A Skyhawk firing rockets in *Sleeping Dogs* (dir. Roger Donaldson, 1977).

Metaphorically speaking, for Donaldson, his adaptation has been contrived, in fantasy, to serve a similar purpose. The film, at a displaced remove, is his way of seeking to explain and justify himself to his estranged father, whose paternal values and role are enshrined in the authority and power of the armed forces depicted in the film, which his surrogate hero resists – just as Donaldson in real life became a refugee to escape them. Uncannily, this complex engagement with the military vocation of his father was symbolically emblematized in real life by the fact that Donaldson himself chose to act as the cameraman for the shots featuring the Skyhawks, which meant placing himself in one of the very machines of destruction that he had fled Australia to avoid, in a kind of make-believe participation of a possibility he had abjured.

There can be no doubt that, whether he were conscious of it or not, in the course of making *Sleeping Dogs* Donaldson exploited the adaptation process as an opportunity to address a number of personal issues that were preoccupying him, especially those relating to his estrangement from his father, and his unwillingness to conform to the social system his father represented. That is why, in his retrospective commentary on *Sleeping Dogs*, nearly thirty years later, Donaldson felt moved to record how his father had come to New Zealand to attend the première, had reacted favourably to the film, and had expressed pride in his son's accomplishment to passers-by. To a son who desired to be understood for what he had done, and to be accepted in spite of it, this had meant that the self-justification embodied implicitly in the film had been accepted by the person to whom, perhaps unconsciously, it had been directed – his father.

In terms of its function as a coming-of-age film, what *Sleeping Dogs* figuratively exemplifies is a process of Oedipal separation and self-assertion that involves the attainment of a sense of personal independence – a sense of self that is felt to be sufficiently precious that it is worth suffering death to preserve. The presence of this Oedipal struggle in the hero is what makes Smithy seem far younger in the film than Smith does in Stead's novel, which contains no hint that this attainment of independence has not already occurred.

The assertion of this hard-earned sense of self, however, entails loss, and something of the plangency of that fact is captured in the lyrics of the song that is heard in the soundtrack as the final credits roll:

And I find myself back on the road again,
There was really nothing there to try;
It don't make much difference,
For the time is surely slipping away.
Turn your back on it all,
  Let sleeping dogs lie.

Metaphorically speaking, Smithy, like Donaldson had done in real life, turns his back on (patriarchal/institutional) authority in order to enjoy an integrity of being that it was not possible to find in the values of order that was being left behind – represented, in the film, by a totalitarian political regime and the armed forces that it used to coerce obedience.

Conclusion

As a coming-of-age film, *Sleeping Dogs* showed for the first time in New Zealand how filmmaking in this genre could be turned into an instrument for imaginative self-projection, even when the film was adapted from a literary source, while simultaneously participating in the youth culture that was increasingly being disseminated from abroad. It also shows how tropes from other cinematic genres could be incorporated into the coming-of-age film and exploited so as to further the idiosyncratic purposes of the filmmaker. As far as its content is concerned, *Sleeping Dogs* attests to the arrival of a new generation of creative artists who would change the terms in which masculinity itself was depicted, displacing the former emphasis on puritan inwardness and self-containment with a new kind of self-assertion and defiance, resulting in a more heroic, less fragilized conception of self in the male hero of the film.

In both its content and manner of expression, then, *Sleeping Dogs* exemplifies the convergence of national and transnational cultural currents in a way that makes it both a distinctively New Zealand film, yet also a film able to assume its place in the international scene. Other young New Zealand filmmakers would soon exploit the same blend of local subject matter and tropes drawn from American genres, notably Geoff Murphy in his Māori western, *Utu* (1984), and the practice would continue in the decades to come, most notably in Taika Waititi's two coming-of-age films, *Boy* and *Hunt for the Wilderpeople*. This deliberate hybridization, with its cinephilic references to American films of the late 1960s and early 1970s, is significant because it reflects the country's changing sense of its place in the world – no longer merely a far-flung province of Great Britain – and of what it wanted to be: that is, an independent country, with its own identity, that was able to assert itself and engage with the external world in its own terms. For this reason, *Sleeping Dogs* can justly be regarded as the inaugural work in a new era of New Zealand filmmaking.

Notes

1. An earlier version of this essay, orientated towards a different purpose, was published in Alistair Fox and Gabrielle Hine, *Cinematic Adaptation and the Articulation of New Zealand Identity*, CRNI Working Papers Series, 2 (Dunedin: Centre for Research on National Identity, 2011), 15–30.
2. *Evening Post* [Wellington], 27 February 1988.
3. 'Review: "Sleeping Dogs",' *Variety*, 31 December 1976, http://variety.com/1976/film/reviews/sleeping-dogs-1200423915/, accessed 31 May 2016.
4. See Cook, 'Auteur Cinema and the "Film Generation" in 1970s Hollywood,' 12–37.
5. Selbo, *Film Genre for the Screenwriter*, 2909.
6. 'The Making of *Sleeping Dogs*,' *The Roger Donaldson Collection:* Sleeping Dogs *and* Smash Palace, directed by John Reid (Magna Pacific, 2006), DVD.
7. C. K. Stead, *Kin of Place* (Auckland: Auckland University Press, 2002), 181.
8. C. K. Stead, *Smith's Dream* (Auckland: Longman Paul, 1973), 12.
9. Ibid., 11.
10. Ibid., 7–8.
11. Stead, *Smith's Dream*, 141–2. I am citing the revised ending of the novel that Stead inserted into the rewritten version reprinted in 1973.
12. 'The Making of *Sleeping Dogs*,' *The Roger Donaldson Collection:* Sleeping Dogs *and* Smash Palace, directed by John Reid (Magna Pacific, 2006), DVD.
13. Quoted by Brian MacDonnell, 'Sleeping Dogs,' in Geoff Mayer and Keith Beattie (eds), *The Cinema of Australia and New Zealand* (London: Wallflower Press, 2007), 104.
14. Ibid.
15. *Sleeping Dogs*, 'Synopsis,' New Zealand Film Archive, Scripts Collection D969, Box 1. MacDonnell notes the existence of this alternative ending, 'Sleeping Dogs,' 106–7.
16. Reid, *A Decade of New Zealand Film*: Sleeping Dogs *to* Came a Hot Friday, 36.
17. MacDonnell, 'Sleeping Dogs,' 102.
18. 'The Making of *Sleeping Dogs*,' dir. John Reid, DVD.
19. Ibid.
20. Stead, *Smith's Dream*, 131.
21. *Sleeping Dogs*, 'First Draft of Screenplay,' New Zealand Film Commission, Scripts Collection, D969, Box 1.

5. AN IMMIGRANT FILMMAKER SUBSTITUTES AN ALTERNATIVE VISION OF ADOLESCENCE: *THE SCARECROW* (SAM PILLSBURY, 1982)

Whereas *The God Boy* exemplified the type of adaptation that maintains an extreme fidelity to its source, and *Sleeping Dogs* represented a second type that seeks to rewrite the original, chiefly by importing elements from other cinematic genres in order to transform it into a vehicle for personal expression, the next New Zealand coming-of-age film, Sam Pillsbury's *The Scarecrow* (1982), demonstrates a third type – the kind of adaptation that suppresses key elements in the source text for the sake of substituting a new vision, or mythos, for that which had informed the original work.

The cinematic version of *The Scarecrow* was based on the 'subfusc' novel of the same name written by Ronald Hugh Morrieson, which was published in 1963. As far as the external events of the fable are concerned, Pillsbury's film adheres closely to Morrieson's novel – at least to outward appearance. The story revolves around a fourteen-year-old boy, Neddy Poindexter (Ned in the film), who lives in a small rural town called Klynham (closely based on Hawera, in the North Island of New Zealand), and the action commences when the hens that Ned and his friend Les are raising get stolen – on the same day, as it turns out, that a serial necrophiliac murderer cuts the throat of a theater usherette in the big city to the south (alias Wellington, in real life). Shortly afterwards, while driving with his father, Ned sees a sinister-looking man at a crossroads, and encounters him again on a train that takes them back to Klynham, his father's jalopy having broken down. This stranger, we learn, is Hubert Salter, the 'scarecrow' of the title (on account of his great height, gauntness, and general appearance), who rapidly inveigles his way into the circle of drunks frequented by Ned's Uncle Athol and Charlie Dabney, the undertaker, and eventually into the Poindexter family itself. Thereafter, the story alternates between Ned's trials and tribulations regarding a loutish gang of youths led by Victor Lynch, and Salter's murderous predations in the town, culminating in his pursuit of Prudence, Ned's beautiful sixteen-year-old sister, who, in an outburst of adolescent sexuality, is attracting the attention of a range of men and boys. Following further murders, the story ends when Prudence disappears, Salter is discovered in his hiding place, is then killed by Ned's brother Herbert, and buried in the town's rubbish dump, and Prudence is rescued, with the 'scarecrow's' eventual fate being kept a secret from the rest of the town.

The film, in fact, makes relatively few changes to the basic story as presented in the novel – compared, for example, to those Roger Donaldson made to C. K. Stead's *Smith's Dream* when adapting it as *Sleeping Dogs* – and most of the changes are minor.[1] As routinely happens in coming-of-age films, the time setting is updated to the period of the filmmaker's own childhood, being shifted from the 1930s to the 1950s (just as Murray Reece did when adapting Ian Cross' *The God Boy*). Several scenes showing Victor Lynch's gang harassing Prudence and her friend Angela are added early in the movie to strengthen this narrative strand in order to lead up to the later episode when they appear about to rape them. Details of some events are altered: Mabel Collinson, the music teacher, is murdered in the movie, whereas in the novel she falls down her stairway under the influence of gin and breaks her neck. There is some reordering of scenes in the sequence of events: Salter's necrophiliac intercourse with the dead body of Mabel Collinson occurs after his meeting with Prudence in the film, suggesting this perverted act is a consequence of the lust Prudence has aroused in him, whereas in the novel this episode occurs before he encounters Prudence; the scene in which Ned and Les encounter the pretty twin girls on roller skates and experience a French kiss for the first time is shifted from earlier in the movie to the very end. Additionally, a number of characters are omitted in order to tighten the structure (Chester Montgomery, Flash Freddy, and the Quinn family); and one new character is added, Chote Fitzherbert, who stands in for a number of other young men who lust after Prudence. Finally, several additional scenes were shot that did not find their way into the final cut: a scene with Prudence chatting with Angela while the latter is in her bath; a scene in which Ned is beaten up by the Lynch gang; and a new ending in which an unseen stranger is shown approaching the young child who was travelling with her aunt at the beginning of the film, with 'an ominous shadow covering her in the last seconds of the movie.'[2] Apart from these fairly modest changes, the story, viewed in terms of its characters and events, remains much the same in the cinematic adaptation as it was in the novel.

This apparent similarity of the cinematic version to its source is nevertheless deceptive. Far more significant than the elements Pillsbury added were key elements in Morrieson's novel that Pillsbury omitted or suppressed. The omission of these elements, in fact, completely altered the nature and meaning of the story, turning it from being the expression of a tormented internal psychodrama on the part of the protagonist, Ned, into an anodyne, conventional coming-of-age tale. To demonstrate how and why this is so requires a careful investigation of both the novel and the cinematic version that was derived from it.

Ronald Hugh Morrieson's Novel

Among New Zealand writers, Ronald Hugh Morrieson (1922–72) was one of the most singular. Apart from short periods in Auckland and New Plymouth, he spent his entire life in the small Taranaki town of Hawera, living with his mother. As a writer, he was an outsider as far as the literary establishment was concerned, given that his novels, in their emphasis on sex and violence, and their exploitation of tropes drawn from cinematic genres, seemed out of sync with prevailing tendencies.

In personality, Morrieson seems to have been fairly troubled. As his autobiographer and certain critics have noted, the relationship between Morrieson and his mother was one of excessive co-dependency, and when she died in 1968, he confessed that he had no desire to continue living and, indeed, did not survive her loss for very long. He was also prey to addictive behaviors, notably compulsive sexuality, and alcoholism – by the time of his premature death at the age of fifty, according to the testimony of Maurice Shadbolt, a friend, 'He had been up drinking, solitary, until two in the morning . . . and was putting away a couple of bottles of sherry before lunch.'[3]

Morrieson's novels are all deeply autobiographical, as his biographer, Julia Millen, makes clear. Klynham in *The Scarecrow* is a thinly disguised version of Hawera, while Morrieson's protagonists, all of whom bear a strong family resemblance, are versions of himself. His description of Cedric Williamson, the lonely teenage hero of *Predicament*, for example, could serve as a self-portrait of Morrieson in his youth:

> . . . we find boredom, unpopularity; a deep interior dissatisfaction with his lot; a brain that sought refuge in the world of fiction he so loved . . . and, on top of these things, all the turmoil of old-fashioned adolescence – *evil passions*; pimples, dandruff; shaving, a brand-new Adam's apple; a voice with a hairtrigger range; unrequited love for a second cousin called Jasmine who might as well have been dead . . ., and a sad, smouldering, savage envy of boys better built and better looking than himself . . .[4]

These are the emotions that provide the raw energy for *The Scarecrow*, Morrieson's debut novel, and the first in which he sought to address his personal issues.

The Scarecrow, in fact, is a symbolic representation through which Morrieson attempts, in fantasy, to confront his demons. To do so, he devised a fiction that was constructed out of tropes drawn from the gothic novel, the horror film, the zombie movie, and the crime thriller – all of which provided material that enabled the expression of perturbed emotions: terror at the thought of unspecified danger lurking in the shadows; guilt at the awareness of illicit impulses one cannot constrain (especially sexual ones); and anger at the circumstances that are felt to have deprived one of the chance to enjoy satisfaction and happiness. As the literary critic Lawrence Jones has recognized, at the heart of the adolescent hero's malaise is the destructive influence of New Zealand puritanism:

> Neddy Poindexter in *The Scarecrow* and Cedric Williamson in *Predicament* experience the pressures of puritan repression on nascent sexuality . . . *The Scarecrow*, despite its finally 'comic' shape, gains great power through the acting out of the narrator's, the community's, and perhaps the author's repressed sexual violence in its textual unconscious . . .[5]

This repressive puritanism leaves the adolescent hero, like Jimmy in *The God Boy*, with a sense of guilt and shame, but in this case, specifically at his inability to subdue his sexual urges. The tension that results leads him to redirect it outwards in the form of various types of transgression. When Neddy and his friend Les Wilson, for example, believing that Victor Lynch has stolen their hens, exact revenge by stealing the Lynchs' fowls, Neddy experiences a kind of liberating exhilaration: '. . . a feeling too delicious by far to be anything but evil. I wanted to make the feeling get worse, so I lit a cigarette.'[6] The 'buzz' that Neddy feels at flouting prohibitions expresses itself in other ways. He and Les steal a bottle of applejack from a drunken woman sitting in the gutter and drink it in their secret hideout, after which they masturbate each other in imitation of what they have seen Don Butcher doing to Peachy Blair – a transgressive act that leaves them feeling acutely 'ashamed.'[7] Similarly, Neddy indulges in an incestuous desire for his sister, Prudence, having seen her 'in her tight and skimpy black knickers, swinging from the beam in the twilit, musky-smelling shed,' which leaves him 'obsessed with the recollection of her legs and the coppery glow beneath the soft skin,' shaking 'from head to toe with a delicious desire.' So powerless is he in the grip of this desire that he plans 'for her to catch me exposed, so that her blood would race as mysteriously as mine.'[8]

It becomes apparent as such moments accumulate – moments in which Neddy reveals awareness that his impulses are transgressive – that he senses an equivalence between Hubert Salter, the 'scarecrow,' and himself. This in turn suggests that Salter is a symbolic personification of the evil and perversion that the narrator fears might reside in himself, the only difference being one of degree.

This imaginatively construed equivalence is revealed in several parallels that surface in the course of the novel. The language Neddy uses to describe the 'feeling too delicious by far to be anything but evil' when he steals the Lynchs' chooks is reiterated in the feelings Salter recalls having had at the time he murdered Daphne Moran: 'So almost unbelievably exciting. Such mad exhilaration, such sexual power the mad, evil moment granted.'[9] The similarity of these reactions to transgression reinforces the parallel established in the famous opening sentence of the novel: 'The same week our fowls were stolen, Daphne Moran had her throat cut.'[10] Hubert Salter is merely the grotesque, ultimate embodiment of the perversion and depravity that Neddy fears may incipiently be present within his own being.

The parallel between the two of them is made even more explicit when Neddy has a dream about Josephine McClinton, the girl whom he lusts after:

> Suddenly I became afraid. Afraid of sleep? No, of death! I could feel my skin tautening over my cheekbones and my blood running cold. The few cells of my brain still unnumbed began to fight like blazes. Jesus, this was no sleep; Josephine was a corpse; I was dying in her blackening arms, falling down a well forever.[11]

Given that earlier in the novel, Sam Finn, the halfwit, has seen Salter in Charlie Dabney's funeral parlor having intercourse with the corpse of Mabel Collinson, the piano teacher, Neddy's dream establishes a parallel between Salter's necrophilia and Neddy's imaginative interpretation of his own impulses, further suggesting that Salter is a projection of what the boy (and, following Lawrence Jones' suggestion, the author) fears in himself.

A further instance of this identification occurs when the body of Angela Potroz, Prudence's friend, is found murdered, strangled, and raped by Salter. Once again, this event triggers a horrified recoil in Neddy when he recollects having desired to kiss Angela:

> That my shell could have ever harboured even a distant cousin of the frenzy which had raged in some murderous fiend seemed unbelievable. Les and I had very little to say. The memory of a thousand conversations about sex hung over us like a pall. We had found and discussed with great animation a beautiful flower in a beautiful garden and now its stench had knocked us flat.[12]

For Neddy, sexual desire is death-dealing, at the same time as it is fearsomely irresistible. The only possible outcome, within this fantasy, is for desire itself to be killed off along with all the illicit feelings that attend it, which is what happens at the end of the novel, with Salter being killed when he strikes his head on a coffin after having been struck by Herbert, Neddy's elder brother, following which he is buried (symbolically) in the town's rubbish tip.

It will be apparent from this account of Morrieson's novel that in terms of its vision it is very different from the cinematic adaptation that Sam Pillsbury based upon it, even though the events that constitute the film's narrative might suggest that the adaptation is a close one.

Sam Pillsbury's Adaptation

In terms of the events that form its plot, as well as in its realization of the sinister evil villain Salter, Pillsbury's adaptation seems very close to its source. Salter, in particular, is given a visual representation that perfectly renders the zombie-like attributes of Morrieson's Salter. The gothic quality of the novel is also admirably captured through the use of expressionist lighting in several scenes, that suggests the lurking presence of Salter and the danger he represents.

Despite the closeness of Pillsbury's version of *The Scarecrow* to Morrieson's original in terms of its plot, however, this apparent closeness is deceptive. Even more important than the superficial similarities is the fact that Pillsbury

Figure 5.1   Hubert Salter, the 'scarecrow' (John Carradine), in *The Scarecrow* (Sam Pillsbury, 1982).

ignored, or suppressed, every single one of the details relating to Neddy's turbid inner emotions in Morrieson's novel that I have highlighted in the account above. The effect of these suppressions is to convert Morrieson's representation of a disturbed inner emotional condition in the narrator of the novel into the depiction of an ordinary boy accomplishing the transition into adolescence, thus rendering the story much more anodyne. In short, during the process of adaptation, Pillsbury turned what had been a highly idiosyncratic and disturbing psychodrama into a fairly conventional genre film.

This shift of vision can be seen in Pillsbury's own description of what he regarded as the themes of Morrieson's novel:

> It is about a boy growing up, learning to see the reality of evil versus good in the people around him, trying to survive the corrupt world he lived in, and making it through his relationship with his sister, Pru. The chooks, the gang, and so on, are actually the mundane things in life which serve to obscure the truth. Salter represents the truth of evil and Ned is the only one who sees through him. This makes Ned superior to the others around him. So Ned matures through the film as his powers of observation *grow*, but he must not *just* observe – he must *act* on his observations to be truly mature. And it takes the example, the prompting of the policeman, Len, to force Ned to act.[13]

Pillsbury's understanding of the meaning of his source was a far cry from Morrieson's tormented vision, replacing the mythos that had informed the novel with a new one, more closely aligned with the type of coming-of-age mythos found in American movies. Whereas the mythos of the original (that is, the pattern of beliefs and prevailing attitudes symbolically represented in the fiction) had its roots in the same kind of repressive New Zealand puritanism found in *The God Boy* and countless New Zealand novels written from the 1930s onwards, the mythos of Pillsbury's version of *The Scarecrow* shifts it away from this ethos of tormented psychic complexity resulting from tensions generated by puritan guilt, towards values that are more typical of the wave of American coming-of-age movies with which Pillsbury was familiar.

That this should be so was not surprising, given that Pillsbury himself came from a different formation. Born in New York in 1946, Pillsbury spent his formative early years in the USA, emigrating to New Zealand with his family when he was already fourteen years old. He therefore grew up in a cultural milieu that did not replicate the circumstances to which native born and bred New Zealanders like Ian Cross and Ronald Hugh Morrieson were responding in the fictions they created, based on their own childhood experiences. The same had been true of Murray Reece, the director of the cinematic version of *The God Boy*, but whereas Reece opted to maintain an absolute fidelity to his literary source, Pillsbury chose to translate the troubled vision of his source into something with which he was more familiar – a story showing a growth into maturity and insight.

The means by which he did so can be traced in subtle alterations he made to Morrieson's novel, beginning with the voiceover narration, which changes the perspective. In the novel, the first-person point of view is that of Neddy, characterized as a youth who is still close to the action. This allowed Morrieson to take the reader deep into his own thoughts and feelings as the events of the novel unfolded. In the film, the first-person narration becomes a voiceover. Initially, Pillsbury had this voiceover delivered by the actor who plays Ned, Jonathan Smith, thus maintaining the perspective of the novel. Subsequently, however, he decided to have the voiceover spoken by an adult man (the actor Martyn Sanderson).[14] The change, as slight as it might appear, had a major impact on the relation of the spectator to the action in the film, compared with the relation that Morrieson had established between the reader and the action in his novel. Having an adult voice deliver the voiceover interposes a much greater distance between the spectator and the main character, Ned, because it invites us to look at him from an adult perspective. We no longer share his innermost emotional perturbations and are not made privy to his secret desires, shame, and guilt. Instead, the voiceover now focuses attention on the external events that comprise the *action*, so that we can gauge Ned's response to them as it evolves. Hence, we see him learning things, in conformity with Pillsbury's personal understanding of the story, such as a growing awareness that it had been wrong for him and Les to steal the Lynchs' hens, and, above all, his realization of the true evil that Salter represents. Ned in the film thus becomes a much more innocent and estimable boy than Neddy in the novel. One might even say that he is idealized.

This altered conception of the character of Ned is reinforced by a number of other changes. The gang of louts led by Victor Lynch is foregrounded to a much greater extent than it was in the novel by the introduction of a new scene early in the film in which the Lynch gang accosts Prudence and her friend Angela Potroz in the street, and a further scene in which they harass the two girls with their unwanted attention during a visit to the local cinema. Pillsbury also has Salter present in this scene, which is absent from the novel, thus creating an equivalence between the youths in the Lynch gang and Salter as predators with sexual designs on Prudence and Angela, rather than the equivalence Morrieson had established between Neddy and Salter.

The effect of this new emphasis on the Lynch gang is to relocate the transgressive impulses revealed in Neddy in the novel into the louts who compose the gang, which sanitizes Pillsbury's Ned by removing his turbid, murky sexual feelings towards his sister and the other girls who excite his desire. This relocating of Neddy's illicit impulses is further reinforced by the introduction of a new character, Chote Fitzherbert, to whom Pillsbury transfers the intention

Figure 5.2 Ned (Jonathan Smith) begins to see through Salter in *The Scarecrow* (dir. Sam Pillsbury, 1982).

of Morrieson's Neddy to let Prudence see him naked in an attempt to arouse her desire, by having the shirtless Chote drop his trousers to expose himself to Prudence while she is cleaning in his parents' house. Once again, the effect is to sanitize Ned, leaving him free to assume the role that Pillsbury wants him to have, which is that of a boy who is learning to see the reality of evil versus good, to a degree that makes him superior to the others among whom he lives.

Pillsbury's new vision, in fact, is much simpler and more conventional in the separation it makes between good and evil, and in its indifference to the idea of corrupting sinfulness and the guilt it entails, which had been such a strong presence in Morrieson's novel. There are recurrent signs of this desire to simplify in order to accommodate the new vision in the film. One instance is the treatment of Mabel Collinson, the music teacher. In the novel, Mabel Collinson is depicted as a drunk degenerate who 'had lost all but six of her piano pupils through breathing gin fumes and cigarette smoke over them, and, at her lowest ebb, making daring suggestions to adolescent boys.'[15] Given that Mabel, at thirty-six, is the same age as Morrieson at the time of writing *The Scarecrow*, and that Morrieson had himself become a music teacher several years earlier, and was by this time seriously addicted to alcohol, one can detect a degree of personal projection in this portrait of a drunken music teacher with transgressive sexual urges. Mabel's fate in the novel suggests a projection of self-loathing on the part of the author:

> At ten o'clock one morning when a very frightened Mabel was feeling so ill [from drinking] she thought maybe she was going to die, she fell down those bloody stairs and broke her neck. This was what killed her of course, but actually she died of everything.[16]

Mabel's fate exemplifies a sordid outcome that Morrieson feared might foreshadow his own destiny.

Mabel is treated very differently in Pillsbury's film, being depicted as someone who plays Debussy's *Clair de lune* with a sentimental beauty that elicits the adoration of Sam Finn, who listens to her each night from outside her house. Pillsbury's Mabel is not allowed to die by falling down her stairs in a drunken stupor, but instead is murdered as yet another of Salter's victims, which serves to magnify his monstrosity at the same time as it removes the taint of drunkenness from the romanticized Mabel, thus enhancing the contrast between good and evil in accordance with the film's simplified schema.

This narrowing of evil into a personified embodiment, in the form of Salter, is supplemented by a change to the sequence of events involving Salter's necrophiliac copulation with Mabel's dead corpse. In the novel, this occurs before Salter has met Prudence, whereas in the film, it takes place after he has met her during his visit to the Poindexters' house. The changed order suggests that it is unsatisfied lust for Prudence that motivates Salter's necrophiliac act, thus rendering it more explicable, rather than a motiveless malignity that is repeatedly presented in the language of the novel as 'devilish.'[17]

Another significant change to the order of events in the plot concerns the encounter of Ned and Les with the two Headley sisters, Marjorie and Beth, who, on roller skates, give the boys their first kiss. As the result of a last-minute decision during the editing of the film, Pillsbury decided to place this episode at the very end, whereas it had occurred earlier in the novel. Again, the effect is to turn the story into a simple coming-of-age tale, one that shows the boys moving on to the next stage in their pubescent development: the discovery of healthy, rather than perverted sex, which leaves them eagerly anticipating the experience that – in the description given to Ned by his brother Herbert, which Ned repeats as the final words of the film – is 'like bluebirds flyin' outa yuh backside.'[18] This is a far cry from the novel, in which the boys' awareness of sexual urges as something sinful has been strongly present from the outset.

Implications of the Shift in Vision

The substantial transformation to which Sam Pillsbury subjected the vision of Morrieson's novel raises several important questions. First, to what extent does the filmic adaptation remain a New Zealand fiction? Second, do the

Figure 5.3 Les (Daniel McLaren) and Ned (Jonathan Smith) receive their first kiss in *The Scarecrow* (Sam Pillsbury, 1982).

changes suggest a waning of the power of puritanism in the national imaginary during the 1970s and beyond? I shall now briefly address these issues.

Despite the shift of the informing mythos from a distinctly New Zealand one to a more generalized international one, the adaptation of *The Scarecrow* remains an important milestone in New Zealand's national cinema because of the fidelity of its mise-en-scène and the excellence of its shooting style – it was the first New Zealand feature film to be screened (out of competition) at the Cannes Film Festival. One of the briefs of the New Zealand Film Commission, which partially funded the film, is to present images of New Zealanders to themselves through the telling of New Zealand stories through the medium of film, and *The Scarecrow* certainly does that. Like *The God Boy*, its re-creation of life in small-town New Zealand during the late 1950s is meticulous down to the last detail of such things as clothing, motor vehicles, household interiors, and streetscapes. This was undoubtedly close to the New Zealand Pillsbury remembered from his arrival in the country as a fourteen-year-old.

The other question is more difficult to answer. Does the adaptation of *The Scarecrow* attest to a shift away, during the 1980s, from the guilt-inducing repressive value system that had prevailed in New Zealand through much of the twentieth century? Quite possibly it did. For the younger generation of writers and filmmakers who began their creative work in the 1980s, the sexual revolution of the 1960s and 1970s, together with an explosion of youth culture, had already taken place, eliminating many of the emotional tensions arising from puritanism that are addressed by writers who were born in the 1930s. On the other hand, the absence of any sign in the adaptation of any awareness of, or responsiveness to, Morrieson's exposé of puritan repression and its toxic by-products, guilt and shame, might simply result from the fact that Pillsbury had been raised elsewhere during his most formative years, and hence had not been exposed to it in the way a native born and bred New Zealander like Morrieson had, as was typical of males of the latter's generation. The issue is complicated by the fact that depictions of the damaging consequences of puritanism, whether in its religious or secularized forms, continued to be produced by writers such as Maurice Gee in *In My Father's Den* and the *Plumb* trilogy, and Stevan Eldred-Grigg in *Oracles and Miracles* and its sequels, in the decades following Morrieson's death in 1972 and well into the new millennium.

It would seem, then, that the two rival value systems represented in the novel and the film may have entered into a competition with one another as the coming-of-age fiction continued to evolve in New Zealand in the last quarter of the twentieth century and beyond. By the time Brad McGann adapted Gee's *In My Father's Den* (2005), the contest between them was unequivocally over, with Gee's vision of puritanism and its consequences, which was reminiscent of that of Morrieson, firmly displaced by a new, more secular perspective.

Notes

1. For a convenient discussion of changes from the novel to the script, and from the script to the final version, see Brian McDonnell, *The Scarecrow: A Film Study Guide* (Auckland: Longman Paul, 1982), 8–19.
2. McDonnell, *The Scarecrow*, 11.
3. See Julia Millen, *Ronald Hugh Morrieson: A Biography* (Auckland: David Ling Pub., 1996), 34–41; Patrick Evans' entry on Morrieson in Roger Robinson and Nelson Wattie (eds), *The Oxford Companion to New Zealand Literature* (Melbourne: Oxford University Press, 1998), 380; and Maurice Shadbolt's preface to Ronald Hugh Morrieson, *Predicament* (Auckland: Penguin, 1986), 11.
4. Morrieson, *Predicament*, 18.
5. Lawrence Jones, 'The Novel,' in Terry Sturm (ed.), *The Oxford History of New Zealand Literature in English*, 2nd edn (Auckland: Oxford University Press, 1998), 119–244, esp. 160.
6. Ronald Hugh Morrieson, *The Scarecrow* (Auckland: Penguin, 2010), 13.
7. Morrieson, *The Scarecrow*, 115–16.
8. Ibid., 116.
9. Ibid., 36.
10. Ibid., 1.
11. Ibid., 128.
12. Ibid., 183.
13. Quoted in Brian McDonnell, *The Scarecrow: A Film Study Guide* (Auckland: Longman Paul, 1982), 26.
14. McDonnell, *The Scarecrow*, 12.

15. Morrieson, *Scarecrow*, 93.
16. Ibid.
17. McDonnell suggests that Salter has sex with Mabel's corpse as a 'second best' option (see McDonnell, *The Scarecrow*, 10).
18. These words are repeated from the novel (Morrieson, *Scarecrow*, 195).

6. ART-CINEMA, CULTURAL DISLOCATION, AND THE ENTRY INTO PUBERTY: *VIGIL* (VINCENT WARD, 1984)

The three films examined so far show two divergent stylistic tendencies that can be observed in the New Zealand coming-of-age film. Whereas *The God Boy* and *The Scarecrow* employ a fairly austere, conventional style to attain a degree of realism, leavened by occasional art-cinema flourishes (such as the surrealistic montage sequence in the former and several intrusions of expressionistic lighting in the latter), *Sleeping Dogs* deployed such devices as fast cutting, handheld camera sequences, and aerial shots to achieve the kind of heightened effects found in American action movies. In contradistinction, Vincent Ward's *Vigil* (1984) moves in a completely different direction, eschewing both realism and the style of Hollywood action movies in order to exploit to the fullest possible extent the stylistic devices and narrative strategies of European art-cinema. It is also the first major coming-of-age full-length feature film made during the New Zealand New Wave to be based on an original screenplay, rather than on a pre-existing literary source.

In terms of its plot, in fact, very little happens in *Vigil*: on a remote farm surrounded by the New Zealand bush, a farmer, Justin Peers (Gordon Shields), dies while trying to rescue one of his sheep off a cliff face, to the horror of his eleven-year-old daughter, Lisa, nicknamed 'Toss,' who witnesses the tragedy; a poacher, Ethan Ruir (Frank Whitten), comes on the scene and is hired as a farmhand, incurring the deep resentment of Toss when she sees him taking the place of her dead father and becoming an object of sexual interest to her mother, Elizabeth (Penelope Kay). At the end of the movie, the three of them, together with Toss' grandfather, Birdie (Bill Kerr), leave the farm to begin a new life elsewhere, with Ethan heading off in a separate direction. In addition to this paucity of action, the film adopts a minimalist style that has remarkably little dialogue, and unexplained temporal gaps between the various sequences. All of this means that the whole burden of the film is placed on its expression of the emotions the characters feel at finding themselves in this situation – especially the emotions of Toss, through whose eyes we see most of the action. The choice of an art-cinema style, with its elliptical narrative, subjective framing of the shots, and symbolic landscapes and evocative objects, was functional to this end.

The Art-film Style of *Vigil*

No other New Zealand film is as heavily laden with art-cinema techniques as *Vigil*. There are several reasons for this. Ward is a graduate of the Ilam School of Fine Arts at the University of Canterbury and is an accomplished painter in his own right, which is evident in the fact that every shot in the film displays a remarkable painterly quality in its composition. In addition, the art-cinema devices Ward uses serve a specific function in the narrative. As Ward puts it: 'I wanted to convey how a child seems to see the real world in oblique glimpses, and like a detective gathering clues, has to work out what is going on about him.'[1]

Vigil makes use of almost every technique characteristic of the work of European auteurs like Ingmar Bergman, Carl Dreyer, and Robert Bresson who had preceded him. In the shooting style Ward chose, we see the minimalist reduction of unnecessary detail as found in the films of Bresson, and also the expressive minimalism of Bergman. This is apparent in Ward's heavy use of close-up shots, and even several instances of extreme close-ups, that serve to register Toss' emotions visibly in her face, and to focus the spectator's attention of what she sees in order to suggest its latent significance. Ward also exploits camera movements and the duration of shots for impressionistic effects, as when he employs an exceptionally long tracking shot to follow Toss' precipitous descent down the hill to get help for her father after his fall – a movement that impressionistically evokes her inner panic. A contrasting use of the camera occurs in the scene where Toss is shown submerged in her bath while her mother flirts with the stranger, when the shot is protracted with an immobile camera to suggest her emotional terror through the arousal of a simulated sensation of drowning.[2] Sounds heard from off-screen space recur frequently, such as the scream of hawks, the crying of lambs, or the raging of a storm, all of which reinforce the visual minimalism of the film at the same time as they enhance its emotive impact.

Devices characteristic of cinematic impressionism abound. Figures are recurrently glimpsed through mediums that tend to distort or obscure them, such as the flames, mist, and smoke through which Toss views her father, and the streaked window pane through which she glimpses the face of Ethan, staring at her.[3] This imprecision, or lack of definition, of vision is amplified by the fact that *Vigil* is shot on 16 mm film stock boosted to 35 mm, which gives the film a slightly grainy look that enhances the oneiric, dreamlike quality it conveys.

Like Bergman, Ward exploits a symbolic landscape as a correlative for the emotions of the characters, and to provide a metaphoric comment on their existential situation. This is seen in stark images of burnt tree trunks, and the roots and branches of dead trees that suggest the brutality of humans' efforts to wrench nature to their purposes, and contrasting shots showing the surrounding bush and pastoral setting, in which, as Helen Martin observes, primary colors are filtered out to give 'a luminous intensity to the grey/green images.'[4] Expressionist use of color also occurs, especially red and blue; for example, when Ethan visits the house and Toss becomes aware of the sexual attraction kindling between him and her mother, unnatural streaks of red light appear on the wall of the darkened hall from where she is watching them, without any obvious source that could have produced them. Conversely, the surrealistic sequences showing Toss' fantasy of Ethan and her father as two medieval knights in combat is filmed through a blue filter, creating an effect of eeriness and emotional dismay, as is a further fantasmatic sequence in which Toss imagines herself being seized by Ethan and dragged into a corner of the shearing shed to be shorn, like a sheep.

Almost all of the mise-en-scène is contrived to arouse an emotional impression. This is particularly true of the farmhouse and its surroundings, which, as the critic Nicholas Reid notes, underlines the isolation of these characters from the rest of humanity:

> The utility truck in which Ethan returns to the farm is a late model, but otherwise all the film's artifacts suggest an earlier, pioneering time when hill farms were often cut off and inaccessible. The decayed, rusted house-roof and the ramshackle, tumbledown shearing yard. The kitchen, lined with tongue and groove, with its coal range, where Elizabeth toils sullenly.[5]

In other words, the farm setting is as much a mindscape as it is a literal location.

Finally, imagistic motifs recur at regular intervals, often functioning as evocative objects both for the spectator and the filmmaker himself. These motifs include the many hawks that appear: literally in nature, mechanically in the metal hawk Birdie has created, and metaphorically in Ethan, the 'hawk-man' of Toss' imagination. Further examples are Toss' pole, which evokes a knight's lance, and Ethan's anorak, which resembles the cowl of a medieval monk, both suggesting a European past that stands in stark contrast to the antipodean post-colonial present of the film's time-setting. Cumulatively, as Reid has pointed out, the combined effect of all these strategies and devices derived from art-cinema is to plunge us 'totally into the consciousness of the child.'[6]

Vigil: A Personal Film

In his fine essay on *Vigil*, Reid suggests further that 'the total film is continuing proof that the most intensely personal works of art are also the most resonant.'[7] Vincent Ward himself has revealed that *Vigil* is indeed a profoundly autobiographical film, which helps to explain the stylistic method he chose to present it, and the haunting, evocative impression it imparts: 'In *Vigil*, I wanted to recreate my childhood perception of the world I had inhabited. I wanted to see a small, intense child on a farm by himself, combating fierce nightmares and fantasizing victories over imaginary foes.'[8]

In this statement, Ward is remembering the farm on which he grew up. His father, after having married a German Jewish refugee woman in Cairo before returning to New Zealand following service overseas during the Second World War, settled with his new wife on a piece of land in Morrison's Bush, near Greytown in the Wairarapa region of the lower North Island, five miles from the nearest town.[9] His wife, who had taken the name Judy, found it particularly difficult to adjust to this new setting after the bourgeois lifestyle she had been used to in Germany before the war:

> It was a hard life. Home was a one-room shack-on-wheels, with small boxes for chairs, a large one for a table. They had no electricity, no water and a patch of gorse for a lavatory. Judy thought how far it was from the servants, the silverware, the classical piano lessons of Hamburg – to her, the farm seemed primeval, at the edge of the earth.[10]

Ward openly admits that the character of Elizabeth in the film (played by Penelope Stewart) is closely based on his mother, 'a woman whose estrangement from the land echoed my mother's sense of isolation and frustration at this strange new country.'[11]

Even more significantly, the main character, Toss, although a girl, is based on Ward himself: her perceptions and feelings are, in fact, those he remembers having had as a boy. Indeed, the film is full of personal memories projected in a series of striking images that serve as evocative objects. Among those that Ward identifies in his autobiographical memoir are the hut on wheels (in which his parents spent their first years on the farm); the image of his father burning stillborn lambs in the fire; the apocalyptic engraved scenes in the family Bible; the derelict woolshed; the 'bloody business of docking and tailing lambs' with his father; the cliff at the far end of the property; and hawks diving from the sky.[12] One can also add to this list his memories of the books that he read:

Figure 6.1 The Father's hand in *Vigil* (dir. Vincent Ward, 1984).

Scott and his *Ivanhoe*, *Grimms' Fairy Stories*, and tales of the Knights of the Round Table.[13] All of these memories are embedded in the mise-en-scène and enrich it with a sense of over-determination – in other words, the latent signification of the images is greater than what their literal appearance might suggest.

Ward's use of this autobiographical material was no casual thing, and the degree of his personal investment is reflected in his images, the power of which derives from the emotional associations they suggest. One such instance occurs early in the film when a shot of the roughened hand of Toss' dead father is shown in close-up. Ward, revealing that 'it was my father's hands that led me to paint and then make films,' explains the feelings that the sight of them aroused in him:

> Even now, I see those hands of his wet with rain, or with blood after an accident with a docking knife. They reminded me of mangled tree trunks and roots during a winter flood, carried down slippery crevices and scarring farmland cliffs, before finally arriving on a flooded river, only to be tossed and broken further.[14]

These mangled trees and roots, too, appear in the film associated with the father for whom Toss is planting a memorial manuka bush. These images are important to the filmmaker because they conjure up how a farmer in this colonial setting is forever set against nature, 'and how nature has its revenge.'[15] His sense of the tension between these two opposing forces – 'the farmer, killing and maiming everything that moves, except his beloved sheep' on one hand,

Figure 6.2 Mangled trees – an autobiographical memory in *Vigil* (dir. Vincent Ward, 1984).

and vengeful nature on the other – provides the motive power for Ward's creativity, which is one of the things that makes him a distinctively New Zealand filmmaker, and *Vigil* a national film.

THE CHARACTERIZATION OF TOSS

In 2010, Ward revealed that in early drafts of *Vigil* the character of Toss had been written as a boy.[16] It was only gradually that the character of the child turned into a girl.[17] Ward admits that he finds it hard to explain this even to himself. The explanation he supplies is tentative:

> When I was young, I didn't mix much with girls, and yet I could remember for a long time fantasising about having a female companion, one I could play with or go hunting with. Perhaps those relationships you miss out on in childhood are those you search for as an adult, and I was giving form and flesh to my imaginary friend.[18]

The events in the fiction, however, suggest that there was much more to it than that, especially given Ward's admission that the character of Toss was created not only from parts of his sister and girlfriend, but also 'from the bones of my childhood,' as is apparent from the autobiographical elements that Toss embodies.[19] The significance of the change of gender begins to become apparent when one takes account of its effects.

Had Ward persisted with his original intention – that is, to create the character of Toss as a boy – the film would have presented an Oedipal scenario very similar to that in Shakespeare's *Hamlet*. In the play, a son whose father has recently died kindles a great hatred for the man who has replaced him in the affections of his mother, along with anger at his mother for what he considers to be her disloyalty and betrayal. Had Toss remained a boy, this situation would have been replicated almost exactly: Toss-as-son, devoted to his father, would have been resentful of Ethan, the 'poacher,' for taking his father's place, at the same time as Ethan displaces the son by attracting his mother's attention and desires. With Toss as a girl, however, this Oedipal situation is converted into one that is marked by an Electra complex – that is, the parallel situation in which the young girl feels attraction for her father and hostility towards her mother, whom she now sees as a rival. By changing the boy into a girl, Ward added a great deal of psychological tension and complexity that is carefully and deliberately worked through in great depth in the movie.

Apart from any personal relevance Ward's characterization of Toss may have had, the way he finally created Toss captures the ambivalence of most childhood attachments to parental figures at the point where the child is struggling to break free of them at the entry into adolescence. The resolution of this ambivalence is what constitutes the action and shapes the narrative of the film.

Toss' Balaclava

One of the most striking symbolic images Ward uses in the film is the dark balaclava Toss wears for much of its duration. The way she treats it provides an index to her inner feelings as she passes through the different stages of her maturation into puberty and sexuality. Toss first puts the balaclava on after the death of her father, when she revisits the cliff where he died, and is shown among tree trunks and roots that serve as an outward visual correlative to her desolate emotional state. The balaclava is thus a psychological defense against the pain of loss in a world that seems indifferent at best, and at worst actively hostile. This sense of retreat into a self-protective defendedness is reinforced soon after when Toss seeks refuge in the shell of a derelict car, which she will visit again several times in the course of the movie.

We can also infer that she wears the balaclava as a defense against what the invading stranger, Ethan, represents, given that during the episode when she dons it, she hears the scream of a hawk, a predatory bird that (symbolically) dives out of the sky to attack 'lambs' (of which, metaphorically speaking, Toss is one). Later in the movie, Toss will explicitly associate Ethan with the hawk soon after she has looked down from her perch on the hill while Ethan and her mother are having sex: 'Hunter, hawk-man, I know who you are.' The predatory hawk, alias Ethan, is associated with sexuality, of which the child unconsciously fears the onset as she is becoming pubescent. Given that her father, Justin, hated hawks and was obsessed with shooting them – a shot early in the film has shown Toss's father leading her up a hill past a dead tree in which dead hawks are hanging – it seems as if Justin and Ethan function as antithetical doubles as far as sexuality is concerned, with Justin representing the 'safe' (that is, non-sexual) father of the pre-pubescent child's imagination, and Ethan the 'dangerous' manifestation of masculine sexuality as perceived by the pubescent child who has become aware of the reality of sex.

Toss' association of Ethan with sexuality is compounded by recurrent images of blood. After the poacher has been hired to take her father's place on the farm, Toss carries a lamb to him to be docked; as Ethan slices off the lamb's tail, blood spurts on Toss' face, after which she smears it over her lips, and spreads it like make-up over her cheeks, in an action that replicates a shot of her mother standing before a mirror in a petticoat, as she applies lipstick to beautify herself in anticipation of receiving the stranger into the house. Through association, therefore, the blood becomes a symbol of the loss of innocence.

The balaclava features again in the scene where Toss visits Ethan in his hut and experiments with her feminine seductive power, and has her first experience of a male eroticizing her. During this sequence, Ethan removes her balaclava – suggesting the lowering of her defenses – and then fondles her face. In response, Toss first bites, and then sucks, his fingers in a provocative action that will be replicated by her mother when the latter and Ethan actually have sex. Significantly, however, during the episode when Ethan and her mother make love, Toss has donned her balaclava once more as she looks down on the house from her hillside perch, imagining what is taking place below. Toss' grief and distress are registered on her face in a close-up shot as if she is a child witnessing the primal scene, even though this is literally impossible, given that she is positioned at a fairly great distance from the house in reality. This taking on and off of the balaclava suggests an oscillation between a desire to experiment and a fear of the consequences in the girl's imaginative sense of the condition that awaits her.

Finally, after Toss has accepted the reality that her mother has given herself to Ethan, and she discovers the menstrual blood of her first period on her fingers, she goes out into the rain at night, takes off her balaclava, and throws it into the water, thus signifying at a symbolic level an acceptance of her transition into adolescent sexuality. In the final scenes of the film, when we see Toss emerging from her grandfather's hut, she is no longer wearing her balaclava. Instead, she is now clothed in a dress, and her hair is starting to grow, as her mother Liz declared she wanted to happen near the beginning of the movie as she was trying to encourage her daughter to switch her interest to ballet. As Liz, Toss, and Birdie prepare to leave the farm, which Liz has sold, Ethan, in his car, bursts through the closed gate in the fence that encloses the narrow world in which they have been living – an action which, apart from suggesting a breaking of the barriers that have limited the scope of the possibilities in their lives, also constitutes an image of defloration, thus foreshadowing the eventual consequence of the sexuality into which Ethan's presence has inducted Toss.

Ambivalent Attachments

One of the most striking aspects of *Vigil* is the degree to which the attachment relationships of Toss to the adult figures in her life are shown to be ambivalent. At the beginning of the film, she is closely bonded with her father and is shown to be eager to desert her mother, who is engaged in 'feminine' activities in the kitchen, for the sake of joining her father in his 'masculine' preoccupations outside on the farm – in this instance, burning the carcasses of stillborn lambs. This male-aligned preference is repeated later in the film when her mother is trying to teach Toss ballet in the very feminine tutu she has stitched for her, and Toss abandons the lesson to run out to Ethan and her grandfather who have erected a pulley attached to the tractor, which they have managed to get working again. Toss' preference for the men's domain would seem to imply a rejection of the mother and what she represents.

On the other hand, Toss imitates her mother in her femininity when she pretends to put on make-up, and when she scrutinizes herself before a mirror in her car-hideaway, in a scene that visually repeats the scene of her mother before a mirror that had occurred earlier. In these respects, she is doubled with her mother, as the similarity between the names 'Lisa' and 'Liz' suggests.

Toss also aligns herself with her mother's nostalgia for the culture of Europe, seen in her fascination with the myth of Satan and the fallen angels engraved in the family Bible, as well as her fantasy of Ethan and her father engaging in combat on horseback with each other as if they were medieval knights, a surrealistic episode showing the extent to which Toss' imagination inhabits her mother's European past.[20] Toss, in fact, is depicted as being in an indeterminate or in-between state as far as her own gender and cultural identifications are concerned – an indeterminacy brilliantly captured in the image of her in her ballet tutu, while wearing gumboots and her balaclava.[21] As already noted, she displays a similar ambivalence to the man who has come to stand-in for her father, alternately behaving seductively towards him and fearing him as a hawk-man to be equated with Satan as a fallen angel.

The Multilayered Symbolic Complexity of the Film

The ambivalence observable in Toss' character points to another layer of complexity in the film, one that may have been developed unconsciously on the

Figure 6.3 Toss (Fiona Kay), in her ballet tutu and gumboots, with Ethan (Frank Whitten) in *Vigil* (dir. Vincent Ward, 1984).

filmmaker's part, if one is to follow a hint implanted in his own reflections on *Vigil*. Ward reports that while the film was being shot, the women members in the crew observed that the girl he had cast as Toss, Fiona Kay, 'bore more than a passing resemblance to me,' causing the director to wonder whether he 'had really scanned the faces of 40,000 schoolgirls unconsciously searching for my clone.'[22] This admission is significant, because it confirms that Ward's own identification with his child protagonist did not end once he had decided to make Toss a girl rather than a boy as he had initially intended. It is worthwhile exploring the implications of this ongoing identification with Toss, which continues despite the change of gender.

We are presented, one suspects, with an instance of the well-known phenomenon that psychoanalysts have identified as intrinsic to the creative process manifest in dreams, fantasies, and, as I have argued elsewhere, in fiction itself.[23] This is the psychic defense mechanism known as *reversal*, which is a form of displacement that allows the ego to deal with a problematical issue while protecting itself from intolerable exposure to it – a device frequently found in fiction (both literary and cinematic).

Ward has been open about his reversal of the gender of Toss' character, but this reversal merely made possible a much more profound one. As I indicated at the beginning of this essay, the change of Toss from a boy to a girl enabled the transformation of what would have been an Oedipal scenario, in which a son feels rivalry with his father as a result of freshly awakened sexual feelings towards his mother, into an Electra one, in which a daughter feels rivalry with her mother whom she seeks to replace in her father's affections. The effect of this profound reversal is to add an additional, underlying dimension to the representation, a dimension that is apparent in the ambiguity that is generated by the presentation of Toss' ambivalent gender identification on one hand, and, on the other, the dominant characterization of Toss as a girl that is maintained throughout the fictional diegesis itself.

Reversal is not the only defense mechanism present in this remarkably richly textured film. As we have seen, there is also splitting of the attributes of the father into two separate, antithetical characters, Justin and Ethan, along with metonymical displacement and symbolic condensation in the imagery. Viewed in this way, a parallel can be detected between Toss' balaclava and the film itself: both serve as a protection against feelings that are possibly too painful or fearful to be confronted directly, until such time as the underlying emotional issues have been successfully processed. This, one might suspect, is the function of the film itself, meaning that by the time the film reaches its conclusion, it has, like Toss' balaclava, served its purpose by offering protection while this processing is undergone, whether on the part of the protagonist, the spectator, or the filmmaker himself.

Together with the minimalist art-cinema style, this ambiguity in the signification of the story is what imparts a dreamlike quality to *Vigil*. The end result is a representation of a coming of age that transcends gender specificity – the passage Toss undergoes from childhood into adolescence, with its conflicted and troubling emotions, is a universal one. At the same time, it is a truly national film on account of its representation of the cultural dislocations entailed in the colonial experience whereby New Zealand became settled by Europeans.[24]

Unsurprisingly, given its artistic excellence and depth of vision, *Vigil* earned much critical acclaim. It became the first New Zealand feature film to be screened in competition at the prestigious Festival de Cannes,[25] and, in the eyes of many, it can hold its own among the best coming-of-age films ever made. As an expression of art-cinema, it certainly remains uniquely accomplished within the corpus of New Zealand cinema.

Notes

1. Vincent Ward, *Edge of the Earth: Stories and Images from the Antipodes* (Auckland: Heinemann Reed, 1990), 69.
2. See Nicholas Reid, *A Decade of New Zealand Film*: Sleeping Dogs *to* Came a Hot Friday (Dunedin: John McIndoe, 1986), 116.
3. See Helen Martin's essay on *Vigil* in Helen Martin and Sam Edwards, *New Zealand Film 1912–1996* (Auckland: Oxford University Press, 1997), 106.
4. Ibid.

5. Reid, *A Decade of New Zealand Film*, 109.
6. Ibid., 109.
7. Ibid.
8. Ward, *Edge of the Earth*, 69.
9. Ibid., 55.
10. Ibid., 56–8.
11. Ibid., 70.
12. Ibid., 73–4.
13. Ibid.
14. Vincent Ward, *The Past Awaits: People, Images, Film* (Nelson: Craig Potton Publishing, 2010), 71.
15. Ward, *Edge of the Earth*, 72–3.
16. Ward, *The Past Awaits*, 150.
17. Ward, *Edge of the Earth*, 69.
18. Ibid., 69–70.
19. Ibid., 70.
20. On the persistence of medieval imagery in *Vigil*, see Stephanie Rains, 'Making Strange: Journeys through the Unfamiliar Films of Vincent Ward,' in Ian Conrich and Stuart Murray (eds), *New Zealand Filmmakers* (Detroit: Wayne State University Press, 2007), 273–88.
21. See Reid, *A Decade of New Zealand Film*, 111.
22. Ward, *Edge of the Earth*, 73–4.
23. See Alistair Fox, *Speaking Pictures: Neuropsychoanalysis and Authorship in Film and Literature* (Bloomington and Indianapolis: Indiana University Press, 2016).
24. For an argument that the representation of the feminine in *Vigil* constitutes an exploration of the post-colonial nation, see Maureen Molloy, 'Death and the Maiden: The Feminine and the Nation in Recent New Zealand Films,' *Signs* 25:1 (1999), 153–70; and Mary M. Wiles, 'Narrating the Feminine Nation: The Coming-of-age Girl in Contemporary New Zealand Cinema,' in Timothy Shary and Alexandra Seibel (eds), *Youth Culture in Global Cinema* (Austin: University of Texas Press, 2007), 175–88.
25. http://www.festival-cannes.fr/fr/archives/ficheFilm/id/0467700E-82C3-43F2-842E-30042FE6BA55/year/1984.html, accessed 15 June 2016.

7. A MĀORI GIRL WATCHES, LISTENS, AND LEARNS – COMING OF AGE FROM AN INDIGENOUS VIEWPOINT: *MAURI* (MERATA MITA, 1988)

If *Vigil* is distinctive in the extent of its deployment of art-film style in a coming-of-age film, Merata Mita's *Mauri* (1988) is equally distinctive as an example of 'Fourth Cinema' – that is, a wholly indigenous approach to the genre. The concept of 'Fourth Cinema' was devised by Mita's fellow Māori filmmaker Barry Barclay (1944–2008) to describe a form of filmmaking that aimed to create, produce, and transmit the stories of indigenous people, and in their own image. Barclay devised the term to distinguish indigenous cinema from Hollywood, art-house, and Third World cinema, expounding this theory in *Our Own Image*, a short book published in 1990. In it, he argued that every culture has a right and responsibility to present its own culture to its own people in ways that answer to its own values and needs. To achieve such an ideal of indigenous filmmaking, Barclay argues, requires a Māori film, for example, to be one that is 'made by Māori' for Māori, with Māori technicians and Māori actors. It also means resisting 'Pākehā plots' when devising a script, given that these inevitably reflect a different value system.[1]

Merata Mita (1942–2010) held a view of, and adopted an approach to, filmmaking that entirely matched Barclay's precepts. The first Māori woman to produce, write the script for, and direct a fiction feature film, and perhaps the first indigenous woman to do so anywhere in the world, Mita considered that by the 1930s the screen had been colonized in New Zealand through the imposition of western perspectives and stereotypes on the Māori people, from the first melodramas made by the Frenchman Gaston Méliès, such as *Loved by a Maori Chieftess* (1913), through the American director Alexander

Markey's *Hei Tiki* (1935), which many Māori view as culturally offensive.[2] For Māori, Mita avers, ever since images of Māori people were first captured by the camera in early colonial days, the reproduced image had *mana* (spiritual power, prestige), meaning that the image is endowed with a sacred aspect. For this reason, a film that shows Māori people is regarded as a *taonga* (cultural treasure), and must be treated accordingly. When a film about Māori is screened in a Māori context, Mita says, the Māori audience 'can find, and themselves express, the spiritual element underscoring our physical world.'[3]

Inspired by these beliefs and convictions, Barclay and Mita both undertook to make films about Māori, by Māori, and for Māori in a way that exemplified the values of Fourth Cinema – Barclay in *Ngati* (1987), the first fiction feature made by a Māori director, and Mita the year following with *Mauri*, which is very important in the history of New Zealand cinema not only because its director is a Māori woman, but because it is also, in Barclay's words, 'the world's first truly indigenous film, first intensively Indigenous film,' given that it adopted an even more purely indigenous perspective than his own *Ngati*, which, by his own admission, was 'set nicely within both the Maori world and the national orthodoxy.'[4]

Equally to the purpose of this book, Mita's film provides a unique perspective on the coming-of-age of a Māori girl; as Mita puts it, *Mauri* is 'a kid's odyssey through life and death and through the grandmother's life and death.'[5] In important respects, the coming-of-age experience that is depicted is very different from that of a Pākehā child.

A Māori Story: Personal Relevance and Structure

In certain key aspects – as with every other coming-of-age film discussed in this book – *Mauri* is a very personal film.[6] Characteristically, the action is set in the 1950s, the time of Mita's own childhood, at a location on the East Coast of the North Island, the region in which Mita was born (at Maketu in the Bay of Plenty). Apart from this autobiographical relevance, the geographical setting has a deeper significance. Mita is from the Arawa confederation of tribes, being Ngāti Pikiao on her father's side, and Ngāi Te Rangi on her mother's side, both from the Bay of Plenty, the traditional landing site of the Te Arawa canoe. It was important for Mita to situate her story on the East Coast because, as she says, it is vital that Māori people know 'who we are and where we come from.' Giving her movie this setting was thus a way of affirming her identity and of locating its story in the context of her own people: 'your ancestors are always there with you, and behind you, guiding the way for you,'[7] which is one of the lessons that the film seeks to impart.

Having chosen this setting and time frame, Mita then projects both her child self and her adult self into two of the main characters: Awatea (Rangamarie

Delamere), who represents her as a young girl (of about ten or eleven years of age), and Ramari (Susan D. Paul), who bears a similarity to her as a young woman. Mita has revealed that Awatea's distressing dealings with a bigoted white racist, Mr Semmens (Geoff Murphy), were based on actual encounters that Mita herself had experienced with an old Pākehā when she was growing up, a man who was even worse, she says, than the caricature presented in the film.[8] Like Ramari, Mita, too, married a Pākehā – the director Geoff Murphy, for whom she had acted the part of Matu in his film *Utu* (1983), and who reciprocated the favor by acting the part of old Mr Semmens in *Mauri*. The role of these younger and older incarnations of Mita is, as Kara (Eva Rickard), the aged grandmother, tells Ramari at one point, to 'listen and learn,' and the various intertwining plot lines of the film constitute the material that presents them with the insights they need to acquire. Kara herself is a very important character, being the guardian of the wisdom of the elders. Her function in the movie as someone who will impart to the other characters the cultural understandings they will need is figured metaphorically in the preliminary scene preceding the credit sequence, in which she is called upon to deliver a baby into the world – while a Pākehā doctor stands by helplessly, unable to assist. Symbolically, this is what Kara will do in the course of the film: she will 'deliver' the child Awatea into a Māori philosophy of life, and a knowledge of life and death.

The main plot lines of the film consist of four interrelated encounters with the Pākehā world that together represent the challenges faced by Māori in their contemporary post-colonial situation. The first is Awatea's encounter with Mr Semmens, a rabidly racist Pākehā who has acquired her tribe's lands by nefarious means, and who hurls verbal abuse at her, calling her a 'tar-baby,' repeatedly threatens her, and seeks to terrorize her by pretending on one occasion to be a scarecrow who comes to life (thus unwittingly presenting in a literally enacted form his real-life status, metaphorically speaking, in the eyes of Māori). Accordingly, Awatea's encounters with Semmens symbolically figure the history of race relations between Māori and Pākehā since colonization as Mita conceives them – a history marked by theft of Māori land, by racial prejudice and discrimination on the part of Pākehā, and by the maintenance of an environment that is hostile to Māori aspirations.

The second encounter is that of Ramari with Steve (James Heyward), the son of old Mr Semmens, who provides a contrasting image of a Pākehā, one who is sensitive to Māori culture, sympathetic and open, and without racial prejudice, having fallen unconditionally in love with Ramari and wanting keenly to marry her. Steve shows his good will by bringing a crate of beer to the camp of Māori men clearing scrub, and wants to join in with them. He also shows cultural sensitivity and respect by using the customary form of address in Māori when greeting Kara, and after he and Ramari have married, against the furious opposition of old Mr Semmens, Steve willingly accepts Ramari's child by a Māori man, Rewi Rapana (Anzac Wallace), to be raised as his own. By embracing these attitudes, he offers an alternative model for relations between Māori and Pākehā to that represented by his father, which, in real life, shadows Mita's own marriage to just such a man in the person of Geoff Murphy, the co-producer of her film.

The third encounter with the Pākehā world is that of Rewi, Willie (Willie Raana), and other young Māori males who have left their rural tribal homeland in order to migrate into the city. Once there, severed from their cultural roots, these young men have sought to create an alternative *whanau* (family) by forming a gang – an action, however, that propels the gang's members variously down the path of robbery, drinking, vicious rivalry, and finally to betrayal, murder, and death, epitomized in the treachery of Herb, who contrives to have Willie, the gang leader, assassinated. The most severe effects of this deracination are experienced by Rewi, whose real name is Paki, a man who has stolen the identity of the actual Rewi Rapana. Given that Rewi had been separated from his tribal family for twenty years, Paki is able to pass off this deception without being detected. As with the other Māori/Pākehā encounters, the events involved in this particular encounter function as a parable that symbolically figures the situation of Māori who have lost their authentic identity, and hence, like Paki, need to simulate a fraudulent one.

The fourth and final encounter is that of the tribe with Government officials about their scheme to build a rehabilitation center on the tribe's land as a means of solving the problem of child delinquency. During this meeting, the Government Minister, after insulting the people with his atrocious mispronunciation of Māori words, further offends their customs by refusing to partake of food and refreshments with them and attend a session at which members of the tribe could ask him questions. To Hemi (Sonny Waru), the *kaumātua* (tribal elder), the Minister admits that the meeting is a sham, a mere exercise in 'public relations.' In attendance is a young Māori cop (Temuera Morrison) in the uniform of the New Zealand Police Force. As such, he is one of the despised 'auxiliaries' who were frequently denounced by Māori activists at this time – namely, a Māori who has gone over to 'the other side' out of personal ambition in order to 'fit into the white system and succeed on white terms with white values.'[9]

Merata Mita has said the story in the film is 'really a parable about the schizophrenic existence of so many Maori in Pakeha society,'[10] and the events generated by these various encounters illustrate what she means. In Mita's view, it is 'only by breaking free of colonial repression and asserting our true Maori identity [that] we ever gain real freedom,'[11] and it is by watching and listening to what transpires as these events unfold that Awatea learns how this liberation may be achieved. Particularly important is the wisdom that she is able to observe in the way her grandmother, Kara, responds to them.

The Form of Mauri

In terms of its form, *Mauri* is equally distinctive as a Māori film, owing to the way its structure reflects a Māori view of time. Given the strong sense Māori have of a spiritual dimension underlying surface reality, and a belief in the living presence of the ancestors, they do not conceive of time in the European linear sense that has been dominant since St Augustine and the early church Fathers.[12] For Māori, as the Māori writer Patricia Grace puts it in her novel *Potiki*, all time is 'a now-time,' centered 'in the being':

> ... the centred being in this now-time simply reaches out in any direction towards the outer circles, these outer circles being named 'past' and 'future' only for our convenience. The being reaches out to grasp those adornments that become part of the self. So the 'now' is a giving and a receiving between the inner and the outer reaches ... .[13]

The way *Mauri* is constructed replicates this sense of now-time reaching out to the outer circles that are named past and future. We see this in the constant flashbacks in which Rewi sees an image of a car crashing down a cliff – the car belonging to the man whose identity he has stolen, and which he pushed over the cliff, with the body of the dead man, into the sea to conceal his theft. The-past-in-the-present and the-present-in-the future is also intimated by a pattern of repetitions and returns. The sacred hill at the beginning from which, Kara tells Awatea, her own grandmother departed for the mythical ancestral home of Hawaiki, returns at the end of the film as the place from which Awatea waves farewell to the departing spirit of her grandmother, anticipating a time in the future when she, too, will depart for Hawaiki in the same manner. This pattern is superimposed over another pattern that begins with birth and ends with death, with the two conflated patterns underlying the circularity of things. The presence of the ancestors is also signaled in the haunting music that accompanies significant moments, which is played on traditional Māori instruments – the *kōauau* (cross-blown flute, made of wood, bone, or a species of kelp), the *pūtorino* (large traditional flute, made of wood), and the *pūtātara* (conch shell trumpet).

Awatea: An Astute Observer

The particular setting and plot lines Mita chose for her story allow her to create a broad panorama that displays many aspects of Māori life from an authentically indigenous perspective, in particular the '*mauri*' of the Māori world – that is, the life principle and essential quality and vitality of the Māori people and the culture that expresses their values and philosophy of life.[14]

Figure 7.1 Awatea (Rangimarie Delamere) observes the adult world in *Mauri* (dir. Merata Mita, 1988).

Moreover, Mita's portrayal of Awatea as an avid listener and observer enables the filmmaker to channel the spectator's perception of this world through the girl's eyes as she registers the impact and implications of what she sees.

Awatea is characterized as a child of boundless curiosity who is keen to learn. Her predisposition in this regard is figured in recurrent scenes that show her examining things in nature through her magnifying glass: when she scrutinizes a stick insect among the flowers in Semmens' garden; when she looks at drops of dew hanging from the strands of wire in a fence; and when she gazes at the intricacy of a spider's web.

Metaphorically speaking, these scenes mirror what Awatea will do with respect to the larger world as the action unfolds. Indeed, Awatea is a witness to almost every major event. She is constantly watching and taking things in, as when she sees the young Māori policeman questioning people on the *marae* as to the whereabouts of Rewi. She takes Rewi and the work gang food at night, and sneaks out her bedroom window when the others think she is asleep, so that she can listen to the conversations of adults. Most of all, she watches how her grandmother reacts to events, asks questions of her, and absorbs her wisdom.

Mita's young protagonist is not merely a passive observer. Another series of shots show her lying in bed, reflecting on the significance of events that have occurred, usually troubling ones, such as the shooting of Uncle Willy. At these moments, she hears the nocturnal cry of the *ruru*, or morepork, a native owl that in Māori mythology is strongly associated with the spirit world and functions as a *kaitiaki* (guardian) with the power to warn of a death in the family – for example, just before news arrives that Rewi's mother has died.

As a result of all this watching, listening, and reflecting, Awatea becomes induced through the course of the film into a deepening awareness of Māori cultural values, customs, and philosophy of life in preparation for her growth into her future adult identity as a Māori, knowing truly who she is.

The Māori World and its *Tikanga*

What, then, does Awatea observe, and what does she learn? Every aspect of the fictional world of the film proclaims the 'Māoriness' of its vision. Many scenes, especially in the earlier part of the film, depict Māori *tikanga*, or traditional practices and the customary way of doing things. In the opening sequence when a Māori girl gives birth, Kara delivers it with the young woman standing up, not lying down as in western culture. Similarly, she insists that the baby's umbilical cord be cut with a piece of paua shell that has been used for this purpose for generations. Following the birth, the placenta must be buried in an appropriate place, in accordance with the appropriate ritual, to reinforce the relationship between the newborn child and the land of its birth.

Other customary practices concern the gathering of traditional food, as when Ramari and Rewi retrieve *tuna* (eels) from pots set in the river, or when Ramari, swimming naked, gathers *kai moana* (seafood) – in this instance, sea urchins. When Willy and the members of his gang arrive, Rewi, even though he cannot show his face to avoid the exposure of his imposture, nevertheless hunts down a pig and prepares and cooks it over a fire in order to present it to the others in fulfillment of his obligation to provide hospitality. Similarly, at Steve and Ramari's wedding, when the members of the tribe hold a communal feast, the food is cooked in a *hāngī*, or traditional earth oven, which uses steam and heat from heated stones.

On another occasion, Awatea accompanies Kara and Hemi up a hill, where her grandmother teaches her how to weave a *kete* (basket) out of flax, and shows her the hill where her own grandmother lived many decades ago in her little thatched *whare* (Māori house).

An important dimension of the Māori world to which Awatea is exposed is its communal nature and the importance of *aroha* (love) as the force that binds its members together. There is, in fact, an enormous difference between the Christian concept of 'love,' which exalts the individual and places personal responsibility on him or her, and the Maori concept of '*aroha*,' which refers to something different. The difference is well expressed by one of the characters in *The Strongest God*, written by the Māori author Heretaunga Pat Baker. Addressing a Christian missionary, the elder, Tiwai, says:

> In your Pakeha religion ... you speak of the individual's duty to God. Then you carry this into our lives as love for the individual, which can

Figure 7.2 Awatea (Rangimarie Delamere) learns how to make a flax *kete* from her grandmother Kara (Eva Rickard) in *Mauri* (dir. Merata Mita, 1988).

mean only one thing, that this person will love only himself and no one else! We think only as a family, as a hapu, as a tribe. We can realize our true selves only through our tribe, and by love of others for us, which teaches us the true meaning of love.[15]

In *Mauri*, this feeling is omnipresent and displayed at every turn. Many of the relationships shown are between individuals who are not immediately connected. Reference is made to Awatea's mother and father, but they are not present in the film; Awatea is being raised by her grandmother, a custom that is frequently adopted in Māori culture. Similarly, Hine's baby is looked after by the family group, and when Steve marries Ramari, he enters into a relationship with her *hapū* (kinship group) as a whole. An outward sign of this commitment is his willingness to raise the baby Ramari has conceived by Rewi as his own, in the full knowledge that one day the boy will be told who his real father is. When Willie, Kara's nephew, arrives, he is treated like a son, and the other members of his gang are received as if they, too, are family members, being embraced with the same kind of *aroha*.

As a witness to all of these cultural traditions, therefore, Awatea learns of the spiritual values and unbroken continuity that binds her into a community that consists not only of those among whom she lives in the present, but all the ancestors who have gone before her in the past.

Rewi/Paki: A Damaged Man

In contrast with the confident sense of identity and fullness of being that is imparted by this communal approach to life, cemented by *aroha* and protected by *tapu* (a set of prohibitions that control how people behave towards each other and the environment), Rewi (actually Paki Selwyn Hemapō), the adult character around whom much of the action revolves, is spiritually a broken man.

In the course of the film, Paki confesses his story to Kara, telling her that he had drifted into petty crime when he moved to the city. On one occasion, acting as a lookout for his gang when it attempted to burglarize a bank, he hot-wired a car to escape when the attempt was botched. As he fled south, he picked up Rewi Rapana, who was hitchhiking home after a twenty-year absence, and who told Paki his own life story. When the car drives off the road and Rewi is killed, Paki sees his chance: he steals Rewi's wallet, removes the medallion and bone carving from around his neck, and takes his coat, after which he pushes the car, with Rewi inside, down a cliff where it explodes and incinerates Rewi at a tideline. After this, he has successfully passed himself off as Kara's nephew, his fraud remaining undetected.

Paki's act, however, constitutes a major transgression of Māori *tapu*: he has stolen Rewi's *wairua*, or spirit, and his *mana*. This theft of another man's identity has left him without a true identity of his own, leaving him the victim of a suite of dysfunctional behaviors. He loves Ramari, but is impeded by guilt from allowing that love to develop naturally into a healthy relationship because, as he tells Kara when she points out that Ramari 'has the hots' for him, he does not think he is the man he needs to be for Ramari. This causes Paki to push Ramari away when she expresses her interest in him, leaving her open to the wooing of Steve Semmens, his Pākehā rival. Nevertheless, Paki is very jealous of Steve, warning the latter to stay away from Ramari. Understandably, Ramari is perplexed by his apparent lack of sexual interest in her, taunting him: 'Are you queer, or something?' To overcome his reticence, she has to challenge and shame him into proving his manhood by having sex with her, which leaves her pregnant with the baby she will have after her marriage to Steve.

Because of the magnitude of his transgression, Paki, as Kara realizes, is 'a troubled man.' He admits as much to Ramari when she follows him to his hideout to tell him he is the father of her baby; Paki explains that he has 'blood on my hands,' and that he has broken 'more than Pākehā laws.' This leaves him haunted by *kēhua*, or spirits that linger on earth after death, as he confesses to the dying Kara: 'Slowly, the shadow of the dead man overtook me until my world was too dark to live in.'

The only way for Paki to recover from this state of spiritual dereliction is for him to rectify the injustice he has committed. Kara tells him what he must do:

> You must remain a fugitive until you have put right the wrong you did to my nephew, Rewi. He's gone – nothing will bring him back. Go to where he is and give back his medallion, his *taonga*, and ask forgiveness. The Pākehā don't understand our *tapu*. Complete the task and you will be a full man. If you fail, you will die. The aura of death is heavy upon you.

Kara's exhortation is reinforced when Paki, whom Steve has helped to escape, subsequently has a vision of a war-party of chanting warriors advancing along a seashore, challenging him to act honorably, and with the courage of his ancestors – which shortly afterwards he does, by returning to the site of the crash, returning Rewi's medallion, and beseeching forgiveness in an expression of harrowing grief and contrition. When the two policemen arrive to arrest Paki, the latter's spiritual restitution is signaled by the fact that the Old Cop performs the *hongi* with him as a sign of greeting and acceptance, and as an act of compassion. His new respect for Paki is also reflected in the fact that when Paki holds out his wrists to be shackled, the Old Cop will not do it, handing the handcuffs to the ambitious, pākehā-affiliated Young Cop. While he may be a prisoner in the white system, Paki is now once again free in the Māori one.

It is highly significant that shots showing the scene of Paki's restitution are intercut with shots of the deathbed scene – watched, as always, by Awatea – in which Kara passes from this world into the next. The juxtaposition of shots from the two sequences implies some relationship between the two scenes, and what connects them is their attestation to the power of the *mauri*, the life force that is manifest in the collective experience of the *hapū* and its culture. Reconnection with it is what heals Paki and sets him on the path to recovering his Māori identity and his wholeness as a man. It is also evident in the presence of Kara's spirit – symbolized as a heron, an image that has recurred several times earlier in the film – as she departs on her journey to Hawaiki, the place of the ancestors. At the moment Kara dies, Awatea runs up the sacred hill to intercept Kara's spirit as it passes. In the most powerfully moving sequence in the movie, from a circular aerial traveling shot, we see the tiny figure, from Kara's perspective, on the summit of the hill, waving goodbye to her.

Although she is dead in body, Kara's spirit lives on, and when Awatea bids farewell to her, no longer having the fear of death to which she confessed earlier, it is a sign that she will one day assume her grandmother's place in the tribe, just as Kara assumed the place of her own grandmother who passed from the same hill.

The Importance of *Mauri* in New Zealand Cinema

Merata Mita's *Mauri* remains unique within the corpus of New Zealand's national cinema. No other film made before or since has been so thoroughly

Figure 7.3   Awatea (Rangimarie Delamere) waves farewell to the departing spirit of her grandmother in *Mauri* (dir. Merata Mita, 1988).

imbued with a Māori ethos, and none has depicted the Māori world so comprehensively, or with such richness. At the time of writing, Mita also remains the only Māori woman to have solely written, produced, and directed a fiction feature film, which means that *Mauri* remains unique in terms of presenting a female perspective on that world.

Other Māori filmmakers have made coming-of-age films showing Māori children and adolescents at different stages in the maturational process, but the ones who have done so adopt a rather different attitude towards the traditional Māori culture, being far more willing to incorporate aspects of non-Māori, western culture. This difference suggests that Mita's film is the product of, and captures the distinctive outlook of, a particular historical moment in the evolution of race relations in New Zealand. The 1980s were a decade that saw the emergence of Māori nationalism and activism following widespread protests against apartheid when the South African rugby team toured the country in 1981, accompanied by a resurgence of pride in Māori culture stimulated by the Te Māori exhibition that toured the United States in 1984. The vision expressed in *Mauri*, with its privileging of 'pure' Māori culture and its demands for self-determination and the return of land appropriated by the Pākehā, is characteristic of the views being expressed by Māori cultural nationalists at the time.

The New Zealand Government's response to this fraught period in race relations was to foster a program of state-sponsored biculturalism, together with a process administered through the Waitangi Tribunal to restore Māori land and other rights accorded Māori under the Treaty of Waitangi in 1840. Māori coming-of-age films made after *Mauri* are strongly marked by the effects of that bicultural ideology, reflected, in particular, in their manifestations of cultural hybridity. Filmmakers like Taika Waititi in *Boy*, or Lee Tamahori in *Mahana*, present coming-of-age characters who want to change, or escape from, traditional Māori culture, rather than embrace it, and both directors expose the dark underbelly of contemporary Māori life (indigence, child-neglect, physical violence) in a way that Mita eschews in her attempt to capture the nurturing, security-imparting aspects of Māori culture as practised in the traditional rural homelands of her youth.

Mauri thus remains one of a kind. Just as Kara imparts a treasure to Awatea by leading her into an understanding of the Māori world, so too has Mita, by contriving the film in the way she has done, consciously sought to create a *taonga*, or treasure, that will be available for subsequent generations.

Notes

1. Barry Barclay, *Our Own Image: A Story of a Māori Filmmaker* (Minneapolis and London: University of Minnesota Press, 2015), 7, 48.
2. Merata Mita, 'The Soul and the Image,' in Jonathan Dennis and Jan Bieringa, *Film in Aotearoa New Zealand* (Wellington: Victoria University Press, 1992), 36–54, esp. 41–2.
3. Ibid., 39.
4. Barry Barclay, 'Exploring Fourth Cinema,' a talk given at the Summer Institute, 'Re-imagining Indigenous Cultures: The Pacific Islands,' East–West Center and University of Hawai'i Center for Pacific Islands Studies, 2003, quoted in Emiel Martens, 'Maori on the Silver Screen: The Evolution of Indigenous Feature Filmmaking in Aotearoa/New Zealand,' *International Journal of Critical Indigenous Studies* 5:1 (2012), 2–30, esp. 7.
5. Julie Benjamin and Helen Todd with Merata Mita, 'Meshes of an Afternoon: An Interview with Merata Mita,' *Alternative Cinema* 11:4 (1983/4), 40; quoted by Geraldene Peters in Ian Conrich and Stuart Murray (eds), *New Zealand Filmmakers* (Detroit: Wayne State University Press, 2007), 111.
6. I wish to acknowledge here my debt to Hilary Radner for long discussions held on *Mauri*, and for benefits derived from reading her essay '*Mauri* (Merata Mita, 1988): Transnational feminism and Colonialism's Traumatic Legacy in Aotearoa/New Zealand,' a paper delivered at the Global Women's Cinema Conference, held at Stony Brook University, New York, on 18–20 September 2014.
7. Karin Williams with Merata Mita, 'Pacific Perspectives: *Merata Mita*' [interview], Pacific Islanders in Communications, Hawai'i Public Television broadcast, 1997.
8. Ibid.
9. I have quoted here the words used by the Māori woman activist Atareta Poananga to denounce such collaborators, reported in Nicola Legat, 'Atareta Poananga and Te Ahi Kaa: Their Message for Pakeha,' *Metro* 5:57 (March 1986), 44–58, esp. 57.
10. Mita, 'The Soul and the Image,' 49.
11. Ibid.
12. On St Augustine's theory of time, see Friedel Weinert, *The Scientist as Philosopher: Philosophical Consequences of Great Scientific Discoveries* (Berlin and New York: Springer, 2004), 149.
13. Patricia Grace, *Potiki* (Auckland: Penguin, 1986), 39.

14. For an account of some of the Māori beliefs and customs depicted in the film, see Bruce Harding, '"The Donations of History": Mauri and the Transfigured "Māori Gaze",' in Alistair Fox, Hilary Radner, and Barry Keith Grant (eds), *New Zealand Cinema: Interpreting the Past* (Bristol: Intellect/Chicago: Chicago University Press, 2011), 217–37.
15. Heretaunga Pat Baker, *The Strongest God* (Whatamongo Bay, Queen Charlotte Sound: Cape Catley Ltd, 1990), 56.

PART 3

THE SECOND WAVE OF THE 1990S

8. CREATIVITY AS A HAVEN: *AN ANGEL AT MY TABLE* (JANE CAMPION, 1990)

Just as Merata Mita's *Mauri* (1988) is unique within the corpus of New Zealand coming-of-age films, Jane Campion's *An Angel at My Table* is similarly unique, but for very different reasons. Astonishingly, with the exception of Vincent Ward's *Vigil* (1984), it is the first feature film to focus on the maturational experience of a New Zealand Pākehā girl, and it is also the first coming-of-age film to be made by a woman. Additionally, it is the first film to blend the coming-of-age genre with that of the biopic, adapting its screenplay from the celebrated autobiography of the New Zealand writer Janet Frame. Finally, it is the only coming-of-age film to depict all three of the main maturational phases of the genre: childhood; adolescence; and post-adolescence. On top of that, *An Angel at My Table* was recognized as attaining a level of excellence that led to its being the first New Zealand film to be screened in competition at the Venice Film Festival.

The most striking aspect of *An Angel at My Table* is how, while outwardly maintaining an extreme fidelity in the representation of episodes described by Frame in her *Autobiography*, the film converts the subjective self-portrait of the original into a vehicle for a complex dual projection on the part of Campion herself. This conversion is made possible by the shift from Frame's first-person narration, which takes the reader deep into the reflections and insights of the author, to a plurimedial filmic narration that places the spectator at an observer's distance from the cinematic version of 'Janet.' Such a shift of perspective indicates a subtle change in the nature and function of the coming-of-age experience.

'My Say': Janet Frame's *An Autobiography*

In a radio interview of 1983, Janet Frame made it clear that her purpose in writing the three volumes of her autobiography – *To the Is-Land* (1982), *An Angel at My Table* (1984), and *The Envoy from Mirror City* (1984), published together in 1989 – was to have 'my say,' that is, to give her account of her experience and correct the myth of herself as a 'mad writer.'[1] To do so, she describes the formative events in her life as a child, teenager, and young adult, retracing the process whereby she came to understand who she was as a person, and the causes and significance of the experience she had undergone. The result, as Michael Holroyd affirmed in his review for the London *Sunday Times*, was 'one of the greatest autobiographies written this century.'[2]

The individual that Frame portrays is one who, as a child, adolescent, and young adult, suffered from an intensifying sense of being a 'non-person' in her own right, which left her with a feeling of existential anxiety that manifested itself in an extreme form of shyness when in the presence of others. In the course of the first two volumes, Frame intermittently drops hints as to the origins of these feelings, and also the stages by which they progressively deepened until she found herself locked up as a committed patient in various mental institutions. Her mother, she tells us, although present and attentive in outward respects, seemed remote and unavailable at a personal level, as though her real existence were in 'another world and other time.'[3] Later, when Frame, during a temporary absence from hospital, visits her parents and sees her mother talking intimately to her sister, she feels 'like a child excluded from her mother's attention,' which brings her to a realization:

> Always in our family there was the struggle between powerlessness and power where closeness to people and the ability to prove that closeness became a symbol of most power, as if each member of the family struggled constantly to move through a wilderness of deprivation, slowly planting tiny cherished blossoms in the waste, and needing to point to them, describe them, rejoice in them, to the other members of the family, who might not be so advanced in their journey through the desert.[4]

This is the language of someone who, as an adult, is suffering the scars of narcissistic deprivation as a child, in this case arising from a feeling of exclusion from genuine intimacy with her mother.

This sense of deprivation is compounded by Frame's relationship with her father. While she 'long[s] to be close with my father,'[5] his puritanical authoritarianism stands in the way, but, as she subsequently learns while undergoing therapy with a psychiatrist in London: 'Dr Miller had said frankly that he thought my father was a bully; he had a similar opinion of Patrick Reilly. My life had been erased almost, by expert bullying while I played the role of victim that like any other repeated role, resists a change.'[6]

Neither of Frame's parents, then, for different reasons, is shown as providing the validation needed for the development of a secure sense of self, and this leaves her, as a child, with a feeling of 'dread and unhappiness that I could not name':[7]

> I remember a grey day when I stood by the gate and listened to the wind in the telegraph wires. I had my first conscious feeling of an outside sadness ... I felt a burden of sadness and loneliness as if something had happened or begun and I knew about it ... I knew I was listening to a sadness that had no relation to me, which belonged to the world.[8]

These feelings of existential sadness and loneliness not only produce 'an anxious child full of twitches and tics, standing alone in the playground at school' – a girl who wants to be invited to join in the skipping games of the rest of the class, but is too shy to ask[9] – but are also compounded by a sense of *shame*. Janet feels the disgrace of getting worms as a child, and suffers humiliation when she is shamed in front of her class for having stolen money from her father's pocket to buy chewing gum, which she has distributed to her classmates. As a teenager, she feels shame when she gets her period, and further shame when she has to wear bulky rags as sanitary protection. At Dunedin, when she is a student training to be a teacher, she is so ashamed of having her periods that she carries her soiled sanitary towels home to put in the washhouse dustbin where she boards, rather than be seen to use the incinerator at the Training College, and then hides them among the tombstones in the Southern Cemetery rather than allow her Aunt Isy to know that she has 'anything to burn.'[10] As an adult, when her teeth become so rotten she has to have them extracted, she suffers shame at her toothlessness.[11] Such a depth of shame attests to a self-sense so fragile in Janet that she cannot risk exposing herself to 'the praising, blaming scrutiny of others' out of a fear of being judged adversely.[12]

In response to this deepening sense of anxiety and growing sense of worthlessness, Janet's initial reaction is to imitate her mother by withdrawing into an inward world that could provide an alternative to the real world: 'I wanted an imagination that would inhabit a world of fact, descend like a shining light upon the ordinary life of Eden Street, and not force me to exist in an "elsewhere" ... I wanted my life to be the "other world".'[13] This takes the form of clinging to literature 'as a child clings to its mother.'[14] Soon, even this is not sufficient protection against the intrusions of the real world, as Janet learns when a school inspector arrives to appraise her teaching and her fear of being exposed to scrutiny is so great that she simply flees. At this stage, Janet sees suicide as the only escape and does indeed attempt, unsuccessfully, to kill herself by swallowing a packet of aspirins, which leads to her being committed to Seacliff Mental Hospital. Frame describes how, for the next eight years, she spent most of her time in various mental asylums, with nothing left but her desire to write: 'I felt hopeless in my plight. I inhabited a territory of loneliness which I think resembles that place where the dying spend their time before death . . .'[15] Early in her stay, there were periods of several weeks when she was allowed to leave hospital, but each time she needed to return, as she felt that 'there was nowhere else for me to live.' After one stay with her sister June and her husband in Auckland, Janet, unable to 'bear the nothingness . . . retreated to an inward state . . . [which] of course, led to my removal to the Auckland mental hospital at Avondale; at least it was a "place" for me where I was believed to be "at home".'[16] In the face of this retreat into inwardness, Frame was only saved from having a leucotomy, for which her mother had signed a consent, by the news that she had won a literary prize for *The Lagoon*, her collection of short stories that had been published.

For Frame, being treated as a person of some basic human worth was a critical turning point: she began writing again, moved back to Dunedin, then to Auckland, where she met the author Frank Sargeson, who provided her with the encouragement and conditions to write her first novel, *Owls Do Cry*, and the rest is history. Following the acceptance of her novel for publication, Frame travelled to Europe on a literary grant to broaden her experience, received further diagnoses that confirmed she had never had schizophrenia – the diagnosis she had been given in New Zealand – and, with the help of a therapist who sees that she 'genuinely needed to write,' and encourages her to do so, she discovers her ability to live her life as herself in the real world: 'No longer, I hoped, dependent on my "schizophrenia" for comfort and attention and help, but with myself as myself':

> I had learned to be a citizen of the Mirror City . . . The self must be the container of the treasures of Mirror City, the Envoy as it were . . . And when the work is finished and the nothingness must be endured, the self may take a holiday, if only to reweave the used container that awaits the next visit to Mirror City.[17]

Frame thus completes her coming of age by discovering, and accepting, her true self: 'I felt I had found my "place" at [a] deeper level than any landscape of any country would provide.'[18]

It will be apparent from this brief outline of Frame's *An Autobiography* that the impression it leaves is both similar in certain respects, but very different in others, from that of Campion's cinematic adaptation.

Jane Campion's Remodeling of Frame's Narrative

As narratologists have shown, all storytelling involves a process of mediation that affects the relative status of the mediating agents – that is, the narrator or presenter and the character(s).[19] In the course of this mediation, one construal of a story world or story scene can be transformed into another as a result of how a number of parameters are manipulated. These parameters include:

(1) What is selected (which determines the scope of the predication).
(2) The observer's distance from the scene (whether it is distal, medial, or proximal).
(3) The way in which a scene is scanned (whether this is static versus dynamic, or synoptic versus sequential).
(4) The scope of what is shown (narrow or wide).
(5) Figure/ground alignment (the extent to which characters and elements are foregrounded or backgrounded).
(6) The degree of granularity (the amount of detail included in the presentation).
(7) The degree of objectivity versus subjectivity.
(8) The spatial and temporal viewpoint (the vantage point and orientation).[20]

Together, the way these parameters are handled creates 'an embodied, spatio-temporally situated perspective on events.'[21]

The effect of Jane Campion's remediation of Frame's narrative is to shift the emphasis away from Frame's introspective self-analysis to a different perspective in which the camera observes events from the outside, at the same time as it approximates the gaze of 'Janet,' thus creating a dual perspectivation that opens up the way for personal projections on the part of the filmmaker.[22]

Autobiographical Investments

As Campion herself freely admits, she had many personal reasons for choosing to make a film adapted from Frame's *An Autobiography*.[23] At one level, as Campion puts it, she could 'really see [her]self' in Frame's story: 'We all feel vulnerable and unchosen, unlovable, uncared about in one way or another.'[24] What she may have meant by this statement may be reflected in her sister Anna Campion's revelation that she found her parents 'distant' and 'secretive,' with a father who was 'uninterested in his daughters,' and a mother 'who took everything personally,' meaning that Anna 'never felt safe.' As a result, in a way that is strongly reminiscent of Janet Frame in *An Autobiography*, Anna retreated into her head, 'into a fantasy haze where the real world didn't impinge.'[25] Jane, on the other hand, according to Anna, 'got on to the idea of projects to save her. She was obsessed by the need to get everything right. She'd write these plays in which she took all the parts – king, servants, the lot. She'd control the projects to have the world appreciate her.'[26] In particular, 'Jane always wanted my father's attention,' and was envious of the special place Anna held in her mother's affection, just as Janet in Frame's *Autobiography* is envious of the intimacy her sister enjoys with her mother.[27]

The parallels Jane Campion sensed between her own experience and that of Janet Frame extended into her adolescence and beyond. Campion confesses that, like Janet, she was very lonely as a student: 'At first, when I went to university, I was unhappy, very alone. I didn't manage to insert myself in any group, in fact I'm a bit twisted ["*tordue*"], and that meant that it took me a while before I could find others who were prepared to share my sense of humor.'[28] Similarly, when Campion, like Janet, went on her 'OE' [overseas experience] to Europe, her experience mirrored that of Janet: she found herself miserably lonely, identified with her aspirations to be an artist, and longed for a man of her own, a boyfriend, or a partner.' Finally, like Janet, she tells us, 'I believed my interior world was reality.'[29] In terms of the way Frame's *Autobiography* held up a mirror to her own experience, then, Campion had ample reason to want to make a film based on it.

Campion had an even more compelling motivation, however: at another level, the filmmaker associated Janet Frame's story as much with her mother, Edith, as with herself. The idea of making the film first came to Jane, she says, in 1982 when her mother sent her the first volume of Frame's Autobiography, *To the Is-Land*, which had just been published.[30] This act on her mother's part had particular resonance for Campion, because when she was a teenager, Jane recalls, her mother had been so badly affected by depression that Jane had offered to assist her to die: 'It really scared me to feel close to her complete lack of hope.' Although her mother turned her down, the experience left 'a deep and lasting impact' on Jane: 'I had to get away, I couldn't breathe, I couldn't see for myself my own optimism any more,' because Edith's way of looking at the world 'seemed almost contagious.'[31] Edith herself had been hospitalized in Porirua Hospital, near Wellington, when Jane was twenty-nine, and had recently been admitted to Ashburn Hall in Dunedin, in 1980, to undergo treatment for her depression, a period during which she compiled a number of writings, papers, and scrapbooks on unipolar depression that are now deposited at the Alexander Turnbull Library.[32] Like Janet Frame, Edith tried repeatedly 'to find some relief from the overwhelming terror and bleakness of her late-life depression' in mental hospitals, as Jane Campion records when describing a visit to her mother in Ward K2 of Porirua Hospital.[33] As a young teenager, Jane used to ask whether Janet Frame, whose novel *Owls Do Cry* she had read when she was fourteen, was in 'the notorious loony bin' at Porirua

Hospital whenever the family drove past on the way to their seaside bach.[34] When her mother sent her a copy of *To the Is-Land* the association with her mother was instant, and had a profound effect on her: 'As I read, I sobbed and sobbed. She had struck a blow right to my heart. But it was not only about Janet's life, I was also experiencing my own childhood.'[35] Quite apart from her self-identification with Frame's childhood experience, then, Campion was equally impressed by the parallels between the psychic condition described by Frame and the terrifying mental state of her own mother. These twinned associative identifications exerted a transformative influence on the way Campion presented her cinematic adaptation.

THE EFFECT OF THE PERSONAL ELEMENT ON THE FILM'S ENUNCIATION

Bearing in mind the eight parameters governing perspectivation listed above, one can see how Campion's personal investments have shaped *An Angel at My Table* both at the macro and the micro level. At the macro level, the *loci* of these investments are most clearly reflected in what she chose to include, omit, and add. In the first part of the film, 'To the Is-Land,' most of the crucial scenes involving Janet as a child survive intact: her theft of money from her father's pocket and her humiliation in front of her classmates; her loneliness in the playground; friendship with Poppy; her poetry writing, which gains her a prize; her voracious reading; her shame when she gets her period; and so on. As the film moves into Part 2, which deals with Janet from the time she leaves home to become a student in Dunedin until she leaves New Zealand to 'broaden' her experience, Campion makes some major cuts and alterations to her source, which, as Lawrence Jones notes in his meticulous examination of the genesis of the film, 'seem to be primarily for emphasis – to reduce Lottie Frame's role in Janet's life, to accentuate Janet's aloneness and the threat hanging over her, and to emphasize the importance of her eventual sexual liberation from a restrictive puritan social environment.'[36] In addition, the rich metacommentary in which Frame reflects upon her view of the nature and function of fictive creativity, as well as not only her own writing, are almost entirely omitted, suggesting that Campion's main interests in the story lie elsewhere. Above all, the scenes involving Lottie Frame, including her poetic vision, her withdrawal into her own inward world, and her writing of poetry are so systematically suppressed and removed that, as one critic has observed, 'the film adaptation blanks out Frame's mother' to the point of a 'virtual disappearance.'[37]

It is not too difficult to work out why Campion erased Lottie Frame in this way, with a corresponding foregrounding of Janet's father, when one recalls the filmmaker's association of Frame with her own mother. Janet in the movie is a stand-in for Edith Campion, and hence *is* the mother, at least at a fantasmatic level: there was no need for Jane Campion to include another mother figure when her associative conflation of Frame and Edith had already supplied one.

This association is greatly compounded by Campion's inclusion of scenes from Frame's earlier novel *Faces in the Water* into her film that depict in harrowing detail the kind of scenes Campion witnessed on the occasions when she would visit her mother in Porirua Hospital. Although Frame had touched lightly in her *Autobiography* on her experiences in various mental institutions, noting that she had described this experience in her second novel, *Faces in the Water*, she was very unhappy about scenes from that novel being included in the film, to the extent that she expressed concern through her agent.[38] Campion's persistence in retaining these scenes, which, harrowing as they are, carry great weight in the film, shifts its center of gravity away from Frame's investigation of herself towards a depiction of the experience of Edith Campion, who similarly underwent electric shock treatment, and participated in dances with the inmates like that shown in *An Angel at My Table*.

Equally, Campion's greater emphasis on Janet's experiments with sexuality, which are only discreetly touched upon in the *Autobiography*, anticipate and reflect the filmmaker's ongoing preoccupation with eroticism, manifest in subsequent films like *The Piano* (1993), *Holy Smoke* (1997), and *In the Cut* (2003), rather than anything that Frame depicts as being centrally important to her own psychic make-up.

At a micro level, Campion's personal investments are apparent in her shooting style. Part 1 of the film, depicting Janet's childhood and early adolescence,

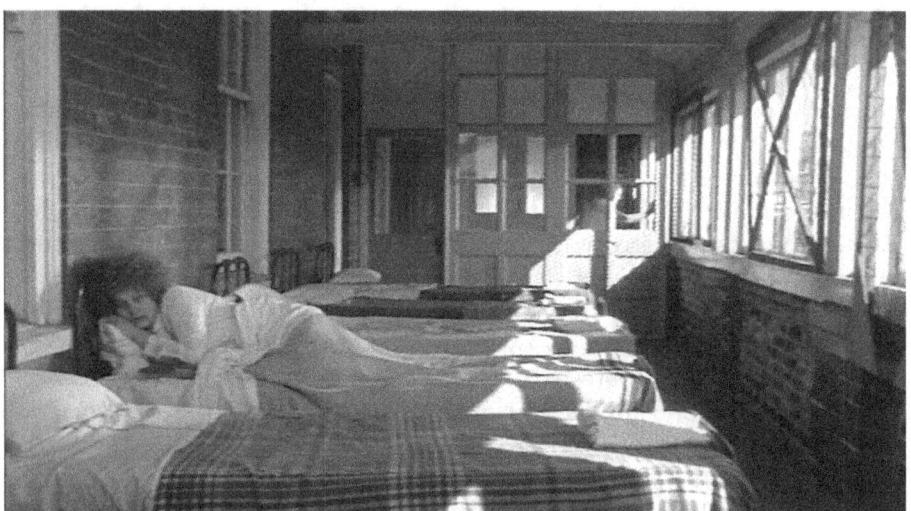

Figure 8.1   Janet (Kerry Fox) in a psychiatric hospital in *An Angel at My Table* (dir. Jane Campion, 1990).

Figure 8.2 Janet (Kerry Fox) experiments with her sensuality in *An Angel at My Table* (dir. Jane Campion, 1990).

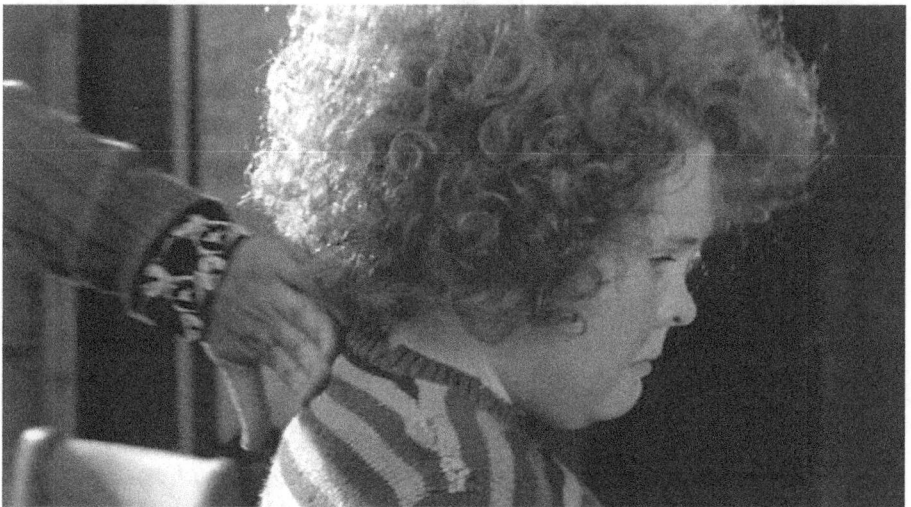

Figure 8.3 Young Janet (Alexia Keogh) shamed in class in *An Angel at My Table* (dir. Jane Campion, 1990).

are where the filmmaker's self-identification with Janet seems to be at its strongest, and this subjective closeness is reflected in the high incidence of close-up shots, such as the one that shows Janet's emotions registering on her face as she stands shamed before a blackboard.

In the later parts of the film, by way of contrast, there is a much greater preponderance of medium long shots and long shots, which puts the spectator at a greater distance, emotionally as well as physically, from Janet in the later phases of her life, which is when Campion identifies her with Edith, her mother, more than herself. One instance, for example, occurs when Janet loses her baby. In Frame's *Autobiography*, this episode occurs while Janet is in Andorra, having left Ibiza, where she became pregnant after a disillusioning sexual encounter with a visiting American poet. In the film, Campion omits the time Janet spent in Andorra altogether, and shifts the episode of her miscarriage to London, after she has returned from the Continent. This change is motivated by more than merely a concern for economy. When Edith Campion was in London in 1949, she, too, lost a baby; by shifting Janet's loss of her baby to London, therefore, Campion introduced yet another parallel between Frame and her mother, which may account for why this scene is presented without a close-up shot that would suggest a deeply subjective identification such as those that are so evident in the earlier parts of the film.

Throughout the film, Campion loads the mise-en-scène with evocative objects that invest its texture with personal associations and reinforce the dual identifications I have identified. In an interview with Marie Colmant, for example, she reveals that the reason she depicts Janet Frame wearing 'gumboots' was because they evoke her childhood past, given that when she was thirteen years old, her own parents moved to the country where everyone wears gumboots because of the mud. Whenever she slips on gumboots, Campion declares, 'it is like a physical memory, an extraordinary sensation . . . I don't know whether Janet actually had them, but I wanted her to wear them.'[39] When Janet is in Ibiza, Campion also shows her wrapped up in a blanket while writing. This, too, derives from a personal memory, based on the filmmaker's own experience of writing in a Tibetan monastery in the Lake District of England.[40] Similarly, one of the reasons she ended *An Angel at My Table* with a shot of Janet Frame writing in a caravan, Campion reveals, was a very personal one: 'My father won a caravan in a raffle . . . and it sits outside his house in New Zealand now . . . I'm still crazy about caravans, and I dream about outfitting one absolutely particularly to me.'[41] At every level and in every respect, then, the way Campion presents the story she found in Frame's *Autobiography* attests to the strength of her personal investments in it, resulting in a transformation that, despite its surface fidelity, turns it into something new. She admits that much of this investment occurred at an unconscious level: 'there is certainly more of me in the final result than I was conscious of when I started.'[42]

The extent and intensity of this personal investment prompts one to wonder what the function of making a coming-of-age film of this sort might have been for the filmmaker. Like most acts of fictive (re)creation, it serves to figure forth symbolically a representation of emotions that have caused perturbation in the past, as a means of externalizing them in a visible, embodied form that enables them to be identified, and hence mastered at a psychic level, however unconsciously. As poets and philosophers from Aristotle to the present have affirmed, the effect of such a process is to 'set the affections in right tune,' to use John Milton's apt phrase.[43]

AN ANGEL AT MY TABLE AS LANDMARK

It remains, finally, to appraise the significance of *An Angel at My Table* within the canon of New Zealand Coming-of-age Films. Merata Mita, writing two years after its release, greatly admired the film, on account of 'its gritty realism, brutal honesty, and unyielding lyricism,' and instantly realized its historical significance: 'Here at last is a film dealing with what it is to be a white New Zealander growing up in this country, without being naïve or romantic. Even though the story is about one particular woman, its truth about repressed, white society in New Zealand is undeniable.'[44] In Mita's eyes, *An Angel at My Table* was symptomatic of a deeper malaise she detected in New Zealand films generally, which she characterized as 'a white neurotic industry': 'what becomes clear in the body of work mentioned is the absence of identity and how driven by repression and fear these films are.'[45]

For Mita, *An Angel at My Table* thus manifested the same syndrome that I have identified in *The God Boy*, but in a feminine, rather than masculine, version. A contrast could be drawn, in fact, between the sense of cultural confidence and protective communal support that surrounds Awatea in Mita's own *Mauri*, made just two years before Campion's film, and the absence of those qualities in *An Angel at My Table*, an absence that poses a threat to the very sense of personal identity of the protagonist until a desperate means is found – in this case, the seeking of refuge in an imaginative world – that can overcome it.

An Angel at My Table also shows why important national stories are important in national cinema. Because they *are* national – that is, they arise out of, and mirror, the cultural conditions of a given society – they are able to act as reflectors that facilitate a process of self-identification and self-(re)definition in other individuals from that society. Frequently, this clarification of identity takes place at a later date, and, in the case of these coming-of-age films, involves members of the next generation. As such, the coming-of-age stories found in national cinemas attest to the importance of this genre not only to the emotional health of individuals, but also the psychic wellbeing of a society at large.

NOTES

1. Janet Frame, 'My Say' (interview with Elizabeth Alley), Concert Programme, Radio New Zealand, Wellington, New Zealand, 27 April 1983; reprinted in Elizabeth

Alley and Mark Williams (eds), *In the Same Room: Conversations with New Zealand Writers* (Auckland: Auckland University Press, 1992).
2. *Sunday Times Review*, 8 December 1985, quoted by Michael King, *Wrestling with the Angel: A Life of Janet Frame* (Auckland: Viking, 2000), 470.
3. Janet Frame, *An Autobiography* (Auckland: Vintage, 2004), 8.
4. Ibid., 217.
5. Ibid., 100.
6. Ibid.
7. Ibid., 41.
8. Ibid., 12–13.
9. Ibid., 38–9.
10. Ibid., 156.
11. Ibid., 213.
12. Ibid., 108.
13. Ibid., 101.
14. Ibid., 157.
15. Ibid., 213.
16. Ibid., 215.
17. Ibid., 405.
18. Ibid., 415.
19. See Peter Hühn, Wolf Schmid, and Jörg Schönert (eds), *Point of View, Perspective, and Focalization: Modeling Mediation in Narrative* (Berlin and New York: Walter de Gruyter, 2009), 1.
20. See David Herman, 'Beyond Voice and Vision: Cognitive Grammar and Focalization Theory,' in Hühn et al. (eds), *Point of View*, 119–42, especially 129–30.
21. Ibid., 129.
22. On the different levels (extratextual, intratextual, extradiegetic, intradiegetic, hypodiegetic) on which perspectivation can be located, see Sabine Schlickers, 'Focalization, Ocularization and Auricularization in Film and Literature,' in Hühn et al. (eds), *Point of View*, 243–58.
23. For a detailed account of the personal elements projected in *An Angel at My Table*, see Alistair Fox, *Jane Campion: Authorship and Personal Cinema* (Bloomington and Indianapolis: 2011), especially Chapter 4.
24. Jane Campion, 'Director's Commentary,' *An Angel at My Table*, DVD, directed by Jane Campion (1990; Irvington, NY: Criterion Collection, 2005).
25. Suzie Mackenzie, 'Beloved Rivals,' *Guardian Unlimited*, 5 June 1999.
26. Suzie Mackenzie, 'Campions Enjoy a Rich Friendship,' *Otago Daily Times*, 2 October 1999, 70.
27. Ibid.
28. 'Dans les premiers temps, quand j'étais à la fac, j'étais assez malheureuse, très seule. Je n'arriverais pas à m'insérer dans un groupe, en fait, je suis assez tordue et ça m'a pris un certain temps pour trouver des gens qui partageraient mon sens d'humeur' (Marie Colmant, 'Jane et Janet, face à face,' *Libération*, 24 April 1991).
29. Campion, 'Director's Commentary,' *An Angel at My Table*.
30. Jane Campion, Introduction to *An Angel at My Table*, by Janet Frame (London: Virago, 2008), xi.
31. Sue Williams, 'A Light on the Dark Secrets of Depression,' *Australian*, 2 May 1995; reprinted in Wexman, *Jane Campion*, 174.
32. Edith Campion, Personal Papers, MS-Papers-6360-119, Alexander Turnbull Library.
33. Jane Campion, Introduction to *An Angel at My Table*, x.
34. Ibid.

35. Ibid.
36. See Lawrence Jones, 'I can really see myself in her story': Jane Campion's Adaptation of Janet Frame's *Autobiography*,' in Hilary Radner, Alistair Fox, and Irène Bessière (eds), *Jane Campion: Cinema, Nation, Identity* (Detroit: Wayne State University Press, 2009), 77–100, especially 87.
37. Maria Wikse, *Materialisations of a Woman Writer: Investigating Janet Frame's Biographical Legend* (Oxford: Peter Lang, 2006), 173.
38. Letter from Tim Curnow, Janet Frame's agent, to Bridget Ikin, 3 February 1988. I acknowledge my debt to Pamela Gordon, Janet Frame's niece, for providing me with this information.
39. 'Quand je les enfile, c'est comme un souvenir corporel, une sensation extraordinaire. Quand je serai très vieille, je me vois très bien dans une ferme avec des *gumboots*. Je ne suis pas sure que Janet en ait eu vraiment. Mais, j'ai voulu qu'elle en porte.' Marie Colmant, 'Jane et Janet, face à face,' *Libération*, 24 April 1991.
40. Campion, 'Director's Commentary,' *An Angel at My Table*.
41. Ibid.
42. Michel Ciment, 'The Red Wigs of Autobiography: Interview with Jane Campion,' *Positif*, April 1991. Reprinted in Wexman, *Jane Campion*, 62–70, esp. 67.
43. John Milton, *The Reason of Church Government*, in Merritt Y. Hughes (ed.), *John Milton: Complete Poems and Major Prose* (Indianapolis and New York: The Odyssey Press, 1957), 669.
44. Mita, 'The Soul and the Image,' 48.
45. Ibid., 47.

9. DESPERATION TURNED OUTWARDS: *HEAVENLY CREATURES* (PETER JACKSON, 1994)

Heavenly Creatures (1994), the film that launched Peter Jackson's international career, was based on a true story. On 22 June 1954, two teenage girls, Pauline Parker and her friend Juliet Hulme, lured Pauline's mother, Honorah Parker (also known as Rieper), on a walk down a secluded pathway in Victoria Park, on the hills of Banks Peninsula near Christchurch, where they bludgeoned her to death by striking her repeatedly on the head with a brick enclosed in a stocking.[1] This horrific matricide, compounded by lurid reports of a lesbian relationship between the girls, left the nation in a state of deep shock. New Zealand at this time prided itself on being 'God's Own Country,' a godly society imbued with a laudable Christian morality that had been rewarded by peace, material prosperity, and a conviction of its ethical superiority to the rest of the world. It was a time when the 'best' qualities of England were believed to have been imported into the British Empire's most recent colony, where they had produced an impeccable respectability – not to mention a genteel sense of class divisions that had taken deepest root in Christchurch, the most Anglican settlement in the country. This was a period when audiences in the cinemas still stood to attention for a clip of Queen Elizabeth, accompanied by 'God Save the Queen,' before the screening of every film, and parents in households still referred to Great Britain as 'home,' even if they were third-generation New Zealanders and had never been to the Old Country.

The reason why the Parker/Hulme murder delivered such a shock to the national psyche was because it blew the lid off New Zealand society's idealized view of itself. Instead of a genteel paradise of moral probity and genteel respectability, what it exposed was the enormous gap between outward appearances and the actual reality they concealed. Decorum in mid-twentieth-century New Zealand dictated that those things should never be talked about: homosexuality, marital infidelity, and a depth of puritan repression that was producing dysfunctional relationships and a range of psychological disorders – even to the extent of breaking out into explosions of homicidal violence when the emotional pressures it generated became too unbearable. This was the social milieu that still prevailed when both Peter Jackson (b. 1961) and Fran Walsh (b. 1959), his partner and the scriptwriter for *Heavenly Creatures*, were born, the meaning of which they were concerned to explore through the exemplum provided by the story of the matricide committed by Pauline Parker and Juliet Hulme.

The Relation of *Heavenly Creatures* to Other New Zealand Coming-of-age Films

Most scholarly studies of *Heavenly Creatures* have tended to focus either on the film's portrayal of lesbianism,[2] or its depiction of class.[3] While both issues are important aspects of the film, to give them exclusive emphasis is to overlook the socio-psychological syndrome that is at the heart of the tragedy, and which links *Heavenly Creatures* thematically to almost every other New Zealand coming-of-age film that had been made prior to it, as well as much of the post-war literature of New Zealand fiction writers up until that time. The repressive effects on children of puritanism, whether secular or religious – as illustrated in classroom scenes, especially – links *Heavenly Creatures* to *The God Boy* and *An Angel at My Table*. The resentment of authoritarianism that this induces similarly ties Jackson and Walsh's film to the rebelliousness depicted in *Sleeping Dogs* and the transgressiveness of Ronald Hugh Morrieson's *The Scarecrow* (and to a lesser extent Pillsbury's adaptation of it), while resentment at parental figures that expresses itself in a fantasy of violence is reminiscent of *Vigil* when Toss aims a rifle at the silhouettes of her mother and Ethan seen through the frosted glass of a door. Equally, the impulse to seek escape into a fantasy world of the imagination as an alternative to reality is strongly reminiscent of Janet Frame's *An Autobiography* (and, consequentially, Jane Campion's adaptation), with the 'Fourth World' of the two girls being very similar to Frame's 'Mirror City.' Even the conversion of frustration arising from repression into an explosion of homicidal violence finds its literary equivalent in Maurice Gee's novel *In My Father's Den* (1972), which would provide the basis of another fine cinematic adaptation, by Brad McGann.

These links show that *Heavenly Creatures* is not anomalous in the corpus of New Zealand coming-of-age films and literature. Rather, the situation it portrays reflects a syndrome that is culturally specific to New Zealand – a syndrome that the writers and filmmakers concerned perceive as exerting such a noxious influence on the self-sense of maturing children, adolescents, and young post-adolescents that they feel compelled to create fictions as a means of resisting and protesting against it. This means that while the film is universal in certain respects, in other important respects it is very culturally specific to New Zealand. As Peter Jackson affirmed: 'we weren't making this film for an international audience. We were very much making it to try and rectify 40 years of misunderstanding about this case within New Zealand. In a way that was our main motivation for making the film . . .'[4] To put it another way, Jackson and Walsh intended *Heavenly Creatures* to be a film by New Zealanders, about New Zealanders, and for New Zealanders, designed to be an intervention capable of identifying the circumstances and psychic pressures that had produced such a tragedy, in order to explain them in terms that could leave their compatriots no room to continue demonizing the two perpetrators of the crime, whom the film depicts as victims rather than villains.

The Personal Dimension of the Film

Like all the other coming-of-age films discussed in this book, *Heavenly Creatures* is imbued with personal investments on the part of both Fran Walsh and Peter Jackson himself. It was Fran Walsh, in fact, who first became interested in the Parker/Hulme murder case as the subject for a film. 'As a young girl growing up,' she says, 'I knew about it,'[5] and, according to Jackson's biographer, the story recalled the intensity of her own teenage friendships in which 'you find someone who represents everything positive and wonderful in the world.'[6] One can infer, then, that from Walsh's point of view one reason for making the film was to explore vicariously the nature of these feelings. As she puts it: 'Our intention was to be true to what we understood of the girls' friendship, and the nature of that friendship and the nature of those families from which those two girls came.'[7] Another reason was a desire to understand the social dynamic that generated the tragedy. Walsh was highly sensitive to the fact that the type of repression reflected in the story was not something that could be merely relegated to the 1950s, and hence to the safety of the historical past:

> That repression is still very much in evidence here: we're not expressive, we're not demonstrative, we're scared of showing, saying too much. When you go to New York, for instance, and people are yelling and the horns are blaring – if that happened here, someone would get out of their car, rip open your door and bash you up. There's a level of violence, a subtext of violence, running through New Zealand society that comes

out in our movies. We have a veneer of being easygoing, but underneath, we're full of rage.[8]

For Walsh, therefore, the making of *Heavenly Creatures* was, at least in part, an exercise in self-understanding and an understanding of the societal milieu she recognized as that in which New Zealanders of her generation were still living.

For his part, Peter Jackson confessed that he could 'relate very much to how they [the girls] had this love of creating fantasy worlds and stories,' just as he had done in his boyhood, which had led to his becoming a filmmaker.[9] As Jackson, who grew up in Wellington as the only child of a local civil servant, said to an interviewer for the *New York Times*: 'If you're an only child you spend a lot of time by yourself and you develop a strong ability to entertain yourself, to conjure up fantasy.'[10] Even more tellingly, he admitted that 'there was a lot of Pauline that I could recognize in myself.'[11]

When one considers the film Jackson had made immediately preceding *Heavenly Creatures*, *Braindead* (1992), it is fairly easy to discern why, given that the genre-bending world of this gore-comedy, or 'splat-stick,'[12] serves as the vehicle for a violent fantasy that is not dissimilar to that in *Heavenly Creatures*, just as the 'Fourth World' of Borovnia provides 'an outlet for violent fantasies' for the two girls in Jackson's next film.[13] *Braindead* revolves around a similar familial situation in which a child – in this case Lionel (Timothy Balme), a young adult – finds life under the tyranny of his cleanliness-obsessed mother suffocating and intolerable. 'Mum' (Elizabeth Moody) seems a pillar of respectable middle-class society, but after she is bitten by a Sumatran rat-monkey she turns into a zombie who creates more zombies. As the movie proceeds, Lionel, who has been, metaphorically speaking, emasculated by his mother, discovers that she murdered his father while Lionel was still a boy, prompting Lionel to slaughter all the zombies with an up-ended lawnmower. In the final scene, the last zombie remaining to be dispatched is 'Mum,' now an even more gigantic monster with massive buttocks and breasts, who tries to suck Lionel back into her repulsive womb, saying 'No one will ever love you like your Mother!' Simultaneously, 'Mum' tries to pry loose the fingers of his girlfriend Paquita (Diana Peñalver), who is dangling from the roof of the house, with the intent of letting her drop to her death. Lionel, however, tears his way out of his mother's womb, voiding her entrails and killing her in the process. He then rescues his girlfriend, displaying the bravado of an action hero, and the movie ends with the two kissing, in a loving embrace.

Clearly, as the critic Helen Martin observes, 'Oedipus drives the narrative' of *Braindead*,[14] but what is equally striking about this film is the way the fantasy that informs it is replicated in important respects in the fantasy of Pauline in

Heavenly Creatures. Both Lionel and Pauline feel suffocated by the oppressive effects of the society within which they live, with its rules and conventions, and both feel intense resentment towards their mothers for their controlling domination, which converts into a fantasy of violence which becomes literally enacted in both films, the former fantasmagorically through the mirth-inducing gore of a splat-stick horror film, and the latter through the genuine horror of a real murder. As Jackson hints in his admission of his identification with Pauline, the coincidence of these two fantasies suggests that they are likely to derive from the personal myth of the filmmaker himself – that is, a recurrent preoccupation that surfaces repeatedly in the form of symbolic configurations that allow it to be addressed at a displaced remove, or what the literary theorist Charles Mauron described as '*métaphores obsédantes*.'[15] In Jackson's case, this myth seems to involve a maternal attachment that is resented on account of its oppressive effects, but simultaneously difficult to separate from, even while the need to do so is pressing, as a precondition for attaining happiness as a fulfilled and individuated adult. One can surmise, therefore, that Jackson and Fran Walsh, who had also collaborated with him on *Braindead*, chose to make a film on the Parker/Hulme case because it provided them with material through which they could confront issues that they recognized as having affected the milieu in which they themselves had grown up, influencing the formation of their own psychic identities.

The Mode of Presentation of *Heavenly Creatures*

Because of the belief he shared with Fran Walsh that an assumption that the girls must have been 'evil' was wrong, Jackson was adamant that he 'didn't want to make a murder movie.' Instead, he invented a highly effective strategy for presenting the 'forces at work within their friendship [and] outside their friendship that led them to this action'[16] – a strategy that involved the mixing of a variety of film styles and generic tropes. To evoke the social milieu of Christchurch in the 1950s, he begins the film with documentary footage in the form of a travelogue, narrated by an unctuous-sounding male voice with a BBC accent, as scenes of the city are shown that display its gentility and 'Englishness': Cathedral Square and Canterbury University College with their gothic-revival architecture; Christchurch Girls' High School in Cranmer Square; and 'the broad acres of Hagley Park, with men dressed in whites playing cricket, while crews of young men row in sculling boats on the River Avon.' The travelogue then turns the camera to a domestic scene of a neat garden in which a bonny toddler crawls on a lawn while his father cuts the grass, and finally to a shot of tidy suburbs viewed from the Port Hills, while the voiceover intones eulogistically: 'Yes, Christchurch . . . New Zealand's city of the plains!' The purpose of this image of a stable, peaceful, civilized society that pictures the ideal of the New Zealand myth is to prepare for the shocking contrast with the next sequence, in which a subjective shot filmed with a Steadicam hurtles down a leafy hillside track while girls' screams are heard from offscreen, before the girls themselves are shown with their blood-splattered legs, until the shot merges seamlessly into a flashback in black and white showing Pauline and Juliet running along the rail of a ship, but this time in a state of ecstatic happiness. The switch to a different shooting style thus underlines the shocking contrast between the superficial appearance of New Zealand society and the reality of the violence that has just (as we later learn) occurred, while the irony generated by the three juxtaposed episodes – Christchurch in its genteel tranquility, Pauline and Juliet in their state of screaming hysteria, and the two girls in a happier potential time that (we later learn) was what they wished could happen, but which in reality never did happen – neatly encapsulates the whole tragedy. Jackson uses movement achieved with a Steadicam on several other occasions to evoke the subjective state of the two girls, and especially to capture their joy and playful energy once the bond between them has become established, as when they chase each other through the woods and strip down to their underwear to the accompaniment in the soundtrack of 'The Donkey Serenade,' sung by their idol, Mario Lanza.

In contrast to this impressionistic art-cinema style, which is associated with the sense of liberation the girls derive from their friendship, sequences showing them at school or at home are filmed in a fairly static style with very little camera movement, which reflects the oppressive discipline and rigidity they encounter in those domains.

For the fantasy sequences that show Pauline and Juliet entering the 'Fourth World' of their imagined country, Borovnia, the style changes again, this time to a full-blown surrealism, obtained through special effects that allow the inclusion of such things as gigantic flying butterflies and animated plasticine figures. In contrast to the other styles, this surrealistic style evokes the 'peace and bliss' the girls feel in this world of the imagination that consists of 'music, art, and pure enjoyment.'

In terms of genre, *Heavenly Creatures* is a remarkable hybrid. As Jackson has affirmed, generic hybridity, in his view, is one of the distinguishing characteristics of New Zealand films:

> In New Zealand we tend to cross genres. In America the film industry is very genre-conscious ... In New Zealand we don't have that tradition. We're really just a bunch of filmmakers making things that interest us, so we end up muddying the genres. We do a bit of this and a bit of that and throw it together.[17]

In *Heavenly Creatures*, generic elements and tropes are mixed for a functional purpose. Barry Keith Grant identifies it as 'at once a teen exploitation movie and art film, simultaneously lowbrow and high culture.'[18] It also has elements of the crime thriller, the female friendship film, the horror film, the fantasy film, the romance genre, and the family melodrama. All of them – reinforced by Jackson's use of the film style appropriate to the particular genre concerned – contribute to a revelation of the inner emotional state of the two girls, or help to convey an impression of their predicament. When, for example, Juliet's mother Hilda visits the Riepers and suggests that Pauline stay with Juliet in the Hulmes' house until the latter leaves to be sent to live with her aunt in South Africa, upon Pauline's arrival Jackson introduces a sequence that combines fantasy with romantic melodrama, by having Mario Lanza sing 'When you are in love, it's the loveliest night of the year' while in the background dance the animated plasticine figures of the girls' imagination. The kitschy song and the sentimentality of the waltz that sweeps the girls along function as expressions of their adolescent joy at being allowed to be together. Conversely, after it is certain that Pauline will not be allowed to accompany Juliet to South Africa, the note turns to tragic with Pauline's decision to find a way to 'remove mother,' and the generic mode shifts accordingly. Instead of a kitschy waltz song, Juliet, after burning her records of Mario Lanza, now sings, (symbolically) unaccompanied, the plangent phrases from the aria 'Sono andati? . . . perché volli con te sola restare' (Have they gone? . . . because I wanted to be left alone with you) of the dying Mimì in Puccini's opera *La Bohème*, culminating in the heart-rending passage 'Sei mio amore, è tutto la mia vita' (You are my love, and my whole life). Commensurately, Pauline tells her: 'I wrote my opera last night – it's a three-act story with a tragic end' – just as the film itself will soon turn out to be. At this moment, the element of condescending fun that had been poked at the girls in the earlier sequence with Mario Lanza on account of their immature sentimentality disappears, to be replaced by a tragic pathos emanating from the real depth of their grief. This pathos is deepened still further in the final scene, in which the 'Humming Chorus' from Puccini's *Madama Butterfly* is heard in the soundtrack as Honorah (Sarah Peirse), followed by the two girls, descends the path that will lead to her death, reminding us that, just as Cio Cio San waited expectantly for a happy reunion with her lover that would never eventuate, so, too, are these girls doomed to have their expectations mocked, with a tragic death being the outcome in both Puccini's opera in the soundtrack, and the real-life opera that Pauline has contrived. Surrounding this scene, in which the murder is presented with horrifying realism, are two contrasting non-surrealistic fantasy sequences in black and white. In the first of them, Pauline, Juliet, and Juliet's parents are seen all happily united on a departing ship. In the second one, we see a shot of the distraught Pauline as a ship pulls away with Juliet on board, separating the two girls forever. The combined working of all these different intermingled generic modes powerfully captures the mixture of passionate attachment, desperation, adolescent naivety, delusional fantasy, and pathetic irony implicit in this tragic situation, in a way that would be difficult to achieve by any other means.

Causes of the Tragedy

For Jackson and Walsh, their professed purpose in making *Heavenly Creatures* was to explore 'What actually happened? What was going through their minds? Why did they do it? What sort of people were they?'[19] In this respect, the film does not disappoint, because Jackson and his partner endow the two girls with fully developed psychic economies that are the product of environmental circumstances in their lives that have a highly destructive effect on their emotional equilibrium.

Both the girls are depicted as suffering from emotional deprivation, as a consequence of their contexts, but for rather different reasons. In the external environment, both Pauline and Juliet feel oppressed by the rigid conformity imposed by Christchurch society. This is imaged early in the movie by scenes showing the girls at Christchurch Girls' High School. As the credit sequence rolls, the sanctimonious Christian piety imposed on the pupils is signaled by the sound of schoolgirls singing the hymn 'Just a closer walk with thee' while we see their stocking-clad legs and neat uniforms as they troop in regimented columns into the school under the stern eyes of the severe Headmistress, garbed, like the other teachers, in her black academic gown. Pauline at once disrupts the order of this scene by being late, and by being shown climbing indecorously over the fence separating the school with its English pretensions from the humble, lower-class dwelling of her parents' home. Soon after, to underline the contrast in class, Juliet is seen arriving at the school in a 'posh' Rover car. Then, once they are in the classroom, the girls are shown being drilled through the imperfect subjunctive in a French lesson. When one girl has the temerity to venture a comment, the teacher snaps back: 'Put up your hand! I will not have girls talking out of turn in class', which neatly encapsulates the rigid discipline imposed by this society that Pauline and Juliet will find so suffocating. Pauline's reaction, in particular, is registered on her face in a recurrent scowl.

The response of both girls to this insistence on conformity is to be defiant and transgressive, as when Juliet, with her superior knowledge of French, deliberately humiliates the teacher before the rest of the class over an error the latter has made in conjugating a verb, and when she draws St George and the Dragon in an art class, instead of a life drawing. This impulse towards transgression progressively escalates in the course of the movie as the girls break one prohibition after another: when they appear stripped to their underwear before the eyes of a shocked farmer; when Pauline sneaks out at night and climbs up a ladder to have sex with the boarder whom she has been forbidden to see;

Figure 9.1 Pauline (Melanie Lynskey), bored and resentful, in *Heavenly Creatures* (dir. Peter Jackson, 1994).

when the two girls are shown naked in bed, locked in a sexual embrace; and, finally, when they perform the ultimate transgression against familial bonds by committing matricide.

The various forms of emotional deprivation that the girls experience at home compound the oppressive restrictions that the social order imposes. Pauline's father has no understanding of, nor sympathy for, her artistic sensibility, as when we see him mock her when she plays a record of Mario Lanza, and her mother, as Pauline complains to a child physician, constantly 'nags her.' This lack of imaginative stimulation makes her long to leave her own family and join Juliet's, which seems to her to inhabit a world that is culturally, as well as materially, richer.

Juliet, for her part, suffers from a fear of abandonment. As a child, she was left alone in a hospital in the Bahamas to be treated for an illness in her lungs, and when her mother, who had promised that the family would never be apart again, announces that she and her husband are going overseas for a conference, the prospect of their long absence reactivates in Juliet the grief and trauma of that earlier separation, which is registered on her face in a lingering close-up shot.

Juliet, like Jimmy in *The God Boy*, also suffers from awareness of her parents' dysfunctional marriage, made starkly apparent to her when she walks in to her mother's bedroom to find her in bed with her lover, Bill Perry (Peter Elliott). Both Juliet and Pauline are acutely aware of the sexual hypocrisy of their mothers concealed underneath their outward probity: Juliet realizes how farcical it is for Hilda Hulme (Diana Kent) to be a marriage counselor while she is having an affair, and Pauline is sensitive to the irony of Honorah calling her 'nothing but a cheap little trollop' for having taken John (Jed Brophy) into her bed when Honorah herself ran off with Pauline's father when she was only

Figure 9.2 Juliet (Kate Winslet) suffers grief at the thought of separation in *Heavenly Creatures* (dir. Peter Jackson, 1994).

seventeen. In the face of these emotional and narcissistic deprivations, compounded by their awareness of the hypocritical hollowness of the respectability of the society in which they live, the two girls cling to their friendship as a comforting compensation, which explains why the thought of being separated is so devastating to them.

Apart from transgression – which, according to psychoanalyst D. W. Winnicott, constitutes a search for a sense of secure holding that is not found in one's family or society at large, in order to sustain hope that some alternative exists to the world that has failed to supply one's emotional needs[20] – Pauline and Juliet seek refuge in Borovnia, their fantasy world of the imagination. Not only is this 'Fourth World' a place that is 'full of peace and bliss,' it is also a place in which, through their surrogate Prince Diello, the 'renegade' child begotten by Pauline and Juliet in their fantasy personae as 'Charles' and 'Deborah,' they can act out, in fantasy, their more violent transgressive wishes. When a sanctimonious chaplain visits Juliet while she is in hospital, for example, Juliet calls upon Diello, who is modeled in plasticine with the features of Orson Welles, to drag him off to the block to be beheaded. Similarly, when Pauline is sent to a child psychiatrist to undergo therapy for her 'unwholesome attachment,' she has Diello murder him when the psychiatrist suggests she spend more time with boys.

As Brian McDonnell has noted, Diello, in his resemblance to Orson Welles, whose movie *The Third Man* the girls go to see in the cinema, is also an ambivalent fantasy who is both repellent and attractive, becoming associated with their burgeoning adult sexuality. This is seen in the way they use a fantasized image of him as a sexual turn-on: 'Pauline becomes Welles straddling

Figure 9.3 The fantasy world of Borovnia in *Heavenly Creatures* (dir. Peter Jackson, 1994).

a responsive Juliet on the bed, Juliet becomes Diello taking Pauline amid an orgy of rutting Plasticine figures.'[21] The fantasy world of Borovnia, therefore, becomes an imaginary world for the girls in which compensatory desires can be attained, repressive forces can be eliminated, and emotional liberation can be achieved.

HEAVENLY CREATURES AS A HISTORICAL MILESTONE

Heavenly Creatures occupies a special place in the canon of New Zealand coming-of-age films because the dynamics of the psychological syndrome it identifies are represented more comprehensively than in any other film that had preceded it. As such, it exposes to critical scrutiny the pervasive value system and social mores that had dominated New Zealand through most of the twentieth century up until the mid-1960s, as well as revealing the emotional damage that this repressive puritanical system had inflicted on children and adolescents growing up under this regime. While certain aspects of the dynamics depicted in the film are universal, such as the ambivalent attachment that many girls feel towards their mother during adolescence,[22] the particular ways in which social and psychological pressures manifest themselves make the experience represented in the film a distinctively New Zealand one – an experience that, despite the horrific nature of its outcome, Jackson and Walsh regard as eliciting sympathy and compassion, rather than unmitigated condemnation.

Heavenly Creatures marks a watershed in the history of the New Zealand coming-of-age film, in that up until 1994 coming-of-age films had been made by filmmakers born in the 1940s and 1950s, whereas after 1994 coming-of-age films would be made by a younger generation of filmmakers born in the 1960s and 1970s. In terms of the thematic preoccupations of these subsequent films, the difference is striking, attesting to significant changes that had taken place in New Zealand society from the 1970s onwards. The entrenchment of a state-sponsored ideology of biculturalism saw Māori filmmakers and Māori subject matter move to center stage, while the waning of puritanism as the dominant value system and growing secularism saw the emergence of a new variety of societal values. In the chapters that follow, I will identify and explore the changes reflected in these films as the country moved towards, and into, the new millennium.

Notes

1. For details of the relationship between the two girls and the murder, see Peter Graham, *So Brilliantly Clever: Parker, Hulme & the Murder that Shocked the World* (Wellington: Awa Press, 2011); republished as *Ann Perry and the Murder of the Century* (New York: Skyhorse Publishing, 2013).
2. See, for example, Karen Boyle, '"Not All Angels Are Innocent" – Violence, Sexuality, and the Teen Psychodyke,' in Alexandra Heidi Karriker (ed.), *Film Studies: Women in Contemporary Cinema* (New York: Peter Lang, 2002), 35–50; and Andrew Scahill, '"Wonderful, Heavenly, Beautiful, and Ours": Lesbian Fantasy and Media(ted) Desire in *Heavenly Creatures*,' *Journal of Lesbian Studies* 16:3 (2012), 365–75.
3. See Davinia Thornley, 'Executing the Commoners: Examining Class in *Heavenly Creatures*,' in A. H. Karriker (ed.), *Film Studies: Women in Contemporary World Cinema* (New York: Peter Lang, 2002), 51–68.
4. Tod Lippy, 'Writing and Directing *Heavenly Creatures*: A Talk with Frances Walsh and Peter Jackson,' *Scenario* 1 (1995), 217–24.
5. Ibid.
6. Ian Pryor, *Peter Jackson: From Prince of Splatter to Lord of the Rings* (Auckland: Random House, 2003), 129. See also Brian McDonnell, 'The Physician Who Assumed His Patient's Fever: Peter Jackson's Narrative Strategy in *Heavenly Creatures*,' *Studies in Australasian Cinema* 1:2 (2007), 161–73.
7. Lippy, ibid.
8. Ibid.
9. Pryor, *Peter Jackson*, 131.
10. Bernard Weinraub, 'Making a Film Out of the Horror of Mother Murder,' *New York Times*, 24 November 1994, http://www.nytimes.com/1994/11/24/movies/making-a-film-out-of-the-horror-of-mother-murder.html, accessed 7 July 2016.
11. Lippy, ibid.
12. On the genre of *Braindead*, see Donato Totaro, 'Your Mother Ate My Dog! Peter Jackson and Gore-Comedy,' *Offscreen* 5:4 (September 2001), http://offscreen.com/view/peterjackson, accessed 7 July 2016.
13. Weinraub, 'Making a Film,' ibid.
14. Helen Martin and Sam Edwards, *New Zealand Film 1912–1996* (Auckland: Oxford University Press, 1997), 161.
15. For the psychocritical theory of personal myth, see Charles Mauron, *Des Métaphores obsédantes au mythe personnel: Introduction à la psychocritique* (Paris: J. Corti, 1963), and the discussion in Fox, *Speaking Pictures*, 215–17.
16. Bobbie Wygant, 'Classic interview: Peter Jackson for "Heavenly Creatures",' *The Bobbie Wygant Archive*, 11 March 1994, http://bobbiewygant.blogspot.co.nz/2011/12/classic-interview-peter-jackson-for.html, accessed 8 July 2016.

17. Jim Barr and Mary Barr, 'NZFX: The Films of Peter Jackson and Fran Walsh,' in Jonathan Dennis and Jan Bieringa (eds), *Film in Aotearoa New Zealand* (Wellington: Victoria University Press, 1996), 150–60, esp. 156.
18. Barry Keith Grant, 'The Films of Peter Jackson,' in Ian Conrich and Stuart Murray (eds), *New Zealand Filmmakers* (Detroit: Wayne State University Press, 2007), 320–35, esp. 322.
19. Barr and Barr, 'NZFX,' 157.
20. See D. W. Winnicott, *The Child, the Family, and the Outside World* (London: Penguin, 1991), 228–9.
21. McDonnell, ibid.
22. See Eva Rueschmann, *Sisters on Screen: Siblings in Contemporary Cinema* (Philadelphia: Temple University Press, 2000), 101.

10. CONFRONTING DOMESTIC VIOLENCE AND FAMILIAL ABUSE: *ONCE WERE WARRIORS* (LEE TAMAHORI, 1994)

At first sight, it might seem strange to include *Once Were Warriors* (Lee Tamahori, 1994) in a book on coming-of-age films when it so clearly belongs to the genres of the family melodrama and the social problem film in its graphic portrayal of domestic violence in a context of poverty and social abjection. Although the fact is seldom mentioned, however, there are three coming-of-age narratives interwoven into the main story that play a crucial role in generating the film's meaning, and for that reason I have chosen to examine those elements here.

The National Importance of *Once Were Warriors*

When *Once Were Warriors* exploded onto the nation's screens in 1994, it attracted audiences on a scale that had never before been seen in New Zealand. With an estimated 1,054,100 admissions,[1] attendance at this film surpassed that for all foreign films released during the previous year, including American blockbusters like Steven Spielberg's *Jurassic Park*, which until then had been the most successful film shown in New Zealand.[2] Even though the box office take for *Once Were Warriors* ($6,795,000) has since been exceeded by those for Taika Waititi's two smash hits, *Boy* (2010) with $9,322,000, and *Hunt for the Wilderpeople* (2016) with $11,809,372,[3] when these figures are related to the cost of a ticket at the time (in 1993, a ticket cost $8.76),[4] the number of admissions remains commensurate. What these figures show is that all three films were national phenomena, which prompts one to speculate on why this was so.

In the case of *Once Were Warriors*, one does not need to look far for the answer; as Rena Owen, who played Beth in the movie, puts it, the film 'had the courage to explore things that no other movie has had the courage to explore.'[5] Lee Tamahori, the film's director, ventures his own explanation for the film's success:

> Everybody saw this film. Maori, who usually ignore things like this in their culture: rape, incest, matricide . . . they don't read a lot, since they're not a culture who had a written language. If you're poor and you're rural, you have an oral history and you watch TV and go to the movies. They went to this film in unbelievable numbers, even though it was a bad rap on themselves. After the movie came out, it was discovered that there was an incremental rise of women getting out of abusive situations and seeking help, and talking about these problems. My own mother's generation, who's a white New Zealander, they might have been knocked around by their husbands, but they wouldn't talk about it. They'd never go by themselves, but in groups of two, three, and four. And it allowed them to talk about and debate these issues that were laid before them. It didn't change the nature of the society, but I said from the get-go, 'If one woman gets out of an abusive relationship because of this picture, I'll be a happy man.' And I'm sure that happened a lot.[6]

Once Were Warriors, indeed, 'spoke unapologetically about the unspoken. It showed lives bathed in violence, a side of New Zealand that had previously [lain] buried in statistics and meager news reportage.'[7] The liberating effect of the film's exposure of this shameful dark secret was reflected in a surge in the number of abuse victims who fled to shelters and a marked increase in reports to the police of domestic violence.[8]

The Source of *Once Were Warriors*: Alan Duff's Groundbreaking Novel

The story that exposed these abuses to view originated in a novel of the same name by the Māori writer Alan Duff, which, prior to being adapted as a film, had been equally successful in its own domain, being the top-selling work of adult fiction to be published in New Zealand.[9] Duff's searing tale describes how Jake and Beth Heke live with their six children in an abject slum, spending most of their time in the local pub or holding drunken parties with crowds of friends. Jake, who is unemployed, prides himself on being able to beat up any other man who challenges his supremacy among the group, and regularly uses his fists on his wife if she irritates him by becoming 'lippy.' Meanwhile, the elder children, emotionally deprived and neglected, respond to the hell they call 'home' in various ways: Nig joins the Brown Fists gang as a substitute family, and ends up getting murdered in a fight with a rival gang member; Boogie takes to stealing before he is caught and placed in a borstal; and Grace takes refuge in her dreams and her friendship with a homeless boy called Toots, until she is raped one night by her Uncle Bully and hangs herself in despair. This harrowing novel ends with Jake homeless, in a dazed and confused state, after he loses a fight to a younger man, and Beth, who has decided that self-help offers a better way, leaving him to initiate a project to help her people. Our last glimpse of Jake is of him alone, concealed in the pines watching the burial of his son and other gang members, while he weeps for his dead child, and himself.

Much of the power of Duff's novel derives from its roots in his own childhood experience, described in detail in his non-fictional memoir *Out of the Mists and Steam* (1999). That childhood, by Duff's account, was traumatic. He portrays his Māori mother as a drunk, 'stinking of beer,' who would appear as a 'foul apparition in her children's bedroom doorway, beer-fuming breath finding her young one's nostrils and standing our hair and every poised nerve on end.'[10] She was also a very violent woman who would attack her husband physically in the children's room, 'or we'd hear the thumping of her hitting and he restraining her down the hallway. Once she even got Dad's rifle from the wardrobe in our room and pointed it at him.'[11]

The effect of this parental discord on the children took different forms. Kevin, the eldest son, assumed the role of their protector. Josie, the oldest in the family, used her 'born decency' as a 'defensive bulwark to protect her sensibilities' and 'lock[ed] the best part of herself away, safe from this woman.'[12] Alan, however, was unable to find any way of protecting himself against an acute sense of shame and distress at the feeling he was not loved: 'Wish she'd just stop, there at the turning, and turn instead back to me and hug me and tell me she loves me. Wish she would.'[13] It is not too difficult to see in these descriptions the origins of the characters that would become Nig, Grace, and Boogie in the novel, and of Beth in her drunken phase before she becomes regenerate, with Duff transferring the mother's violent rages to Jake, who is modeled on other adult Māori males in his family circle:

> I have the most vivid memory of one mid-year school holiday staying with another aunty out of town, and her head being held under a tap over a sink and the blood being washed from her face. My uncle held her by the hair like this, after he'd beaten the hell out of her in front of us, his own children and myself and another visiting first cousin from Rotorua, right in the middle of the meal aunty had just served us. Words had been exchanged. He demanded she shut her mouth. She wouldn't. So he beat

her up. We knew to sit there and to act like we were still eating, as that was the way demanded of children witnessing violence.[14]

In incidents such as this, one sees the source of what in the film, via the novel, would become one of the most horrific episodes of spousal violence ever depicted on the screen.

As Duff himself says, 'so many of the settings and characters of my novels are from my childhood.' Referring to a two-storey mansion owned by a Pākehā family that was visible from his own family's state house, he says:

> It was not difficult when writing *Once Were Warriors* to recall myself in spying witness on that Bertram family, the Tramberts in the novel, and like the character Grace Heke I have at times throughout my life considered suicide. A little part inside me knows the feeling of that grey blanket coming down and turning to the blackest black that engulfs reason. You just have to be stronger, if that's the way your mind and emotions get inclined at times.[15]

From this we can see that not only do all the characters in *Once Were Warriors* have their origins in Duff's own personal experience, but that he also projects aspects of himself into several of them. Grace is his sensitive, vulnerable part, the part that would become a writer. Boogie, on the other hand, is the delinquent part who would act out and end up, like Duff himself, being placed in a borstal as a Ward of the State. Even Beth is turned into a projection of Duff, representing his belief in self-help as a remedy for the socio-economic abjection he depicts in his novel, with her project to help her people recover their pride shadowing Duff's own 'Duffy Books in Homes foundation,' which is a literacy-focused charitable organization.[16]

I have emphasized the autobiographical dimension of Alan Duff's novel at some length because it is from the depth of his personal investment in the story that its emotional power and force arises. And the essential point is this: that emotional force derives from the anguish of a terrified, emotionally deprived, and traumatized child whose perspective lingers on the adult author – a perspective that is reactivated in the film by a shot showing the terrified Heke children huddled together on a bed upstairs while they hear their father beating up their mother down below.

The Genesis of the Adaptation

As Lee Tamahori has confirmed, while the basic conception of the characters and episodes in *Once Were Warriors* remained firmly that of Duff, he and his team 'grafted our own experience onto it.' In particular, they 'included

Figure 10.1 Terrified children listen to their parents fighting in *Once Were Warriors* (dir. Lee Tamahori, 1994).

more from a female perspective.'[17] The idea of making a film adaptation of Duff's novel came from Robin Scholes, a principal at the television company Communicado, who had been searching for a project that reflected her own experience: Scholes says that she had been grievously beaten by a serial rapist, Mark Stephens, in the early 1980s.[18] When Tamahori was asked whether he wanted to direct the film, his first thought was that it was unfilmable: 'I had read the book and said that I didn't see how you could make it into a movie. I thought it was too dark, too depressing ... it was like a Fassbinder movie or something, you'd want to slit your wrists.'[19] Moreover, the New Zealand Film Commission repeatedly turned down the project's applications for funding, and it was only an impassioned speech by the Māori politician Rana Waitai, at that time a police commander in Gisborne, that persuaded the Film Commission to change its mind.[20] Meanwhile, Tamahori had approached a Māori woman friend of his, Riwia Brown, to rewrite the script from a woman's point of view.[21] Brown says that she enjoyed writing the screenplay 'because my whole kaupapa for writing is number one with Māori women ... This gave me a huge opportunity to make Māori women the heroine of the story and to write about what affects us as Maori – the good, the bad, and the ugly.'[22] As a result of these combined investments on the part of the producer, the director, and the scriptwriter, the story, which had been Jake Heke's in Duff's novel, was recrafted to be one that was told from the mother's and the daughter's perspective: 'I think that made a huge difference,' Tamahori says.[23]

For the violence in the film, the director drew upon his own experience. The son of a Māori father and a Pākehā mother, Tamahori reveals that 'I had grown up amongst a lot of that, seen a lot of it in my sort of "young man drinking" days.'[24] While his own family was not like that – Tamahori says he had a poor, but loving working-class upbringing – he nevertheless 'came out of a young man's hard drinking culture with fights erupting in bars all the time. I knew street violence, not from taking part in it, but from dodging it all the time. I also know my own east coast Maori community pretty well.'[25] Thus, on top of the passionate indignation emanating from Alan Duff's personal experience, there was superimposed a further layer of emotional investments that helped to influence the reshaping of the story in the process of its transposition from page to screen.[26]

The Genrification of *Once Were Warriors*

In order to adapt Duff's novel, Tamahori was faced with a need to find ways of making it more cinematic. Whereas Duff had painted on a very broad canvas, contrasting the lives of the Māori who live in the abject squalor of the Pine Block housing estate with the affluent and genteel lifestyle of a Pākehā family who live in a mansion at the top of the hill, and included a whole series of interior monologues as the narrative perspective shifts from one character to another, Tamahori achieves a tighter unity of action by narrowing the focus to emphasize family issues more, and by reconstructing the novel so that it becomes more concerned with Beth's personal growth.[27] At the same time, 'in the film, the young people are clearly portrayed more positively than in the novel,[28] which helps to give the movie an "up" ending,' as Riwia Brown puts it.[29] This is why it is important to acknowledge the role of the coming-of-age elements in the film, even though the graphic depiction of adult violence may tend to overshadow them.

Tamahori's adaptation is, in fact, a generic composite, illustrating once again the tendency of the coming-of-age genre to hybridize with other genres, as well as the inclination of New Zealand filmmakers to combine elements from different genres, illustrating Peter Jackson's contention that 'in New Zealand we tend to cross genres ... we end up muddying the genres. We do a bit of this and a bit of that and throw it together.'[30] In Tamahori's case, this genre-mixing is particularly evident: one can identify in *Once Were Warriors* a blend of elements drawn from the family melodrama and its sub-genre, the maternal melodrama; the social-problem film of the sort exemplified in the films of the British filmmaker Ken Loach, for whom Tamahori professes his admiration;[31] the action movie; the coming-of-age film; and the film style of the spaghetti westerns of Sergio Leone. Because Tamahori believed that 'you couldn't have it be a story about a mindlessly violent thug,' he shaped Duff's narrative into a family melodrama centering on the mother: 'I was more fascinated by a story of a mother who makes efforts to rise above her circumstances and create a life for her children.'[32] Moreover, recognizing that an exercise in social realism could potentially be off-putting for a cinema audience, Tamahori adopted a number of tropes, along with a pace and editing style, that were also drawn from a range of genres: 'In some ways it was made in the spirit of an action movie. It was social realism, meets Sergio Leone, meets action movie.'[33]

The director describes how as a youth he had become hooked on the films of Robert Aldrich, Don Siegel, and Sam Peckinpah – 'really solid, professional, American testosterone movies!' – explicitly mentioning *Ulzana's Raid* (Robert Aldrich, 1972) as one of the films he particularly admired,[34] a film that depicts a war party of Apache Indians fighting back against invading settlers, with extremely graphic violence. There was a difference, however, because Tamahori knew he was dealing with real violence, not 'mindless, cartoon violence of the sort found in the films of Aldrich and "Bloody Sam" Peckinpah':

> With *Warriors*, this was about real violence, in your face ... unlike Sam's stuff, I wanted to do it so fast and vicious and over before you know it with your cameras right in there amongst it with a certain style and selection of lenses so the audience has no choice but to get dragged along into this sort of screaming morass ... something you should remember if you're ever doing this, the more you can pull off in one shot, the more horrible it's going to seem, because subliminally the audience knows about cuts.[35]

There was a further major difference; whereas Aldrich had shown a native people directing violence against their alien oppressors, Tamahori, following Duff, showed them inflicting on their own kind a brutality that enabled the screen violence in *Once Were Warriors* to convey a social message that was far more arrestingly meaningful than the visceral entertainment offered in the movies that supplied Tamahori's models for the action-movie dimension of his own film, even though traces of that entertainment motive remain – as, for example, the glamorization of the film's gang, which, as McDonnell notes, emerges 'as an idealised modern-day warrior group.'[36]

This blending of elements drawn from a variety of genres within an overarching family melodrama, which itself contains aspects of the maternal melodrama as well as being a social-problem film, enhanced with the style and tropes of the action film, provides a frame within which the three coming-of-age sub-plots are located, assuming a much greater prominence than they had occupied in the novel. Within the rhetorical and thematic structure of the film, this greater prominence was necessary because it is the mother's perception of the effects on her children of the violence and drunkenness within her household, and of the abject circumstances in which they live, that triggers in her a process of self-actualization that leads to her moral, emotional, and cultural rehabilitation, and hence to the possibility of a remedy for the situation for her children.

The Three Coming-of-age Sub-plots

The three coming-of-age narratives that form the film's sub-plots are interwoven with the main narrative concerning Jake (Temuera Morrison) and Beth (Rena Owen), so that they resurface at regular intervals to punctuate and provide an implicit comment on it. Together, these three narratives exemplify the array of possible outcomes for children confronting such a situation.

Grace (Mamaengaroa Kerr-Bell) is a sensitive, gentle idealist whose romantic outlook on the world stands in sharp contrast to the disillusionment of her two brothers. At first, she wants to think the best about everyone. Early in the movie, when she and Boogie are upstairs listening to Jake and Beth, who are cuddling and singing happily in the midst of the party taking place down below (before things turn ugly), she exclaims: 'Aren't they beautiful when they're like that!' To Boogie's cynical reply, 'They're just drunk, that's all,' she answers, 'People say what they think when they're drunk.'

This benevolent outlook on the world motivates her to be a comforter and a helper. When we first see her, she is reading a story to her younger brother and sister. She takes food to Toot, the homeless boy who lives in a wrecked car, cleans up the trashed house the morning after the party, and feeds the other children, thus supplying the role that her mother should be fulfilling, but is not. When Jake is beating up Beth downstairs, it is Grace who comforts her terrified siblings as they huddle together on a bed upstairs, Grace who accompanies Boogie to the courtroom for his hearing, and Grace who comforts her mother after her brother is remanded in Social Welfare custody.

Like Boogie, Grace is sensitive and vulnerable, seeking refuge – like so many children in other New Zealand coming-of-age movies – in a fantasy world of the imagination, reflected in the stories she writes in an exercise book that she is seen clutching at key moments, as if it is a lifeline. The other source of refuge for Grace is her friendship with the homeless boy, Toot. As she says to him on one of her visits, 'You're the only one I can talk to, you know that, Toot?', to which he replies, 'Yes, I do. Best mates.' It is only when she fears that she can no longer trust in that friendship, after she has been betrayed by her own uncle and her father, that she succumbs to despair.

Grace's breaking point arrives when she is no longer able to defend herself against the reality of how morally and emotionally bankrupt her father is, and how hellish the circumstances of her family life actually are. This occurs when, having rented a car at Beth's urging so that the family can visit Boogie at the

Figure 10.2 Grace (Mamaengaroa Kerr-Bell) and Toot (Shannon Williams) in *Once Were Warriors* (dir. Lee Tamahori, 1994).

borstal, Jake stops at a pub and gets caught up in a drinking session with his buddies, meaning that they never get to see Boogie, with Beth having to take the children home in a taxi: 'I hate you! I hate you both!' cries Grace. Soon afterwards, once the session at the pub has become extended into yet another party at the house, Uncle Bully, fired with drink, enters Grace's bedroom and rapes her, leaving her with the words: 'It's our secret, Grace. Keep your mouth shut!'

The effect on the girl is to remove the possibility of sustaining hope. 'Why is everything so black, Toot?' she asks her friend, while seeing if he has any glue to let her sniff: 'You never see black in a rainbow, do you? Just bright colors.' For Grace, the colors have disappeared, and when Toot goes to kiss her, she repels him, saying: 'You're just like everyone else around here!' While Toot cannot understand what he has done to cause this reaction, we, as spectators, can: Bully's sexual molestation of Grace has destroyed her ability to believe in the goodness of men.

The catastrophe finally occurs when Grace returns home to find Jake and his mates drinking and partying, and Bully beckons her, 'Come on, give your Uncle Bully a kiss goodnight.' When Grace refuses, her father, committing the ultimate betrayal of his daughter, flies into an abusive rage, rips up her exercise book, and throws her violently on to the couch, following which Grace, sobbing, runs out of the house and hangs herself. Grace's story, then, provides a tragic, horrifying exemplification of the damage that can be inflicted on a child emerging into adulthood when raised in the kind of familial environment that is so graphically depicted in *Once Were Warriors*. Mercifully, the two other sub-plots reveal the possibility of alternative, more positive outcomes.

Nig, the elder brother, seems at first to be heading down a comparably self-destructive path when he joins a gang, having decided to get 'out of this fuckin' hole!' when his mother slaps him violently across the face. For Nig, the gang serves as a substitute family, a fact that is ironically underlined when the gang leader tells him, 'Bro, now you've met your new family.' Ironically, this new family replicates the violence of Nig's former, real family, as he learns when his initiation involves him in being beaten up by the other gang members.

In contrast to the novel, however, in which Duff's Nig ends up being killed in a gang fight, Nig in the film version eventually decides to move in the opposite direction. The change between the two versions of this character is evident in the contrast between two parallel moments when he stares down his father. The first occurs when Nig's gang enters a pub in which Jake and his mates are holding court, and Jake goes to pick a fight with a gang member who stands at the bar with his back facing towards him. When this gang member turns around, Jake is shocked to find that it is Nig, who dares his father to pursue his intention. At this stage in his developmental itinerary, Nig has only one side of his face tattooed, which figuratively symbolizes the fact that he has progressed only half way in his identification with the gang and its values. The second occasion also occurs during a scene at the pub, when Beth, having learnt the truth, screams at Bully 'You fuckin' animal... You raped a 13-year-old girl!', incurring the wrath of Jake. At this moment, Nig steps between Jake and his mother to protect her, which reflects the entrenchment of a new sense of personal responsibility. The first signs of this emergent new sense occurred earlier during Grace's funeral when Nig addresses his dead sister, saying, 'Sorry. I should have been there for you, Sis.' By the end of the movie, Nig has come back home, both literally and figuratively, and his *hongi* with his uncle, who is an elder from the tribal *marae*, signals that, like Beth, he is going to re-embrace the traditional values of pride and *aroha* (love) that characterize the customary culture of Māori, and thus recover his *mana*, self-respect, and sense of dignity.

Boogie (Taungaroa Emile), his younger brother, traverses a similar trajectory. At the beginning of the film, he has already slid down the slope into delinquency, leading to his removal to a reformatory school run by the Welfare Department. Like Grace, he is sensitive, which leaves him vulnerable; as Beth observes, he is 'not strong like the others,' which is why Jake's failure to turn up for a visit at the boy's home is devastating to him. A crucial turning point in Boogie's personal evolution, this episode was based on a real-life incident, in which Alan Duff's mother, having been waylaid by a 'booze session,' failed to turn up for a pre-arranged visit at the Boys' Home to which he had been remanded.[37] In the novel, it is not just Jake who is responsible for this callous indifference to the feelings of his son; his dereliction is compounded by that of his wife when

Beth joins her husband in the pub and also falls off the wagon. Duff expresses his indignation, grief, and anger at this parental betrayal by giving the narrator of the novel version of *Once Were Warriors* an intensely emotional outburst:

> Oh, and this poor kid, eh, the one in the Boys Home up in Riverton, waitin all day for his [Jake's] visit. All day. And the housemaster on the evening shift coming up to him: Mark Heke, it appears your visitors are not coming. And the kid saying, Yes they are. Yes they are. How kids get when they won't face the truth . . . Any fuckin wonder they grow up still mostly a kid in their hearts; it's because people, adults, the fucked-up society they come from, don't take any notice ofem . . . and when they get sent away to these Boys Home places for being bad, the people working there think the first and only thing they gotta do is straighten the kid out . . . Yet they wouldn't treat a dog like that a dog was sent to em been kicked and abused all its life . . .[38]

In both the novel and the film, however, the Boys Home nevertheless does have a beneficial effect on Boogie, owing to the presence of an impressive Māori welfare officer, Mr Bennett (George Henare), who, like Chief Te Tupaea (Te Whatanui Skipwith) at the *marae* ceremony for Grace's *tangi* (funeral), manifests the pride and the magnificence of traditional Māori culture, and is able to transmit it to Boogie by teaching him the *haka* (war dance), and how to handle a *taiaha* (fighting stick), thus imbuing him with the prowess of a true warrior, not the degenerate version that Jake represents. As Bennett says to Boogie, 'When I have taught you, your mind will be [your weapon]. You'll carry your *taiaha* inside you' – a prophesy that is confirmed at the end of the movie when Boogie declines to get a tattoo like Nig's: 'I wear mine on the inside.' By reversing the downward trajectory he is on and reforming himself in this way, Boogie shadows the major rehabilitation that will take place in Beth, his mother.

Beth's Self-actualization

In the course of the film, as in the novel, Beth undergoes a major transformation that itself could be considered a belated coming of age, justifying McDonnell's suggestion that in some ways the film presents 'a feminist re-reading and re-construction of the novel.'[39] Like Boogie and Nig, Beth experiences a personal growth in the course of the film that leads to a reversal of her earlier assumptions. At the mid-point, when she is sharing Grace's distress at the realization that Jake is beginning a boozing session that will prevent them from seeing Boogie, Beth says to her daughter: 'It's just a woman's lot, that's all. One day you'll understand.' By the next morning, after Jake has brought his drunken

COMING-OF-AGE CINEMA IN NEW ZEALAND

Figure 10.3 Boogie (Taungaroa Emile) exercises newfound pride in his culture in *Once Were Warriors* (dir. Lee Tamahori, 1994).

buddies home for another party and Beth has had time to think about the effect it is having on her children, she finds the courage to defy him, saying: 'You're not going to hurt my babies any more. Not while I can do something about it.' By the end of the movie, when Beth has decided to leave Jake and return to her people, along with her children, her final speech sums up its ideological message:

> I've found something better, Jake, and I'm going to make sure my kids have it all. From now on, I make the decisions for my family . . . You've got nothing I want. Our people once were warriors, but not like you, Jake. They were people with *mana*, pride, people with spirit. If my spirit can survive living with you for 18 years, then I can survive anything.

As well as recovering her sense of maternal responsibility, Beth has also discovered the strength and resolution of her true self, and in the face of it, Jake can only rave impotently, 'Fuck off, go . . . Fuck you! You'll be back!' – which we know she will not. When we last see him, Jake is alone, as ineffectual and powerless to make any meaningful impression as the axe whose head he broke off when trying to chop down the tree in which Grace hanged herself.

THE IDEOLOGICAL VISION OF THE FILM

Whereas Duff in the source novel allows Jake the possibility of redemption once he has hit rock bottom, which the author would subsequently explore in the two sequels that followed – *What Becomes of the Broken Hearted*

(1996), and *Jake's Long Shadow* (2002) – Jake in the film is permitted no such prospect, because he remains locked in the mindset of a slave, as Beth points out to him. Instead, the film presents a return to the values of traditional Māori culture as the solution to the social ills it portrays, and to convey this message it erases virtually all traces of the presence of Pākehā, making them 'irrelevant to the conflicts, aims, and hopes of the film's story.'[40]

Duff had taken a different tack by including a Pākehā family, the Tramberts, to represent a style of life and material prosperity to which he believed Māori should aspire, and by enunciating a self-help doctrine as the means whereby they could get there. This perspective, seen as aligned with right-wing neoliberal economics, provoked a storm of outrage in some quarters; the Māori academic Ranginui Walker, for example, denounced Duff as 'irrelevant' to Māori 'because he is not part of the people's struggle for emancipation and social advancement.'[41] Others, to the contrary, took issue with the film's embrace of Maoritanga as the solution for the social ills depicted in *Once Were Warriors*,[42] objecting to the way in which 'the idea that something needs to be done about poverty in life elides into its resolution in art, rather than in life.'[43] Just how the discrepancy between these rival perspectives would play themselves out within subsequent coming-of-age films on Māori subjects is a topic that I will explore in the chapters to follow on *Whale Rider* (Niki Caro, 2002), *Boy* (Taika Waititi, 2010), *Mahana* (Lee Tamahori, 2016), and *Hunt for the Wilderpeople* (Taika Waititi, 2016).

Notes

1. This figure is reported by Pivac and Stark, *New Zealand Film: An Illustrated History*, 297.
2. Brian McDonnell, 'Once Were Warriors: Controversial Novel Becomes Blockbuster Film,' *Metro Magazine: Media & Education Magazine* 101 (1995), 7–9.
3. These figures are derived from 'Top Twenty New Zealand Films Released At New Zealand Box Office (to 15 July 2016),' NZ Film Commission, http://www.nzfilm.co.nz/sites/nzfc/files/Top%2020%20July%202016.pdf, accessed 12 August 2016.
4. 'A Trip to the Flicks: Watching Cinema Admission Prices in the CPI,' Statistics New Zealand Tatauranga Aotearoa, http://www.stats.govt.nz/browse_for_stats/economic_indicators/prices_indexes/watching-cinema-admission-prices-in-the-cpi.aspx, accessed 12 August 2016.
5. Elizabeth Beattie, 'Throwback Thursday – 22 years on, Once Were Warriors is as relevant as Ever,' *The Spinoff*, 28 January 2016, http://thespinoff.co.nz/featured/28-01-2016/throwback-thursday-22-years-later-once-were-warriors-is-as-relevant-as-ever/, accessed 10 August 2016.
6. Alex Simon, 'Lee Tamahori: Along Came a Filmmaker,' *The Hollywood Interview.com*, 3 December 2012, http://thehollywoodinterview.blogspot.co.nz/2008/03/lee-tamahori-hollywood-interview.html, accessed 10 August 2016.
7. Beattie, 'Throwback Thursday.'
8. See Kirsten Moana Thompson, 'Once Were Warriors: New Zealand's First Indigenous Blockbuster,' in Julian Stringer (ed.), *Movie Blockbusters* (London: Routledge, 2003), 230–41, esp. 233.
9. 'The Top 20 Bestselling New Zealand Books,' *New Zealand Listener*, 15 May 2004.

10. Alan Duff, *Out of the Mist and Steam: A Memoir* (Auckland: Tandem Press, 1999), 32.
11. Ibid., 35.
12. Ibid.
13. Ibid.
14. Ibid., 76.
15. Ibid., 48.
16. See Michael Dickison, 'Author's Campaign to Boost Reading Marks 15th Birthday,' *New Zealand Herald*, 21 August 2010.
17. Anon., 'An Interview with Lee Tamahori,' *Stuff.co.nz*, http://movies.interactives.co.nz/tamahori.php, accessed 10 August 2016.
18. Greg Dixon, 'Once Were Warriors: Twenty Years On,' *New Zealand Herald*, 16 August 2014, http://www.nzherald.co.nz/canvas-magazine/news/article.cfm?c_id=532&objectid=11308911, accessed 10 August 2016.
19. Alex Simon, 'Lee Tamahori: Along Came a Filmmaker,' *The Hollywood Interview.com*, 3 December 2012, http://thehollywoodinterview.blogspot.co.nz/2008/03/lee-tamahori-hollywood-interview.html, accessed 10 August 2016.
20. Dixon, 'Once Were Warriors: Twenty Years On.'
21. Simon, 'Lee Tamahori: Along Came a Filmmaker.'
22. Beattie, 'Throwback Thursday.'
23. Anon., 'An Interview with Lee Tamahori.'
24. Simon, 'Lee Tamahori: Along Came a Filmmaker.'
25. Anon., 'An Interview with Lee Tamahori.'
26. Detailed accounts of changes made between the novel and the film adaptation are given by McDonnell, 'Once Were Warriors: Controversial Novel Becomes Blockbuster Film,' and Emiel Martens, *Once were Warriors: The Aftermath: The Controversy of OWW in Aotearoa New Zealand* (Amsterdam: Aksant, 2007), 39–43.
27. See McDonnell, 'Once Were Warriors,' 8.
28. Ibid., 7.
29. Dixon, 'Once Were Warriors.'
30. Jim Barr and Mary Barr, 'NZFX: The Films of Peter Jackson and Fran Walsh,' in Jonathan Dennis and Jan Bieringa (eds), *Film in Aotearoa New Zealand* (Wellington: Victoria University Press, 1996), 150–60, esp. 156.
31. 'I was a great lover of Ken Loach and British social realism' (Anon., 'An Interview with Lee Tamahori').
32. Ibid.
33. Anon, 'An Interview with Lee Tamahori.'
34. Simon, 'Lee Tamahori.'
35. Ibid.
36. McDonnell, 8.
37. Duff, *Out of the Mists and Steam*, 119–20.
38. Alan Duff, *Once Were Warriors* (New York: Vintage, 1995 [1990]), 107.
39. McDonnell, 'Once Were Warriors,' 8.
40. Ibid.
41. Ranginui Walker, 'Eat Your Heart Out, Alan Duff,' *Metro* 145 (1993), 136–7.
42. Pascale De Souza, 'Maoritanga in *Whale Rider* and *Once Were Warriors*: A Problematic Rebirth through Female Leaders,' *Studies in Australasian Cinema* 1:1 (2007), 15–27.
43. Ruth, Brown, 'Closing the Gaps: "Once Were Warriors" from Book to Film and Beyond,' *JNZL: Journal of New Zealand Literature* 17 (Summer 1999), 141–55.

PART 4

PREOCCUPATIONS OF THE NEW MILLENNIUM

11. AN ADOLESCENT GIRL EXPERIMENTS WITH SEXUALITY: *RAIN* (CHRISTINE JEFFS, 2001)

If Peter Jackson and Fran Walsh's *Heavenly Creatures* marks a watershed, it is because the next significant coming-of-age film made in New Zealand, *Rain* (Christine Jeffs, 2001), shows that the prevailing value system that had dominated society through the mid-twentieth century had been replaced by a new one. Instead of depicting children and young people wrestling with the destructive effects of puritanism and the oppressive social rigidities that it enforced, a younger generation of filmmakers born in the 1960s was beginning to make movies that reflected the move into hedonism and permissiveness that had followed the sexual revolution, together with a progressive dismantling of systems of domination in all domains of life. If the coming-of-age films of the preceding generation had shown the rigidity of the social values and practices of puritanism to be incapable of providing sensitive children with a 'sense of secure holding,' to use D. W. Winnicott's term, those made by the younger generation would show the new 'liberated' society to be equally defective in terms of furnishing children with the emotional security needed for wellbeing. While the environmental circumstances may have been different, their effects on children were equally disruptive, if for different reasons.

The first of the younger filmmakers to tackle these emerging new circumstances from the perspective of a young teenager undergoing a rite of passage was Christine Jeffs (born 1963), who attracted worldwide attention with her first feature film *Rain*, which had its première in the Director's Fortnight at Cannes. Jeffs adapted her film from an equally acclaimed first novel, *Rain*, published in 1994, by the New Zealand writer Kirsty Gunn (born 1960).

While the film and the novel share a similarly critical view of the 1960s New Zealand society in which both Jeffs and Gunn had grown up, and the film replicates the basic story of, and a number of key events in, the novel, the way in which the film auteur and the literary author construe the meaning of the experience presented in these two works is significantly different. On one hand, Gunn sees the world she depicts as exposing children to dangers in the external world that attest to a metaphysical condition – a human situation that is inherently tragic; Jeffs, on the other hand, sees that world as the backdrop to a stage in human development – the onset of sexuality – that will launch the maturing teenager into relationships with other adults that, being impacted by stresses and disturbances, will simply involve 'holding on' as one traverses an adult experience that is, as the words of the concluding song in the soundtrack affirm, 'a long way to travel.'

The difference in the nature of their respective visions had a profound influence on the form and mode of each of these works. Indeed, in the course of adapting Kirsty Gunn's novel, Christine Jeffs, as usually happens with coming-of-age adaptations, completely transformed the original, investing it with a different view of the nature of things.

The Poetic Vision of Kirsty Gunn

Kirsty Gunn's rendering of the story in *Rain* is, above all, a poetic evocation of the significance of the world as understood by the heroine of the story, Janey, who is looking back as a thirty-year-old on the experience of her earlier twelve-year-old self during a summer vacation at her family's bach, situated at the edge of a lake. Left to themselves by their parents, who prefer partying with friends, Janey and her younger seven-year-old brother Little Jim amuse themselves, with Janey trying to teach her brother how to swim, until Janey falls prey to a child abuser, and, while she is absent during a sexual encounter with the predator, Little Jim, who has been left alone, drowns.

The significance of the story in Gunn's version is conveyed through a pattern of reiterated images that imbue it with a richly symbolic texture. The lake itself, around which all the action revolves, is invested with a sense of death and drowning in terms that prefigures the death of the little boy at the end of the novel, as well as the inevitability of decay and the transience of things:

> All the trees were drowning. They reached their long skinny branches into the lake, leaning so far that their gnarled roots could barely hold the clay. You knew it was only time before whole bodies would be dislodged, allowed to drift, then sink. The water would seal over them again and that's how it would end: you would never know there had been trees there at all.[1]

The lake is also associated with fear. When Janey swims out into it, she hears her young brother cry out from the shore: 'Don't go! . . . Come back to where I am, it's scary there.'[2] On the other hand, the part of the lake where the two siblings swim, being 'a tray, where you walk out for miles,' seems deceptively safe: 'Nothing bad could happen. There were no hooks to catch or lines to bring you down, no deep ledges or treacherous currents could tug your body away' – or so it seems.[3] The lake, in other words, as would be the case later in Jane Campion's moody TV series *Top of the Lake* (2013), takes on a metaphysical significance, symbolizing dark aspects of the world, through which human beings have to make their way.

Within this world, Janey and Jim derive no sense of protection or safety from their parents, who represent 'a coupling of glamour and decay . . . with their yellow lawn, their stained chairs,' mother 'wet with oil, tanned in all her parts,' and 'our poor father, crusted.'[4] Rather than look after their children, the parents prefer partying and drinking, and to play bridge with their friends, leaving Janey and her brother to look after themselves: 'It was almost as if we'd been born unparented.'[5] Despite the hedonism of their lifestyle, the parents are not happy. The mother occupies a 'sad, cruel place where she lived, her unhappiness,' spending many hours alone in her darkened room, while the father's life 'was shrunk by now up onto dry land': 'He took so many hours, so much sun for her pretty sake he was desiccated with waiting. All his young life was gone.'[6]

In response to this parental neglect, the two children long to escape in a boat to a far-off place, in which they fantasize living an Edenic life in the bush, living off the land: 'In our boat we could be safe, quite sure of our destination. It was where we needed to be.'[7] Janey, however, realizes that this fantasy is unattainable in the world of adult reality: 'I was growing up. I think I knew already the whole sad fact of children trying to escape.'[8] Aware that she is 'nearly teenaged,' Janey is fearful of the prospect of becoming a sexual being, which is why she clings to her preoccupation with her little brother: 'I'm not like those puberty girls, I don't want any of those other things happening to me. I've planned it, I'll never know a boy. It will always be only my brother I'll care for, he needs all my attention and I have no time for the other part.'[9] To sustain her attachment to Little Jim, which is itself a compensation for parental neglect, is to remain within a state of innocence, protected against latent realities of which Janey is aware, but which she fears admitting into her full knowledge.

Those realities, however, impinge upon her in all their fearfulness when a thirty-year-old neighbor, Bill Cady, one of her mother's friends from the house down on the point, enters Janey's bedroom during one of her parents' parties and is only prevented from sexually abusing her by the arrival of her mother. Shortly after, Cady actually does abuse her when he intercepts her swimming, on an occasion when she has left her brother to play on his own, and takes her into the bush:

> 'Don't be shy . . .'
> It was just once at first, letting myself be taken, then more times, over and over until it was me myself going back for more. Leaving my family, leaving my little brother playing while the tides in the river were rising.[10]

For Janey, it is sadly ironic that these episodes in the bush, satisfying the lust of a sexual predator until she herself becomes corrupted by it, become the reality that substitutes for the idealized utopian vision of an innocent Edenic life in the bush that she had shared with her brother. When, as a result of Jim's having been left alone during one of these sexual assignations, Janey returns to the place where he was playing to find his drowned body, the boy's death represents, at a symbolic level, the death of her own childhood innocence as much as it constitutes a literal death. Significantly, Janey cannot revive him, just as she cannot revive the cocooned state of innocence out of which she has been ripped by her seducer.

At the end of this haunting story, it is the water of the lake, with all that it symbolizes about life itself, in Kirsty Gunn's vision, which prevails:

> The water has them, those people you pretend were your life. It has you. It's water's pulse beating in your wrist now. You know it too. The lake, she's your lovely body now, with all her openings. Close your eyes, she's still there. Some days the surface of water is pulled over like satin, others it's rumpled and bony. There's your memory. Pure images of tide and depth and the colour of the water . . . Who you were, who you are now, your people . . . They're drowned in her. All the rest is water.[11]

The novel turns out, then, to be a metaphysical parable about the condition of the world itself: what it means to grow up, and the sad realities – broken marriages, failures of responsibility, and tragic accidents – that one is likely to encounter when one does so.

Changes of Mode and Genre in Christine Jeffs' Adaptation

In adapting Kirsty Gunn's novel, Christine Jeffs turned it into something quite different. The most fundamental change was the transformation of what had been a lyrical meditation on a situation exemplifying the human condition into a fairly conventional family melodrama with a clearly defined three-act structure. Together with this major shift in genre, Jeffs abandoned Gunn's retrospective narrative, in which Janey as a thirty-year-old adult looks back at her experience as a child, and also updated the setting from 1967, the exact age of Kirsty Gunn at the time when the novel's action takes place, to the 1970s when Jeffs herself was a teenager, like Janey in the film. In addition, she shifted the location from Lake Taupo in the central volcanic region of the North Island, Gunn's setting, to the Mahurangi Peninsula in Northland, where Jeffs has a home – a sign that, as one might anticipate, the film contains personal associations like all the other coming-of-age films discussed in this book.

The change of genre into a cinematic melodrama was motivated, in part, by the difficulties Jeff encountered in getting the film funded. As she has revealed in an interview, she was turned down many times because the funding bodies 'didn't think there was a narrative in the book.' Moreover, 'they didn't think that anyone wanted to see a film about a 13-year-old girl who was the main character,' and 'were looking for a feel-good comedy.' In short, 'It just didn't fall within the genre films they thought they wanted to make.'[12]

In her alterations to the source novel, what Jeffs does, in effect, is to convert the story into a genre film – in this case a melodrama – that would be more likely to meet box office expectations. The first thing she does is to develop two new characters that allow the emphasis of the film to be placed on the issue of sexuality, both for Kate (Sarah Peirse), the mother, and her daughter Janey (Alicia Fulford-Wierzbicki), rather than on the metaphysical implications of the human situation, as it had been in Gunn's novel. Whereas Bill Cady is only briefly mentioned in the novel, and is not given any physical description, Jeffs develops him into a fully rounded character in the film, turning him into a handsome photographer who moors his cabin-cruiser in the bay where the family has their bach. This allows her to trace the development of a full-blown affair between Cady (Marton Csokas) and Janey's mother, which Janey observes, and which intensifies her sexual curiosity.

Jeffs also introduces a new character, Sam (David Taylor), who is a boy the same age as Janey, for the purpose of contrasting him with Cady. Whereas Cady is sexually experienced, leading a freewheeling, promiscuous lifestyle, Sam is sexually inexperienced, which allows Jeffs to use his presence to highlight Janey's aggressive sexual curiosity. Thus, in a reversal of what occurs in the novel, Jeffs, instead of having Cady come to Janey's bedroom, transfers this action to Sam, in order to show how he flees when Janey takes the initiative to kiss him (itself a reflection of her emerging interest in sexuality) – a retreat he will repeat later in the film. Cady, on the other hand, readily complies with Janey's seduction, even though he knows she is a minor.

To strengthen this shift of focus onto the issue of sexuality, Jeffs also introduces a range of new episodes. We initially see scenes of Kate flirting with Cady when the family are out with him on his boat on a fishing trip, and we see Cady going skinny dipping with others during a party, and then going off with Joy (Claire Dougan), another young woman, for the night, which sketches in his promiscuous lifestyle. Subsequently, we get two new scenes in which Janey observes Cady and her mother kissing, and two further scenes showing Kate going to visit Cady on his boat, in dry-dock to be painted, on the second occasion of which they have sex. Additional new scenes show a series of encounters between Janey and Cody, culminating in a lengthy new scene depicting Janey's aggressive seduction of him in a pine plantation.

The end result is the remodeling of the original story into a classic three-act structure as found in the majority of genre films: Act I introduces the major characters and the world they live in and provides a 'hook' in the form of the sexual interest in Cady that develops on the part of Kate and her daughter; Act II presents the rising action, which consists of the flirtations pursued by both mother and daughter; and Act III consists of the resolution, involving Janey's sexual initiation and the tragic death of her brother, followed by the break-up of the family, which is reported in Janey's final voiceover.

The shift from a densely figurative symbolic parable in the original novel to this fairly conventional cinematic family melodrama is accompanied by a film style that is perhaps best characterized as 'artful realism.' In terms of the choice and length of shots, the film is fairly classical, except for the fact that Jeffs and her cinematographer John Toon eschew the formality of dollies in favor of a hand-held camera for much of the movie, and include several slow-motion takes at key moments to emphasize what is happening to Janey and her mother.[13] The film also switches to black and white for the climactic moment when Janey loses her virginity.

The style of the film is very distinctive, however, in the careful framing of its shots and the way it selects and focuses on objects. These aspects of Jeffs' style have been highly praised, for reasons that are well summed up in A. O. Scott's review for the *New York Times*:

> Ms. Jeffs, directing her first feature film after many years of making commercials, uses the physical world – small, homely objects like lemons or ice cubes, as well as the brooding seaside landscape – to suggest the emotions her characters cannot express directly. Her gorgeous, fluid compositions, underlined by Neil Finn and Edmund McWilliams's melancholy music, are charged with metaphor, but rarely easy, obvious or self-indulgent. The visual beauty of the film, rather than distracting from the troubling story, makes it more troubling still.[14]

What makes the imagery of Jeffs' film very different from the imagery in Gunn's novel is that Jeffs' images, as signifiers, become literalized as emblems of a lifestyle and its values, rather than symbolic figurations of metaphysical realities or spiritual states. As Philip Matthews puts it, the film presents us with 'raw kiwiana ... processed through a clear and deliberate arthouse

Figure 11.1 Janey (Alicia Fulford-Wierzbicki) imitates her mother's glitzy ostentation in *Rain* (dir. Christine Jeffs, 2001).

aesthetic.'[15] At a banal level, we see this in close-up shots of, for example, a lawnmower, sewing machine, and Kate's hands in rubber gloves doing the dishes in a sink, all of which suggests the mundaneness of her domestic life that is responsible for her boredom. At a more elevated level, we see endless shots of whiskey, wine, and beer bottles, spirits being poured, glasses full of champagne, cigarettes being smoked, and the gaudy jewelry Kate wears, which Janey imitates when she goes to her assignation with Cady, donning multiple bangles, as we have seen her mother do. The veteran New Zealand filmmaker Ian Mune rather unkindly dismissed *Rain* as a '90 minute commercial' on account of its surface glossiness,[16] but to make this assumption is to miss the thematic functionality of the images on which Jeffs chooses to focus.

Many of the shots are exquisitely framed and composed, as, for example, the shot of Little Jim (Aaron Murphy) running happily through the water, or the contrasting shot of Kate walking disconsolately back through the rising tide after having sex with Cady on his boat. The function of such shots is to highlight the pathos as well as the ordinariness of the family melodrama that unfolds before the spectator's eyes.

Janey's Entry into Sexuality

All of the changes mentioned so far, including the newly developed episode showing Kate's affair with Cady, serve to foreground the centrality in the film of Janey's coming-of-age experience, which involves the loss of her virginity as

Figure 11.2 Little Jim (Aaron Murphy) in *Rain* (dir. Christine Jeffs, 2001).

a rite of passage. To achieve this new emphasis, Jeffs subjects the character of Janey to another major transformation. Instead of a fearful girl who variously wishes to escape with her brother into an idealized fantasy world of Edenic innocence, and to remain within the cocoon of her pre-pubescent child's self, Janey in Jeffs' version is a precocious, rebellious teenager who proactively seizes the initiative to become sexual. This is seen in her aspirations to become a fashion model, which provide the pretext for her to arrange an assignation with Cady so that he can take a photo of her for her 'portfolio.'

An entirely new element in Janey's desire to explore her sexuality is the motivation, in Jeffs' redaction, that she derives from her mother. In the first instance, her mother provides an example Janey wishes to emulate. We see this on several occasions when Janey flaunts a cigarette in imitation of what she sees as the suave sophistication of her mother, who is repeatedly shown smoking and drinking. When Sam, the teenager, approaches Janey during one of her parents' parties, she lights up a cigarette to indicate her *savoir faire*. Soon afterwards, when Janey encounters Cady the following day, she asks him for a cigarette to signal transgressiveness as a means of suggesting her sexual availability.

Janey's mother provides an example in more explicit ways. Twice Janey sees her kissing Cady, the first time on the darkened beach during the party when the revelers frolic naked in the water, and the second on the occasion of yet another party when Janey opens the door of the bathroom to see Cady and her mother locked in a passionate embrace. Witnessing these scenes alerts Janey to the power of sexuality, motivating her to try it out on Sam, whom she similarly kisses on two occasions, just as her mother kissed Cady.

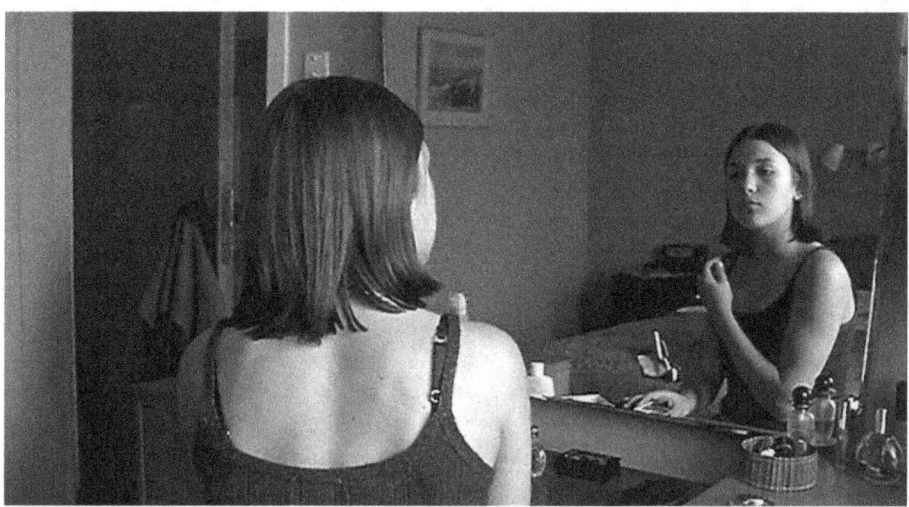

Figure 11.3　Janey (Alicia Fulford-Wierzbicki) puts on her mother's make-up in *Rain* (dir. Christine Jeffs, 2001).

A number of other scenes show Janey imitating her mother in ways that underline the parallel between them. In one scene, Janey is seen before a mirror putting on her mother's make-up. Soon after this, she tries on one of her mother's gaudy, floral summer dresses, asking if she can wear it. This is the dress that Janey will wear when she swims out to meet Cady on his boat, smoothing the wet garment against her so that it outlines the curves of her pubescent body.

Unlike the indifferent mother of Gunn's novel, Kate in Jeffs' version is complicit in all of this. She happily alters the dress so that it fits snugly against Janey's form, and during a scene in which Janey asks her anxiously, 'Is Daddy still your boyfriend?,' Kate encourages her to experiment with boys by saying 'kissing is fun.' Kate thus sets the tone for Janey as well as a pattern to imitate – a fact that Cady wryly observes under his breath when Janey comes on board his boat and surprises him in bed: 'Like mother, like daughter!' To Janey, he says directly, 'Don't come dressed like that – you look like your mother.'

This characterization of Janey as a precocious would-be seductress is manifestly a far cry from Gunn's comparatively innocent, frightened twelve-year-old. Indeed, Jeffs depicts her as being animated by an Electra complex that is even more powerfully in evidence than in the case of Toss in Vincent Ward's *Vigil*, which never seems far from this director's mind (although the impressionistic film style of the earlier film is very different). Janey enters into a rivalry with her mother in which she aims to supplant the latter by taking away her lover – an Aegisthus figure, as in the Greek myth, whom, in one part of her mind, Janey resents as the cause of her mother's betrayal of her father. Kate herself is presented as being aware of this competition, as well as the fact that she cannot, in the long run, hope to win it – a realization she confesses to her daughter: 'Everything's in front of *you* now, not me.' There is thus a strong element of culpability in the sexual encounters with Cady of both women: Kate betrays the fidelity she owes to her husband, and Janey betrays her loyalty to her mother. Two further parallel scenes in which the mother's behavior is mirrored in that of the daughter underline this shared culpability. The first occurs immediately after Kate has committed adultery with Cady, after which she returns to the house to take a shower. The second occurs following Janey's discovery of her drowned brother's body after her seduction of Cady, when she, too, is seen taking a shower. In both cases, the taking of a shower seems as if it is an attempt to cleanse oneself of guilt, an action that further serves to equate the two females.

The sense of guilt that Kate and Janey share, which derives from their awareness of where their sexuality has led them, and what consequences it has produced, leads, in Jeffs' vision, to understanding and redemption. As Jeffs herself puts it: 'there's the whole cleansing of the shower at the end. The shower becomes a kind of a metaphor for cleansing and renewal for mother and daughter.'[17] This renewal is reflected in the way they comfort each other after the tragic death of Little Jim, and how they end up together, as Janey notes in her final voiceover that reports what subsequently happened: 'Mum and Dad split up . . . Well it's strange, because it's just me and Mum, no Jim, and not much of Dad.' Janey, in fact, by the end of the movie, has moved into her mother's place: 'And now it's my turn, holding on, it's holding on.' Rather than showing a girl who grows into an awareness of the aspects of the world that cause the experience of it to be inflected with sadness, as Kirsty Gunn does in her novel, Jeffs' film shows a teenager who assumes her destiny as a woman whose chief goal is simply to endure in the face of the disappointments, frustrations, and tribulations that one encounters in life. Thus, while Jeffs' *Rain* presents a vision that is very different compared with that found in Gunn's novel, the film nevertheless offers a very compelling portrayal of an adolescent girl's sexual initiation, perhaps the most fully developed that has yet appeared in New Zealand cinema.

RAIN AS SYMPTOMATIC OF A TREND

While *Rain* is a film that is highly accomplished in form, with its carefully crafted parallels and contrasts and deliberate three-act structure, as well as the art-house beauty of its cinematic style, it is also more facile in substance than many of the coming-of-age films that preceded it, and certainly less rich in symbolic implication than its literary source. This is because of its generic conventionality, which deprives the film of its cultural specificity in terms of the mores that are shown, as distinct from the superficial 'kiwi-ness' that is created by its mise-en-scène.

Rain, in fact, inaugurates a trend that will become increasingly apparent in a number of the coming-of-age films that would follow it: a trend whereby the commercial imperatives of funding bodies like the New Zealand Film Commission would push filmmakers further towards making genre cinema than they might wish to do of their own accord. Such a tendency is starkly evident in the next film I shall discuss, Niki Caro's adaptation (2002) of *The Whale Rider*, a novel by the Māori author Witi Ihimaera. This was an adaptation that caused a storm of protest from Māori at its distortions of Māori culture, which were themselves a consequence of the generic tropes and conventions that the filmmaker imported into the realization of a story that was, in its origins, distinctively indigenous, but which, when turned into a film, ceased to be so, at least not to the same degree.

Notes

1. Kirsty Gunn, *Rain* (London: Faber & Faber, 1994), 1.
2. Ibid., 2.
3. Ibid., 6.
4. Ibid., 69.
5. Ibid., 14.
6. Ibid., 72.
7. Ibid., 11.
8. Ibid., 19.
9. Ibid., 47.
10. Ibid., 81.
11. Ibid., 94.
12. 'Rain Woman: Christine Jeffs Interviewed by Lynette Read,' *Illusions* 33 (Autumn 2002), 3–8, esp. 6.
13. See 'Rain Woman,' 8.
14. A. O. Scott, 'Drowning in Fear of Certain Disaster' [review], *New York Times*, 26 April 2002.
15. Philip Matthews, 'High-water Mark,' *New Zealand Listener*, 14 October 2001, 50–1.
16. Stan Jones, '"Kiwi as . . .": Ian Mune and Filmmaking as Cultural Expression,' in Ian Conrich and Stuart Murray (eds), *New Zealand Filmmakers* (Detroit: Wayne State University Press, 2007), 169.
17. 'Rain Woman,' 8.

12. ASSERTING FEMINIST CLAIMS WITHIN MĀORI CULTURE: *WHALE RIDER* (NIKI CARO, 2002)

The most important New Zealand movie of 2003, Niki Caro's *Whale Rider*, first shown at the Toronto Film Festival in September 2002, where it was voted *People's Choice*, and released elsewhere the following year, was one of the most successful fiction films made in this country, winning twenty-nine international awards. Apart from being highly successful in New Zealand, with ticket sales of 752,941,[1] making it the fourth most popular locally made movie to date, even more significantly, it was a huge hit internationally, with foreign box office earnings of $20,662,227.[2] In addition, it was the first feature-length film to be adapted from a novel by Witi Ihimaera, the most prominent Māori writer of fiction, inaugurating several other adaptations based on his works, including *Nights in the Gardens of Spain* (Katie Wolfe, 2010),[3] a coming-out drama, and *Mahana* (Lee Tamahori, 2016), based on the novel *Bulibasha: King of the Gypsies*, with further plans under way to film his major novel *The Matriarch*.

Despite *Whale Rider*'s popularity with audiences, however, within New Zealand its reception was mixed. In particular, some Māori found the film culturally offensive, and objected to the fact that a Pākehā director had presumed to make it. The scholar Brendan Hokowhitu, for example, saw *Whale Rider* as 'a problematic and even dangerous film for the project of Māori decolonization,' on the grounds that 'Pākehā have embraced this movie because it promotes a conscious paternalistic narrative of nurturing a savage culture while repressing the role of Pākehā in the oppression of Māori.'[4] In similar vein, Tania Ka'ai denounced the film as misrepresenting various tribal traditions, arguing that 'the patriarchy/feminism division operates very differently in the Ngāti Porou tribe, where *Whale Rider* is based, than it does either in the film or in Eurocentric feminisms.'[5]

What such criticisms point towards is the fact that Caro and her producer, John Barnett of South Pacific Pictures, deliberately reworked the source story of *Whale Rider* for the sake of making the film appeal to an international audience. Barnett, who optioned the book fourteen years before the film was actually made, became interested in the story because he felt

> ... that this is a universal story, that these themes of inherited power and the clash between the contemporary and the traditional, the familial love and the obligations that Koro the chief has that get in his way of exercising that familial love, the role of a woman in society – those were things that it didn't matter where you came from in the world, you were familiar with these things. I really saw it as a story that people would understand wherever they were.[6]

For Barnett, in other words, cultural specificity is unimportant compared with the potential for the story to have universal appeal, no matter what society in the world a spectator comes from.

For her part, Niki Caro was attracted to the project because she saw 'a coming-of-age story in a young girl that wasn't about a sexual awakening, but was a spiritual awakening, and I thought that was really new, very compelling for me.'[7] She also opined, however, that 'although the book is beautiful it doesn't present itself immediately as an adaptation'; consequently, when presented with the treatment that had already been prepared by the producers, Caro 'asked if I could write my own draft that would apply my vision to the film.'[8]

We are confronted, then, with a film that was purposefully directed away from the source story as it was in order to be converted into a film that would appeal universally across cultures – in other words, a recognizable genre film – and a film that would also serve as a vehicle through which the filmmaker could project her own personal 'vision.' This is precisely the trend that is evident in Christine Jeffs' *Rain* when compared with the source novel by Kirsty Gunn upon which it is based, and it reflects both the advent of an increasingly strong commercial imperative in New Zealand filmmaking from the 1990s onwards, as well as the growing influence of a globalized international culture. The end result was a cinematic version of Ihimaera's *The Whale Rider* that presented, in Hokowhitu's words,[9] a 'simulacrum' of Māori culture and the original story, while transubstantiating its inner meaning in the course of converting the source into a conventional coming-of-age genre film.

Ihimaera's Novel: Mode and Meaning

In terms of certain aspects of its cultural content and manner of presentation, Witi Ihimaera's *The Whale Rider* displays a close resemblance to Merata Mita's *Mauri* as an authentically indigenous work – that is, one that views the world from a Māori perspective and invests it with attitudes that derive from a Māori value system and belief system. At the heart of Ihimaera's story is the same importance that the character Kara in *Mauri* attributes to the transmission of knowledge through generations, as well as a strong awareness of the line of descent from ancestors. There is also the same sense of time as a spiral, reflected in the frequent return of episodes from the past into the narrative of the present, and the close connection Māori have with the natural environment and its creatures. Above all, in both Mita's film and Ihimaera's novel, there is the same sense of a union between the natural and the supernatural, and a belief in the importance of respecting *tapu* (prohibitions) and the *mana* (prestige, status, spiritual power) of others.

The omnipresence of these values in Ihimaera's story is conveyed through a variety of means. At the beginning of the book, the arrival of the gigantic *tipua* (supernatural being) in the form of a whale is accompanied by magic realism as Paikea, the man who is riding him, 'began to fling small spears of mauri seaward and landward': 'Some of the mauri in mid flight turned into pigeons which flew into the forests. Others on landing in the sea changed into eels. And the song in the sea drenched the air with ageless music and land and sea opened themselves to him, the gift long waited for: tangata, man.'[10] When the ancient whale returns near the end of the book, there is 'a dull booming from beneath the water, like a giant door opening a thousand years ago,' and 'streaks of blue lightning came shooting out of the sea like missiles.'[11] Such eruptions of magic realism are not simply decorative: they serve to intimate the presence of a spiritual, supernatural dimension inherent in the nature of things.

The union of the natural and the supernatural and the communion of Māori with the natural world is also seen on the occasion when Kahu, the girl (named Paikea in Caro's film), dives into the sea to retrieve the carved stone her grandfather Koro has thrown there as a test to identify the boy who is destined to carry on the leadership of his people in the new generation. As Kahu is searching the reef for the stone, 'white shapes came speeding out of the dark towards her.' They are dolphins who 'seemed to be talking to her,' and speed her to another area of the reef, where she finds the stone and returns it to the surface.[12] Later, near the end of the book, after Kahu has ridden the great whale, when she is found unconscious, 'floating in a nest of dark lustrous kelp in the middle of the ocean,' dolphins are guarding her, keeping her safe until she is rescued.[13]

Equally present is an overarching sense of the importance of *whanaungatanga*, or the kinship network that binds the members of the tribe into a larger unit, rather than placing the primary emphasis on the individual and the nuclear family, as occurs in Pākehā culture.[14] The existence of this larger network, which encompasses both past and present, and extends over distance and time, is reflected in the inclusion of many plot strands concerning a variety of characters. It is also apparent in the comings and goings of those who are part of the *whanau* (family group), including the great whale himself, to Whangara as the home-place of the tribe. This is not just Kahu's story; it is also the story of Rawiri, the narrator of the story, who is aged twenty-four. He is a bikie who leaves home to live in Australia for four years, and then two years in New Guinea, with Jeff, his white flatmate (who foreshadows Jason, the white lover of Michael, the narrator in Ihimaera's *The Uncle's Story*), during which time he grows into an understanding of himself as a Māori, not least as a result of encountering the racism of Jeff's parents. It is also the story of Koro, who is described as 'like an old whale stranded in an alien present,' as he struggles to find a way to understand his role in a changing world.[15] Not least, it is the story of the 'handsome and virile' bull whale himself, who loves the human who became his master, and who suffers heartache at being separated from him when, having been taken by the whale to Aotearoa, his 'golden master had met a woman and had married her.' Thereafter, the bull whale yearns to be reunited with his handsome young master in 'the dangerous islands to the south-west,' being unable to dislodge him from his thoughts.[16] The homoerotic overtones in the passages describing the relation between the bull whale and Paikea provide a reminder that, for Ihimaera, this is a very personal novel: it was written for his daughters, Jessica and Olivia, and embodies personal projections, some of them relating to his experience as a gay man, and some of them displaced into the story of Kahu herself, as he intimates in an interview. Despite being someone who has inherited all the expectations of leadership, he says, 'I have been able to live a life away from the iwi [tribal kinship group] somewhat inconsistent with that normally ascribed to any successor: I married a Pākehā woman, I am now a gay man, I have had daughters (not sons), and I don't live with the iwi.'[17] Thus, just as in the novel Kahu disappoints traditional expectations by being the eldest child of an eldest son, but born a girl, Ihimaera in real life, by being a gay man in a culture that one of his characters describes as 'among the most homophobic in the world . . . [in which] I am not supposed to exist,'[18] similarly contravenes the expectations of the kind of man a leader should be. Ihimaera's main purpose in the novel, therefore, was to open up a space within Māori culture for those who are not recognized within its patriarchal structures. In the case of *The Whale Rider*, this space involves acceptance of females as being equal in worth to males, but behind the claim for recognition of this right, one suspects, was the further claim for acceptance of gay males that Ihimaera would go on to assert in several of his later novels.

The underlying thought – merely obliquely hinted at in the yearning of the bull whale for his golden master – is summed up by Sam's recollection of the hierarchical values of Māori society in *The Uncle's Story*, written a little over a decade after *The Whale Rider*: 'The male was high and sanctified. Woman was low and common. How much lower were men who loved men—.'[19] Within the structures of *whanaungatanga* (sense of family connection) and *manaaki* (caring for others), these are the values that Ihimaera, through the fiction of *The Whale Rider*, is seeking to change. The point I would emphasize, though, is that in Ihimaera's version of the story, this is a space that he wants to see opened up *within* a Māori tribal perspective, not created by the superimposition of alien values imported from a different culture and imposed upon the Māori one from without. That is the fault that many Māori saw as vitiating Caro's cinematic adaptation of what, in Ihimaera's version, is quintessentially a Māori work.

Caro's Conversion of the Source Story into a Genre Film

In the course of adapting Ihimaera's novel for the screen, Caro, even though, as she rightly claims, 'the most important events in the film are very faithful to the book,'[20] transformed it utterly. In accordance with her view that the most appealing aspect of Ihimaera's story was a coming-of-age element involving a 'spiritual awakening,' she stripped out any material that did not directly contribute to the depiction of the girl's coming of age. Hence, the observing presence of Rawiri is eliminated in order to substitute Paikea (Keisha Castle-Hughes) as the narrator through her intermittent voiceovers. Similarly, the whole story involving Rawiri's sojourn overseas and his relationship with Jeff is suppressed, and his role as the one who leaves the *iwi* is given to Porourangi (Cliff Curtis), Koro's eldest son, thus investing Porourangi with similar issues to those of Paikea, given that he is an artist with a German wife, and hence also contravenes the traditional expectations of his culture of origin. In Ihimaera's version, to the contrary, Porourangi does not rebel against expectations in this way; instead, he dutifully remarries a Māori woman, Ana, after Kahu's mother has died, and begets another child, which Koro also hopes will be a son. The acceptability of Porourangi in the novel is reflected in the way Koro identifies him as 'the one' in his generation to carry on the leadership of the people, unlike his namesake in the film, whom Caro's Koro (Rawiri Paratene) regards as a disappointment.[21] In Caro's version, a character called 'Uncle Rawiri' (Grant Roa) still remains, but he is given an entirely different character, being presented as the stereotype of a fat and lazy Māori, lying outdoors on a couch in the sun with his marijuana pipe, so that he can be set up as a foil for Paikea to reform and rehabilitate in her role as incipient leader.

Just as Caro leaves out the major plot strand involving Rawiri in the novel, so too does she omit any allusions to the bull whale's yearning for his master, or the whale's grief at their separation and desire to be reunited with him. In the film, the whales are literally whales, and nothing more – neither *tipua* nor *taniwha* – which is consistent with a general moving of the story towards a mode of literal realism, with the episodes of magic realism in the novel being almost entirely eliminated from the film, apart from a vague intimation that somehow Paikea can communicate empathically with the whales, as when she says, after the whales are beached, 'I called them and they came, but it wasn't right, they were dying.'

Along with the disappearance of Ihimaera's magic realism, Caro also omits anything that suggests the presence of the supernatural. Hence, there are no dolphins to guide Paikea to the *rei puta* (whale-tooth ornament) at the bottom of the sea as there are to guide Kahu to the carved stone in the novel, and neither does a female consort persuade the bull whale to return Paikea to the surface as happens to Kahu; instead, Caro's Paikea simply lets go of the whale and floats naturalistically to the surface. In the absence of these magical elements, the whole sense of a numinous world in which human beings are in communion with the ancestors and the creatures of the natural world virtually disappears, to be replaced by a literalized form of realism that represents a different world view altogether.

This is not to say that the film does not seek to depict Māori life in its cultural specificity; indeed, the movie is full of scrupulous care in that regard, showing a range of cultural practices, such as several instances of a *waiata tangi* (song of mourning) and *karakia* (prayer), a *pōwhiri* (welcome ceremony), a *haka* (posture dance), and the launching of a *toiere* (war canoe with carved stem and stern), all rendered with realistic detail. Despite this attention to external verisimilitude, which is filmed with exceptional beauty by Leon Narbey, the cinematographer, the Māori sensibility with which the novel is so pervasively imbued is absent. One only need compare this film with Merata Mita's *Mauri* to detect the difference. Take, for example, the music, for which Mita uses traditional Māori instruments – the *kōauau* (cross-blown flute), the *pūtorino* (large traditional flute), and the *pūtātara* (conch shell trumpet) – to suggest the presence of the ancestors at significant moments. In *Whale Rider*, Caro aims for a similar effect in the music that accompanies each shot of whales swimming, declaring her satisfaction that the composer, Lisa Gerrard, had been able to find 'indigenous Māori sounds within her equipment.'[22] In the absence of a sense of a living connection with the ancestors, however, and of the past in the present, together with an unbroken continuity of values, such as imbues the whole texture of *Mauri*, these simulated 'indigenous sounds' lack the full signifying function that they have in the earlier film, serving more as an emotive mood-setting device. There is a certain symbolic pertinence in the fact that the 'indigenous' music of *Whale Rider* was made on an electronic synthesizer, bearing the same relationship to the authentic instruments used by Mita as the Māori world presented in Caro's film does to Māori culture in the real world.

The end result of these major omissions – leaving aside for the time being the numerous new scenes that Caro added – is to focus attention almost exclusively on Paikea's coming-of-age experience, turning the film into a classic genre film in the process, albeit one that uses Māori life and customs as a colorful, exotic backdrop.

A Feminist Vision in a Cross-cultural Context

Caro has been open about her desire to apply her own vision to a girl's coming-of-age story that involves 'a spiritual awakening.' What does the film show to be the nature of this vision, and what kind of 'spiritual awakening' does it imply? It is in this respect that, as several commentators have recognized, Caro implants into the story a feminist vision of female emancipation drawn from globalized western culture at large.

To some extent, this assertion of the right of females to be accorded equality with males in Māori culture was already present in Ihimaera's novel, in the idea that it should make no difference whether the first-born child in the line of succession to lead the tribe is a boy or a girl. This is what Koro himself comes to understand at the end of the novel when he tells Kahu to take her 'rightful place' among her people: 'You're the best mokopuna in the whole wide world,' he said. 'Boy or girl, it doesn't matter.' Caro, however, pushes this notion a whole lot further, presenting Paikea not simply as a female who deserves to have her place acknowledged, but as a reformer who is prepared to defy and challenge the whole Māori cultural system.

Paikea, in Caro's vision, has a leader's mission and competence from the outset, as her name reflects. In Ihimaera's version, Kahu only becomes 'Paikea' when she rides the whale, just as Kahutia Te Rangi, the ancestor after whom she is named, was given another name, Paikea (humpback whale), to commemorate his voyage to Aotearoa; in other words, it was a name that was earned by the performance of a heroic deed.[23] In contrast, Caro's heroine in the film is called 'Paikea' from the beginning, suggesting that in the filmmaker's conception she already has those outstanding qualities.

This reformulated conception is reflected in a series of new episodes that Caro invented to show Paikea's leadership in action. On several occasions, she is seen chastising members of the tribe for smoking (a health issue among the Māori population), as when she rebukes her grandmother, Nanny Flowers (Vicky Haughton), and two of her older women friends for smoking, or when she upbraids Hemi (Mana Taumaunu) for the same misdeed, having caught him smoking outside their school. She also shames Rawiri, who has become

Figure 12.1 Paikea (Keisha Castle-Hughes) reproaches Hemi (Mana Taumaunu) for smoking in *Whale Rider* (Niki Caro, 2002).

'fat and ugly' through indolence, into jogging to regain his health, and performs the role of a comforter to her own father when she explains why Koro regards him (and her) with disapproval.

Furthermore, Caro's Paikea is given additional exceptional competencies that illustrate her superior qualifications for assuming leadership of the tribe. In one new episode, for example, when Koro is trying to get an outboard motor to start and the starter-cord breaks, Paikea uses her ingenuity to join it together again and succeeds in starting the engine. The symbolism of this scene is obvious: whereas her grandfather cannot start the motor that will propel his people forward, his granddaughter, with her superior skills, is able to do precisely that.

This use of a boat as symbolizing the tribe itself is duplicated in the central

Figure 12.2 Paikea (Keisha Castle-Hughes) fixes her grandfather's outboard motor in *Whale Rider* (Niki Caro, 2002).

symbol of the whole film, a half-built canoe that has been left abandoned and unfinished, stranded, like the whales will be, high and dry, unable to travel. Caro explains that she invented the *waka* (canoe) to serve 'as an image to speak for a community, for a people, for a culture that were without constant sustenance, which is still magnificent, but runs the risk of falling into decay.'[24]

The logic of using the canoe as a symbol of the tribe and its future requires that Paikea, as leader, take control of it and, indeed, at regular intervals through the movie she is shown standing in the middle of the *waka*. On one of these occasions, as Caro points out, 'Pai's blanket, when she is standing in the waka, chanting, starts to look like a *korowai*, the cloak of a leader; she is starting to feel literally like the chief she is becoming.'[25] Finally, at the end of the film, once the *waka* has been completed and is 'reborn, flying,' we see Paikea 'in what is known as the *rangatira* position – the chief's position, the most prestigious position' as the boat heads boldly into the future on a new journey of discovery.[26]

As satisfying as Paikea's occupation of Caro's invented *waka* might be in terms of the feminist ideology of the filmmaker's vision, in real life to have the girl trespass into the space of the canoe, let alone assume the chief's position, amounted to a breach of *tapu* in terms of Māori spirituality. Caro herself was highly aware of this, as she explains in her commentary: 'women traditionally should not be in these canoes, and we had to have a *tapu*-lifting ceremony to make it safe for her to be in there, for me to be in there.'[27] Caro's willingness to breach *tapu* in this way, in a manner that Ihimaera scrupulously avoids in his version of the story, attests to the zeal with which she promotes a distinctly Europeanized feminist agenda in the film – the personal 'vision' that she declared she wanted to 'apply.'

It is small wonder, then, that many Māori were offended by the movie, especially as the strict rules of *tapu* were repeatedly breached in a number of the new scenes Caro invented to augment Ihimaera's fable in order to convert it to her purpose. Regarding a new scene early in the film, in which children present a pantomime version of the story of the whale's arrival at Whangara, Caro notes: 'There was some discussion about how appropriate it was in this sacred place [Whitireia, the meeting house] to have the whale farting, but as we know, farts are funny.'[28] *Tapu* is further breached twice during the scene of the *pōwhiri* to welcome the boys: first, when, at her grandmother's instigation, Paikea leads the boys on to the *marae* (the open area in front of the meeting house), which is a man's role; and, second, when she takes a seat on the *paepae* (orators' bench), the front row of seats occupied by the visitors. Again, Caro was aware of how culturally provocative this addition was: 'When you watch the film with a Māori audience and she sits down there, you can hear an audible gasp – it's so transgressive, what she does.'[29] Similarly, she adds several scenes showing Paikea's determination to learn how to fight with a *taiaha* (long wooden weapon), and

Figure 12.3 Paikea (Keisha Castle-Hughes) breaches *tapu* by sitting on the *paepae*, reserved for men, at a *pōwhiri* in *Whale Rider* (Niki Caro, 2002).

depicts her defeating Hemi in a confrontation, prompting the angry Koro, who has been instructing his *wānanga* (school) of boys in the art of the *taiaha*, to exclaim: 'What have you done? You have broken the *tapu* of this school!'[30]

The insistent provocativeness with which Caro challenges Māori customs in the furtherance of a white feminist agenda explains the indignation expressed by a Māori woman scholar such as Tania Ka'ai. For Ka'ai, the depiction of Māori culture in *Whale Rider* was a travesty that reflected misunderstanding of certain assumptions and practices that diverged from Pākehā ones. She particularly objected to the scene showing Paikea delivering the *karanga* (call), traditionally executed only by a *kuia* (elderly woman) during the *pōwhiri*:

> This is simply inconceivable in Māori society, for her grandmother was exposing her to the risk of *kanga* [curses]. Regardless of Paikea's inherited status, she is vulnerable because she has not yet reached puberty and therefore a prime candidate for such practices. Furthermore, Paikea behaved as if she was a child brought up by her father in Germany, with no knowledge of Māori culture, when she sat on the front pew with the men. A child raised by her grandparents would simply not behave in this way. This is an example of the Eurocentric feminist belief that women can challenge a supposed male hegemonic practice that appears to discriminate against Māori women and, therefore, relegates them to lesser positions in Māori society. The disregard for the cultural significance of the *marae* and the protection of women is masked by this Eurocentric feminist challenge, thus portraying Māori as a 'barbaric' people who have no respect for women.[31]

Ka'ai also took exception at the way Caro showed Hemi striking Koro on the back during a *taiaha* lesson: 'it is simply inconceivable that a child, male or female, would beat an elder let alone a tribal leader with their *taiaha* (a weapon and oratory staff). To do so would be to commit a *hara* (a cultural offence of the worst order).'[32] In the light of Ka'ai's objections, therefore, one can see that, as fervent and committed as the film was, Caro, in the course of altering her source to fit the agenda of her personal vision, whether wittingly or unwittingly, transposed the story from being a Māori one, to one that is seen through Pākehā eyes, and not without a degree of condescension.

This difference of vision is reflected in a radical contrast that exists between the respective endings of the novel and the film. Ihimaera's Koro finally accords Kahu the acceptance that she has always craved, in spite of her gender, by telling her that, 'Boy or girl, it doesn't matter.' This prompts Kahu, in return, to reciprocate by saying that he is 'the best koro in the whole wide world.'[33] Caro's Koro, in contrast, is punished for his patriarchal assumptions by being humbled, a diminution of status that is reflected in his last words addressed to Paikea – 'Wise leader, forgive me. I am just a fledgling new to flight' – which imparts a different message altogether by elevating Paikea to a status above her grandfather. The difference is highly significant. In Ihimaera's version, Kahu, in order to receive the acknowledgement she longs for, needs to pass a test that demonstrates her connection to the *mauri*, or life force, in the natural world; this is what will equip her to lead her people. In contrast, Caro's Paikea already has superior leadership qualities, and the test is transferred to Koro, for whom passing the test amounts to conceding that his granddaughter has those qualities, and hence can supersede him as a 'wise [for which read "wiser"] leader' whose feminist enlightenment is superior to his benighted patriarchal blindness. Caro thus passes a boundary of disrespect that Ihimaera was not prepared to transgress.

One further aspect of the cinematic version needs to be noted. As film scholar Bruce Babington astutely observes, the historical markers in the novel that evoke the history of Māori race relations with Pākehā, such as Koro's involvement in politics and references to Waitangi Tribunal settlements, have been completely erased from the film, which makes the issues presented in the film non-specific and hence readable 'in terms of both the indigenous community and the larger society, thus catering not only to national desires, but also international ones.'[34] The only presence of Pākehā in the movie occurs in the fleeting glimpse we get in the final sequence of Porourangi's German wife, which implicitly suggests, as Māori scholars like Hokowhitu have argued, that the film sees the future for Māori as one in which Māori cultural distinctiveness is assimilated into a merging of the races under an 'enlightened' Eurocentric set of values. While this erasure of difference between the races through the elimination of historical markers of the relationship between Māori and Pākehā may have made the film palatable to Pākehā and overseas audiences, commensurately, it made it less than satisfying to Māori. As the

Māori filmmaker Barry Barclay wryly observed, to the extent that *Whale Rider* is a Māori film at all, it is an 'indigenous film for beginners.'[35]

Māori Films after *Whale Rider*

Although Caro stepped well beyond where Ihimaera had felt he wanted to go in claiming the right to equality of women in Māori culture, crossing boundaries with respect to *tapu* that his fiction shows him as having been careful to observe, she was not alone in seeing a need for Māori culture to change. Indeed, Ihimaera himself would soon go on to write subsequent novels that would challenge the traditional culture even more aggressively, especially in *Bulibasha: King of the Gypsies* (1994), and *The Uncle's Story* (2000). In these two later novels he would depict protagonists who stand up to the patriarchal tyranny and bullying of a grandfather and a father, respectively, who are far more despotic than Koro is presented as being in *The Whale Rider*. Ihimaera's challenge to traditional Māori culture in these later novels is direct and explicit: in *The Uncle's Story*, for instance, he would also assert the right for a Māori man to be both Māori and gay, without relinquishing 'the mana, the tapu, the ihi or life force and the wehi or dread that the dynamic of being a man depended on.'[36] Both of these themes – the rejection of patriarchal authoritarianism, and the right to be gay without loss of *mana* or sacredness – would in turn be developed in subsequent films adapted from Ihimaera's works – *Mahana* (2016) and *Nights in the Gardens of Spain* (2010) – suggesting a move away from the ideal of a 'Fourth Cinema' embodying traditional Māori values, as exemplified in *Mauri*.

At the same time, subsequent films by Māori, on Māori subjects, display the same trend towards international genre cinema that is evident in Caro's *Whale Rider*. This tendency, which is particularly apparent in the two coming-of-age smash hits directed by Taika Waititi, *Boy* (2010) and *Hunt for the Wilderpeople* (2016), attests, as I shall demonstrate in later chapters, to two forces that would influence Māori filmmaking in the future: the incursion of globalized popular culture on one hand, and the effects of the development in New Zealand of biculturalism as a state-sponsored policy on the other. Whereas the former would supply a whole banquet of tropes from a variety of genres that filmmakers could draw upon, the latter would license the incorporation of certain Pākehā practices and values. Both, as I will demonstrate, encouraged the evolution of new forms of cultural hybridity as a dominant characteristic of coming-of-age films in the second decade of the new millennium.

Notes

1. Diane Pivac and others (eds), *New Zealand Film: An Illustrated History* (Wellington: Te Papa Press, 2011), 297.
2. This figure is taken from *Box Office Mojo*, http://www.boxofficemojo.com/movies/?page=intl&country=NZ&id=whalerider.htm, accessed 17 July 2016.
3. The title of this film for its American release was *Kawa*.
4. Brendan Hokowhitu, 'The Death of Koro Paka: "Traditional" Māori Patriarchy,' *The Contemporary Pacific* 20:1 (2008), 115–41, esp. 132, 128.
5. Tania M. Ka'ai, 'Te Kauae Mārō o Muri-ranga-whenua (The Jawbone of Muri-ranga-whenua): Globalising Local Indigenous Culture – Māori Leadership, Gender and Cultural Knowledge Transmission as Represented in the Film *Whale Rider*,' *Portal* 2:2 (July 2005), 1–15, https://epress.lib.uts.edu.au/journals/index.php/portal/article/view/92/59, accessed 17 July 2016.
6. Denis Welch, 'The Producer,' *New Zealand Listener*, 5 July 2003.
7. 'Interview with Niki Caro, Writer/Director of *Whale Rider*,' *The Movie Show*, Episode 12, 11 May 2003 [online].
8. D. Kehr, 'At the Movies,' *New York Times*, 6 June 2003, E23.
9. Hokowhitu, ibid., 125–6.
10. Witi Ihimaera, *The Whale Rider* (Auckland: Heinemann, 1987), 6.
11. Ibid., 92–3.
12. Ibid., 74.
13. Ibid., 117.
14. See Ka'ai, 5.
15. Ibid., 59.
16. Ibid., 10, 80, 11.
17. Margaret Meklin and Andrew Meklin, 'This Magnificent Accident: An Interview with Witi Ihimaera,' *The Contemporary Pacific* 16:2 (Fall 2004), 358–66, esp. 363.
18. Witi Ihimaera, *The Uncle's Story* (Auckland: Penguin, 2000), 22.
19. Ibid., 219.
20. Niki Caro, 'Director's Commentary,' *Whale Rider*, DVD (Buena Vista Home Entertainment, 2004).
21. Ihimaera, *The Whale Rider*, 58.
22. Caro, 'Director's Commentary.'
23. Ihimaera, *The Whale Rider*, 27.
24. Caro, 'Director's Commentary.'
25. Ibid.
26. Ibid.
27. Ibid.
28. Ibid.
29. Ibid.
30. Ibid.
31. Ka'ai, 8
32. Ka'ai, 11.
33. Ihimaera, *The Whale Rider*, 122.
34. Bruce Babington, *A History of the New Zealand Fiction Feature Film* (Manchester: Manchester University Press, 2007), 228–9.
35. Peter Calder, 'Riding High on "Whale" Tale World Report: New Zealand Success of Whale Rider Promotes New Zealand Film Industry,' *Variety* 393:5 (2003), A2.
36. Ihimaera, *The Uncle's Story*, 156.

13. FAMILY SECRETS AND THEIR DESTRUCTIVE CONSEQUENCES: *IN MY FATHER'S DEN* (BRAD MCGANN, 2004)

Following the outstanding international success of *Whale Rider*, the next New Zealand coming-of-age film to attract critical acclaim and attention, both nationally and abroad, was Brad McGann's adaptation of an iconic novel by Maurice Gee, *In My Father's Den*, originally published in 1972. Hailed as being one of the best films to come out of the Antipodes, this film won a host of awards at international film festivals, including the prestigious International Critics' Award at the Toronto International Film Festival, with praise given for the emotional maturity, striking performances, and visual grace displayed in its story of a damaged young man who returns from overseas to his family in New Zealand and gradually comes to terms with the traumatic aspects of his childhood experience that he has repressed, having sought to evade them by retreating physically overseas, and emotionally into a self-imposed form of detachment. In terms of its status as a coming-of-age film, *In My Father's Den* constitutes a post-adolescence coming of age on the part of the main character, Paul (Matthew Mcfadyen), that has been forestalled and delayed by earlier trauma, while also containing a second coming of age on the part of a teenage girl, Celia (Emily Barclay), that in certain respects mirrors the first, but has a tragic outcome.

Apart from being one of the most accomplished of all New Zealand films, McGann's *In My Father's Den* (2004) reveals more clearly than any other the two main functions of the coming-of-age genre in the context of a national cinema. At one level, it accomplishes a radical updating of the cultural perspective of its literary source, thus serving to register shifts that had occurred in

New Zealand society between the period in which Gee wrote (the 1960s and 1970s) and that in which McGann made his film (the 2000s). Whereas for Gee the cause of the tragedy at the heart of the story – the murder of an innocent seventeen-year-old girl – lay in the damaging effects on two brothers of a repressive upbringing under the influence of a harshly repressive Presbyterian mother, for McGann, it arose from 'the harbouring of family secrets' and the effects of lack of communication and of miscommunication.[1] Being born in 1964, McGann belonged to a different generation from that of Gee (born 1931), and felt that the New Zealand in which he had been brought up was not the same: 'Maurice Gee was writing about a New Zealand which for me no longer existed . . . The New Zealand I'd grown up with was more secular, more open-minded. I felt they [the issues] had to be reimagined in order for it to work with a modern day audience.'[2] Consequently, McGann updated the setting from the 1930s and 1960s to a more contemporary one (with flashbacks to the 1980s), and eliminated most of the 'religiosity' of the book.[3] Instead of focusing on the psychic damage caused by puritan repression, as Gee had done, McGann emphasized themes such as 'how the past impacts on the present, living with complicated and fractious familial relationships and the effects of being cut off emotionally from family members.' As McGann puts it, 'I wanted to work with material that had a strong thematic core, but with the licence to change that material in order to make it work as a modern day film.'[4]

At another level, the film strikingly demonstrates the personal negotiation that takes place, both for the filmmaker and the spectator, as a result of the dialogue that occurs between national cinema and the nation's literature whenever a filmmaker adapts an iconic literary work. A comparison of *In My Father's Den* with Niki Caro's *Whale Rider* illustrates the different ways in which this negotiation can be conducted. For Caro, the negotiation is a *transcultural* one, in which the values of an alien culture (in this case Māori) are subjected to transformation through the imposition of values deriving from another culture (in this case, global feminism) as a means of advocating for social change. For McGann, by way of contrast, the negotiation is an *intracultural* one, involving the displacement of an older set of societal values in order to replace them with a different, updated set. In both instances, the purpose of the substitutions is to achieve a new type of self-definition – in Caro's case, through projection, and in McGann's case, through exploration and reconstruction. Ultimately, the end effect of these negotiations with the source materials is to enable an expanded sense of self-experience, both for the auteur who is making the film, and for the spectator who responds empathically to it and identifies with what is being shown in the fictive representation.

As always, the best way of revealing how these twin preoccupations are at work in a coming-of-age film adapted from a literary source is to compare the two versions and their thematic content in order to speculate on the significance of any alterations to the source material. Such a comparison between Gee's version of the story from 1972 and McGann's version from 2004 shows that while McGann, as he professed in an interview with Gordon Campbell, may have believed that 'The way we tell it is different, but essentially it's the same story,'[5] the changes he made in the course of adapting Gee's novel facilitated the depiction of a coming-of-age experience that was fundamentally different in kind.

Maurice Gee's Account of the Causes of Psychic Damage

Central to Gee's understanding of the causes of the dysfunctions he depicts in *In My Father's Den* is the role of the mother. We learn this through the retrospective narration of the main character in the novel, Paul Prior, a 34-year-old man who is prompted to look back over his previous life as a means of working out how an adolescent girl he has befriended, Celia, could have ended up being murdered violently by his younger brother, Andrew. In the course of this reconstruction, he comes to realize that his mother's joyless religion, and the oppressive view of life promoted by its morality, is responsible for emotionally crippling both her sons, himself included, and is ultimately responsible for the tragic event that caps the story.

Mrs Prior's vice, Paul tells us, was 'spirituality,' deriving from a Presbyterianism that was 'grim and fundamental': 'She knew her soul was of the common grey. Her life was a struggle to scrub it clean. One of the dim understandings of my childhood was that mother was less kind than good.'[6] Her Calvinist conviction of the corrupting power of the body makes her recoil from her husband's physical grossness, and promotes an asceticism that leads her to deny pleasure both to herself and her children, as when she orders her children to spit out the sweets they have won in a lolly scramble at a picnic held by Rationalists.[7] In short, 'the demon of godliness would not let her rest' as she moves towards ever stricter observances,[8] which eventually leads her to cut her luxuriant wavy brown hair when a mongoloid son, John, is born, and then to move into a separate bedroom under the pretext of looking after him.

The impact of their mother's religious severity on Paul and Andrew as children is to drive them to develop in opposite directions. Paul rebels, becoming allied with his father, a libertarian, who has his own form of rebellion that consists of covertly reading subversive books in his secret den, concealed in the orchard's poison shed. Paul also takes refuge in acting out: 'I began to enjoy guilt the way one can enjoy a toothache. I began to steal; then added cruelty to my sins.' When he steals a packet of cake papers and sails them over the waterfalls in the local park, 'the orgy of pleasure and remorse I enjoyed . . . remains unequalled in my life for depth of emotion.'[9] Later, in adolescence, he extends his transgressive impulses to include sex, acquiring a reputation as 'rakehelly, popular, randy Paul.'[10] As an adult, he has affairs with many women, but without emotional involvement.

Andrew, on the other hand, becomes progressively more dependent on, and close to, his mother, becoming 'closed-in, private,' and seeming to live 'with his senses dulled.'[11] At school he wants to play games with the other children (like Janet Frame in *An Angel at My Table*), but doesn't know how to join in, and suffers bullying. When he enters puberty, replicating his mother's abhorrence of things carnal, Andrew is tormented with guilt by his inability to prevent himself from masturbating, and as an adult he expresses extreme disapproval of Paul's penchant for exotic foods and expensive wine, and his reading habits, which he sees as a betrayal of their mother: 'Nothing but dirt and filth. How do you think she would have felt?'[12] For Andrew, who desperately needs to cling to his attachment to his mother even after she has died, Paul represents everything that she stood against: 'Nothing but self-indulgence and pleasure. Women, drink, the stuff you call art. No discipline, no belief, no order. It's as if our mother had never existed . . . You gave in to every appetite you ever had.'[13]

Although each of the brothers responds in antithetical ways to the life-denying emotional deprivation inflicted on them by their mother, they end up being equally damaged. Whereas Andrew tries to keep his mother alive by becoming the guardian of her moral legacy, Paul, in his adolescence, tries to find a substitute for her in the first girl with whom he dares to share intimacy, Joyce Poole. When Joyce breaks off the relationship, Paul's response is to retreat into a pose of detachment that long practice turns into the real thing: 'Detachment, self-sufficiency. Den-living,' stroking his side-burns and sipping his whisky.[14] It is only when he meets Celia, the daughter of his former lover Joyce Poole and Charlie Inverarity, his former best friend, who married Joyce after Paul's departure for a seventeen-year absence overseas, that his detachment and fear of intimacy is in danger of breaking down, with Celia, whom he contemplates 'worshipping,' becoming a substitute for the religion he has discarded, the absence of which has left him feeling 'incomplete' and 'hollow.'[15] But even then, part of his motive in cultivating a relationship with Celia is to 'pinch' her back from her father by encouraging her intellectual curiosity and her desire to go to university, in order to requite Charlie for the way he 'pinched' Joyce from him when he had informed her that Paul had a mongoloid brother. Then, when the catastrophe occurs and Celia is killed, Paul retreats back into his books, rebuilding his library, in a new den, in a new house, in a new place.

For his part, Andrew cannot sustain the psychological pressure generated by the intensity of his identification with his mother. During the climactic confrontation between the two brothers, Paul surmises that Andrew killed Celia because he had needed to make himself feel clean again after 'all those dirty thoughts' the sight of her had aroused in him.[16] It was the sight of Celia's hair unplaited that pushes Andrew over the edge, given that Celia had the same wavy brown hair that their mother did. The combination of the memory of his mother aroused by Celia's hair with the sexual desire that the sight of the nubile Celia herself aroused, with 'a button of her collar ... undone,' was too much for Andrew, who had become overpowered by his need to extirpate her as the evil agent of the defilement she represented. As Paul observes: 'The whole of his life overflowed into the killing,' depicted by Gee in its extreme, graphic violence.[17]

As far as coming-of-age experiences go, the itineraries and destinations of Paul and Andrew are equally tragic illustrations of the destructive consequences of being raised in a dysfunctional family, in which the dysfunction arises, in Gee's depiction, from the imposition of the excessively rigid and oppressive religious code that had been dominant in the New Zealand of his own youth.

Brad McGann's Reformulation

Given McGann's belief that the New Zealand in which he had grown up was no longer the same as the one that has shaped the formative experience of the two boys in Gee's novel, it is not surprising that he felt a need to subject it to some radical changes.[18] These changes are designed to serve two main purposes: first, to give the relationship between Paul and Celia much greater prominence, placing it at the center of the film in order to show how this relationship is instrumental to resolving the psychological problems that have left Paul a damaged man; and, second, to show how, rather than any one person being responsible for Celia's tragic fate in the story, 'everyone and no one is culpable,' in McGann's words, with the tragedy being 'a collective result of the lies and deceit that surrounded her.'[19]

McGann's reason for giving the relationship between Paul and Celia much more centrality is because, as he puts it, 'she becomes a kind of conduit for him to unravel parts of himself that he would possibly not share with anyone else.'[20] Because 'Paul recognises a part of himself – who he used to be – in this sixteen year-old girl,'[21] his developing relationship with her highlights the contrast in his awareness between the hopeful child he once was, curious about the world and eager to explore it, and the adult he has become, who is someone that has ceased to engage with it emotionally. As his friendship with her grows, it makes it possible for him to rediscover intimacy and, as a result of that, confront some of his own demons.

Giving Celia a more central role also enabled McGann to unify the film both structurally and thematically. Structurally, it made it possible for him to underline the similarities between Celia and Paul by introducing a number of parallel

Figure 13.1 Celia (Emily Barclay) imagines the excitement of traveling overseas in *In My Father's Den* (dir. Brad McGann, 2005).

scenes. Paul first meets Celia in his father's den, which she has discovered after his death, listening to music and beginning to write her story, thus furnishing a mirror reflection of his own childhood fascination with the den and the expanded realm of possibilities that its books seemed to intimate. Another repeated scene shows Paul as a boy looking with wonder at his father's illuminated globe of the world, which is paralleled by a comparable scene in which Celia gazes at the same globe while telling Paul of her dream of traveling to Spain. The parallels established by these scenes lend substance to the statement Paul makes to the police when he says 'I remember being her,' as well as establishing the relationship between the past and the present.

A number of other changes in McGann's treatment of the story help to reinforce the shift in his vision. In Gee's novel, Paul is under no illusion that Celia is his biological daughter, as she was conceived and born well after he had left to begin his travels overseas; he simply takes satisfaction in knowing that she is his daughter in a metaphoric, wishful sense because, in naming her 'Celia,' her mother, Joyce, was recalling her romantic encounter with Paul in the orchard, during which he recited Ben Jonson's poem to her, 'Come my Celia, let us prove, / While we may, the sports of love.'[22] In the film, both Paul and Celia come to believe that she might be his daughter, owing to the fact that she was born eight months after his departure, and that a photo is discovered with her name on the back. This change brilliantly complicates the plot, contributing to the misunderstanding that leads to Celia's death, and illustrating the dangers of the lies, dishonesty, and concealment involved in the maintenance of family secrets.

One major transformation concerns the source of the damage Paul suffered in his childhood upbringing. In Gee's novel, Paul is damaged first by the life-denying puritanism of his Presbyterian mother, and then by the disloyalty of Joyce, the girl to whom he risked opening his affections; in other words, the damage arises from a withholding of emotional nurturance on the part of his mother, and then an emotional betrayal on the part of his lover that has propelled him into inwardness and a pose of detachment. In McGann's reformulation, Paul's damage arises from a different source of trauma: instead of losing his girlfriend, Jackie (Jodie Rimmer), to his best friend, Charlie Inverarity, as in the novel, Paul now loses her to his own father, Jeff (Matthew Chamberlain). In the film, Paul's father walks in on Paul and Jackie while they are making love in the den, and indulgently condones it: 'Nothing to be sorry for, as long as you're being cautious,' which indicates his lax moral attitude. Subsequently, this situation is reversed when Paul, in his turn, walks in on his father having intercourse with Joyce in the den. As an inversion of Oedipal competition on the part of the protector who should be his guide and model, this betrayal is doubly devastating. Worse than that, when the adolescent Paul comes on the scene, he sees his mother also witnessing her husband's infidelity, which causes her – already diagnosed with manic-depression – to wade into a river with a shotgun and shoot herself, again witnessed by Paul.

The combined effect of his father's betrayal and his mother's desertion-through-suicide delivers a far greater psychic blow to Paul than Gee's Paul has to suffer, and his response to it is not just simply to withdraw into detachment, but, in addition, to disavow and repress his memory of what happened altogether. That is why the reawaking of intimacy that his relationship with Celia opens to him is so important, because it is what makes it possible for him, by degrees, to readmit his memories of those tragic events. The process of recovering these memories is only fully attained with the death of Celia, because, as McGann puts it, 'Something of sufficient enough magnitude had to occur, to be sufficiently cathartic to bring all that shit out into the open.'[23] This cathartic function is why Celia's death is placed at the end of the film instead of the beginning: its repositioning allows the revised conception of Paul's coming-of-age experience to be developed through the juxtaposing of scenes showing the past and the present, at the same time as it shows how family secrets can foster miscommunications and misunderstandings that can have tragic consequences.

The Personal Elements in the Story

As almost invariably occurs in a coming-of-age film, there is a strong element of personal investment and projection on the part of the filmmaker that enters into *In My Father's Den*. McGann recounts that when his producer, Trevor Haysom, first offered him Gee's book as a prospect for adaptation, he turned it down because he did not want to spend eight months on a work that was going to be shown only once on television, despite the fact that he responded to its themes. He changed his mind, however, when he had a dream that prompted him to think about it in a different way.[24] The filmmaker explains the nature of this dream in his director's commentary accompanying the DVD release of the film:

> The story of the ocean going out originated from a dream I had about these two characters who were standing in this barren landscape that looked like a place where the ocean used to be, and I guess in a way it was one of the things that, for me, allowed me to bring my own voice to the project ... the story ended up becoming a spine that kind of went through the film.[25]

This dream, then, became the short story that Celia writes, and, as such, supplies the frame narrative for the whole film, with extracts from it recurring at regular intervals through the movie.

In nature, this surrealistic dream-narrative is highly symbolic, especially as it is elaborated in Celia's voiceovers in the film. The tide goes out leaving 'a desert of unimaginable magnitude'; the people become worried and decide to send a small group to search for it 'in the hope of bringing it back'; the ocean, however, has vanished without trace, and 'the quiet land, once bountiful, had become hard and unyielding'; finally, realizing that the sea has disappeared for good, the people 'had no choice but to face each other in their loss' and 'learnt to live in the space the ocean had left, although it lingered in their dreams.' In terms of symbolic connotations, the images in this story suggest a spiritual condition in which the ocean figures a sustaining life force and the desert a state of emotional aridity and impoverishment, while the memory of a lost condition of happiness lingers that is longed for, but which is felt to be impossible to reclaim. As such, Celia's story symbolically figures Paul's experience and the itinerary he will follow as he seeks to recover the missing part of himself that he recognizes in Celia's curiosity, eagerness to explore the world, and her hopes for the future.

The fact that this symbolic story originated in McGann's own dream suggests further that the two figures in his dream represent an unconscious prefiguration of the Celia/Paul pairing. This identification is most clearly evident in the scene in which Paul and Celia drive through the Central Otago landscape and stop to observe it. Here, the image of the two captures their status as doubles, while showing them against the backdrop of the arid landscape of McGann's dream and Celia's story, suggesting that the fiction of the film is presenting the relationship between his older and younger self through the relationship between Paul and Celia.

IN MY FATHER'S DEN

Figure 13.2   Symbolic use of landscape in *In My Father's Den* (dir. Brad McGann, 2005).

The very shift of location from Gee's Henderson to Central Otago originates in McGann's own personal associations with the region:

> ... it's just an area that, I don't know, it just resonates with me for some reason. I lived in the South Island for six years and years later I would have dreams about Central Otago. I don't know what the reason is, but I always had a yearning to go back there and asked Trevor if we could set it there ... where the environment had these allegorical connotations.[26]

There are many other elements in the film that embody personal references for McGann, especially the various evocative objects he includes, which are invested with an over-determined significance. For example, the atlas Paul's father gives him as a boy, which is a symbol of his desire to spread his wings, and which he later, in turn, gives to Celia, is, McGann informs us, 'very like the one I used to have as a kid.'[27] Similarly, many of the musical items in the soundtrack, such as the track that plays while Celia is riding her moped over a bridge, and the songs sung by Patti Smith (one of which gave rise to the white horses in Celia's story that the people mistake for the ocean coming back), derive from McGann's own youth in the 1980s. The reason he gives the character of Jonathan (Jimmy Keen), Andrew's son, which is greatly expanded from the novel, his own secret den in the form of an abandoned car is because, McGann confesses, 'as a kid I always wanted something like that. I like the idea of having your own van in the middle of nowhere where you can pig out.'[28]

Jonathan, in fact, functions, like Celia, one suspects, as another projection of McGann's sense of his own earlier self, especially in his love of photography, which shadows not only Paul's vocation as a war photographer, but also McGann's own vocation as a filmmaker. This may account for why, as

169

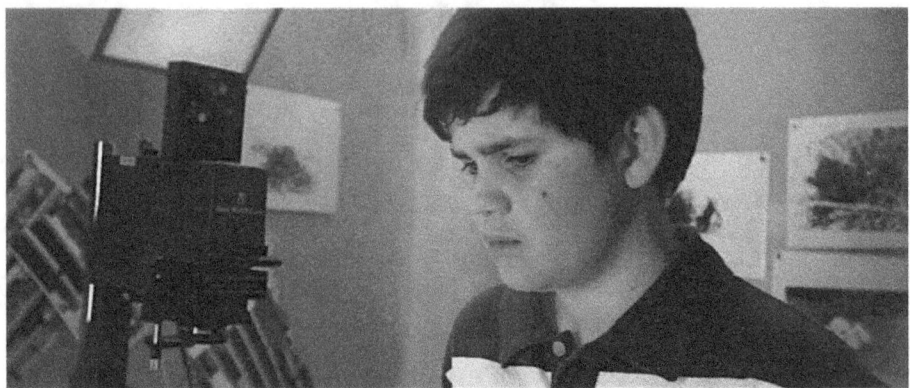

Figure 13.3 Jonathan (Jimmy Keen), in his own version of a den, in *In My Father's Den* (dir. Brad McGann, 2005).

McGann professes, 'I do love the character of Jonathan,' who only makes a very brief appearance in Gee's novel.

If one compares *In My Father's Den* with the four short films McGann made prior to making his one and only feature film, it becomes apparent that he was drawn to Maurice Gee's novel because it furnished him with a vehicle through which he could explore, in a more complex way and in greater depth than he had been able to do before, the dilemma that constituted his 'personal myth,' to use the term proposed by Charles Mauron.[29] The common, recurrent element in all McGann's films is 'the outsider and isolation.'[30] His first film, *A Home Away from Here* (1989), is a psychological drama that deals with a power struggle and the subsequent isolation within a family; his next film, *Come as You Are* (1997), explores issues of identity and isolation by tracing the lives of three people who, like Paul, have created a second self; and his third short film, *Possum* (1997), depicts an outsider and 'the emotional quest for a sense of place and belonging.'[31] Viewed in the light of this recurrent theme, therefore, Paul's search for a reconnection that he does not consciously know he wants, or needs, constitutes the main preoccupation of McGann's own personal project. As he puts it, 'There are parts of myself that I've brought to the film,' and that 'I had to go into myself and explore the way my past has impacted the way I behave as a human.'[32] Elsewhere, he has admitted, 'I think the subtext of any story is very much your own subtext.'[33] In my view, it is this personal element, and the richness of imaging it promotes, that gives this coming-of-age film its peculiar power.

The Relation of Style and Structure to the Film's Themes

It may already be apparent that the structure and style McGann adopts in *In My Father's Den* is admirably suited to the complexity of the vision he presents of the psychological process that his central character, Paul, undergoes in the course of the film. The use of a fragmented narrative, and flashbacks in particular, not only facilitates a juxtaposition of the past and the present so that the two may be compared in order to underline the relation between cause and consequence, but also enable the psychological process whereby Paul confronts, and comes to terms with, his demons, to be enacted in the sequencing of the film's presentation of its story.

McGann also exploits a location-based, art-school film style that is heavily influenced by Robert Bresson, among others, including Bernardo Bertolucci, Terence Malick, John Cassavetes, Kieslowski, and Tarkovsky.[34] This art-cinema style involves the use of symbolic landscapes. At the time of Paul's youth, when he was in the first flush of romancing Jackie, the orchard is shown in full bloom, as it is again in the scene where Celia, with whom he is developing an emotional closeness, prepares a nighttime, candle-lit picnic to celebrate his birthday – which, normally, we are told, he never celebrates. At other times, Paul is shown wandering through the orchard in a state of bare, winter starkness, which symbolizes the emotional sterility of the detachment within which he has cocooned himself.

Similarly, a recurrent series of shots showing Celia crossing a bridge is metaphorically suggestive. At one point in the film, Paul says to her: 'We're all out there on a bridge, eh?,' suggesting the metaphysical condition – of being precariously suspended over an abyss – that Paul is desperately trying to negotiate, and with which, the image implies, Celia will eventually be confronted.

The use of impressionist style appears, too, in the filmmaker's use of color. The scenes in the respective dens (that of Paul's father and Paul, and that of Jonathan) are shown in colors that distinguish them from ordinary scenes. The den in the poison shed is depicted in deep shadow illuminated by points of light, as, for example, the light that illuminates the globe of the world that excites the imagination of both the young Paul and, later, Celia.

In Jonathan's case, the illicitness of his interest in photography – at least in his puritanical parents' eyes – facilitated by the camera Paul gives him, is signified by the red filter that colors the scene in which he is shown in the darkroom developing the photos he has taken of Celia. Conversely, a blue filter is used to suggest Paul's internal perturbation and depression whenever he is shown in a state of distress, as in the shot of Paul sitting in a bath, under a running shower, after his sexual encounter with the Scottish girl, during which he was unable to allow himself to make connection with her.

Finally, the shooting style of *In My Father's Den* displays the expressive minimalism advocated by Bresson as a means of making visible 'what without you might never be seen', a precept that McGann tells us he kept preserved in his diary.[35] Hence, the screen is often occupied by close-up shots that linger on the faces of the main characters in order to register their unspoken emotions.

In terms of exploiting art-house style to achieve his thematic goals, then, McGann can hold his own with the great European auteurs.

Generic Hybridity and its Impact on the Meaning of the Film

As one has seen with many of the films already discussed in this book, New Zealand filmmakers display a marked penchant for the mixing of genres to achieve their expressive ends. The same is true of *In My Father's Den*, which begins by looking as if it is going to be a family melodrama, but converts into a fully fledged tragedy by the end, and concludes with a comedic (in Dante's sense of a work that has a happy ending) coda. The one thing it is not, and might very well have been, had McGann followed Gee's version more closely, is a murder mystery; like Peter Jackson in *Heavenly Creatures*, McGann eschews the easy generic option in order to conduct a more profound exploration of the psychological dimension of the experience depicted.

The shift in genre from melodrama to tragedy is registered in several ways. First, the lighting of the film becomes progressively colder, and this is reinforced by the use of a hand-held camera in the sequences that show the confrontation between the two brothers and the search for Celia's body along the river bank, thus lending a raw edginess to the representation that intercepts the possibility of its sliding into melodrama. Second, the reiteration of the image at the opening, which shows Paul's mother wading into a sunlit river with sparkling water and then pointing to a hawk that is wheeling above in a clear blue sky, underlines a dramatic change in the significance of this scene. Whereas the first time it is shown the scene seems as idyllic as it is beautiful, when it recurs late in the movie, as Andrew (Colin Moy) forces Paul to remember what actually happened, the sequence is extended to show the actual way the scene ended: with their mother putting the barrel of a shotgun under her chin, after which we hear the blast of the gun off-screen as she pulls the trigger, while on-screen a flock of white birds is shown taking flight out of fright at the noise, as Paul, who has witnessed the suicide and sees his mother's body floating in the river, screams hysterically. With great economy, then, the repetition of this episode in an extended version neatly juxtaposes the idea of hope, suggested by the mother pointing to the hawk in the sky, with that of the extinction of hope, figured in the ironic contrast between the bird wheeling in unfettered flight above, and the despairing action of the mother down below. Metaphorically, these sequences link to the painting of *Hope* that has been seen several times during the film, personified as a woman who is blindfolded and seated in an abject posture, which associates her also with the titles of several books upon which the camera has lingered in close-up: *The Cloud of Unknowing*, and *Owls Do Cry*. Through this complex web of associations, combined with the shifting of the note to tragic, McGann does not flinch from showing the unforeseeable eventualities in life that harm the innocent along with the culpable, making the human situation an inherently tragic one.

Then, McGann does something remarkable by inserting at the end of the movie a flashback to the final encounter between Paul and Celia, in which they are reconciled, with him giving her an air ticket to Spain, along with his prized atlas, and her departing happily to pursue her adventure. In his director's commentary, McGann explains the reason: 'I really didn't want to kill the character of Celia. I struggled with that . . . I wanted to find a way out for her.'[36] In one earlier version of the film, he even did an edit where he took Celia's death out of the film: 'She just disappeared, vanished like the ocean in her story, and you didn't know what had happened to her.' He concluded, however, that this was unsatisfying, given that the film needed Celia's death to 'bring everything to the fore.'[37]

What, then, does Celia's death bring to the fore, and why, in that case, did McGann end the film with a scene of reconciliation and her happy, hopeful departure? If one allows oneself to respond to the emotional rhythm that is generated by the ordering of the components in the fragmented narrative of the film, what is conveyed is a suggestion that regeneration is activated through the very experience of tragedy. This is evident in the way Paul reopens himself to human emotion, and in the compassion that the characters now display towards one another, as in the shot showing Paul comforting Jackie in her grief. It is this spiritual regeneration, McGann seems to be saying, expressed in forgiveness and a compassionate acceptance of one's humanity, that makes it possible – in the terms of Celia's allegorical story – to learn how to live in the space the ocean has left, even while the idea of a world of unvitiated bounty lingers in their dreams. What the complex, multilayered fiction of *In My Father's Den* symbolically figures, therefore, is McGann's feeling that a true coming of age means growing into a realization and acceptance of this fact, while allowing the understanding that arises from it to condition one's response to life, and one's conduct towards others.

Notes

1. Shonagh Lindsay, 'Brad McGann – In My Father's Den,' *Take* 36 (July 2004), 26–9.
2. Marisol Grandon, 'Q&A: Brad McGann,' *The Telegraph*, 24 June 2005, http://www.telegraph.co.uk/culture/film/3644197/QandA-Brad-McGann.html, accessed 19 July 2016.
3. Lindsay, 'Brad McGann.'
4. Ibid., 26–9.
5. Gordon Campbell, 'Point Proven,' *New Zealand Listener*, 3 July 2004, http://www.listener.co.nz/uncategorized/point-proven/, accessed 24 July 2016. See also Lawrence Jones, '. . . Essentially It's the Same Story': Maurice Gee, Brad McGann and the Creative Adaptation of *In My Father's Den* (2004),' in Alistair Fox and Gabrielle Hine (eds), *Cinematic Adaptation and the Articulation of New Zealand Identity* (Dunedin: Centre for the Research on National Identity, 2011), 43–53.

6. Maurice Gee, *In My Father's Den* (Auckland: Penguin, 2004 [1972]), 14.
7. Ibid., 21.
8. Ibid., 20.
9. Ibid., 16.
10. Ibid., 58.
11. Ibid., 51.
12. Ibid., 86.
13. Ibid., 145.
14. Ibid., 115.
15. Ibid.,140, 131.
16. Ibid., 163.
17. Ibid., 165–70.
18. For an excellent account of the genesis of McGann's film and an appraisal of its themes and style, see Duncan Petrie, 'From the Cinema of Poetry to the Cinema of Unease: Brad McGann's *In My Father's Den*,' *Illusions* 37 (Winter 2005), 2–8.
19. Lindsay, 'Brad McGann.'
20. Ibid.
21. Ibid.
22. Gee, *In My Father's Den*, 95.
23. Lindsay, 'Brad McGann.'
24. Nick Grant, 'Reel Authenticity' [interview], *Onfilm* 21 (September 2004), 13.
25. Brad McGann, 'Commentary,' *In My Father's Den*, DVD (Icon Home Entertainment, 2004).
26. Grant, 'Reel Authenticity.'
27. Brad McGann, 'Commentary,' *In My Father's Den*, DVD.
28. Ibid.
29. Charles Mauron, *Des Métaphores obsédantes au mythe personnel: Introduction à la psychocritique* (Paris: Librairie José Corti, 1963, reprinted 1995), 209–26.
30. Raskin, 'An Interview with Brad McGann.'
31. Brad McGann, 'Bio,' *P.O.V.* 7 (March 1998). [Adapted from the press-kit for *Possum*.]
32. Grandon, 'Q&A: Brad McGann.'
33. Richard Raskin, 'An Interview with Brad McGann on POSSUM,' *P.O.V.* 7 (March 1999), http://pov.imv.au.dk/Issue_07/section_2/artc3A.html, accessed 24 July 2016.
34. Grant, 'Reel Authenticity.'
35. Raskin, 'An Interview with Brad McGann.'
36. Brad McGann, 'Commentary,' *In My Father's Den*, DVD.
37. Lindsay, 'Brad McGann.'

14. A GAY BOY COMES TO TERMS WITH HIS SEXUALITY: *50 WAYS OF SAYING FABULOUS* (STEWART MAIN, 2005)

While all of the films discussed in this book express gender in one way or another, the first feature film made in New Zealand for theatrical release about gay adolescent masculine sexuality, *50 Ways of Saying Fabulous* (Stewart Main, 2005), is also one of the first, along with Niki Caro's *Whale Rider*, to foreground gender issues explicitly as the main preoccupation of the movie. Based on a novel by the expatriate New Zealand gay writer Graeme Aitken published in 1995, the film was 'really a very brave one to make,'[1] just as the novel had been a bold one to write. As the author himself states of the film that was based on his work:

> *50 Ways of Saying Fabulous* is ... very distinctively a New Zealand film ... When I was growing up in rural New Zealand in the 1970s, there were no positive representations of gay men anywhere ... I can't imagine such a film being made back in the Seventies when it is set, so it is also a testament to the fact that times have changed.[2]

Both the book and the film are extremely courageous, not merely because the subject of gay sexuality and love between young men was a taboo subject in New Zealand until well into the twenty-first century, but also because the approach that Aitken took to the subject was unflinching in its realism – a quality that was appreciated by at least one reviewer when the film was released overseas:

Billy (Andrew Patterson), the hero of our story, is overweight, fey, fickle, treacherous to his friends, unfaithful to his lover, and cursed with an EQ low enough to assume he can seduce aforesaid farmhand [Jamie, the handsome young man hired by the hero's father] by jumping on him. In other words, he's the selfish, brainless brat most of us once were. He's a wonderful character *because* he's so realistically imperfect.[3]

Predictably, the combination of taboo subject matter and a de-romanticized approach meant that neither the novel nor the film was well received by critics in New Zealand and Australia. Concerning the novel, for example, while recognizing that '*50 Ways* was hailed as a breakthrough book and was, in queer fiction terms, a bestseller,' the scholar Dean Kiley denounced it as 'fatuous,' dismissing its success as merely the product of a 'subcultural whinge-cringe factor which deals with such novels not as text but as event.'[4] As for the film version, the verdict of Peter Calder, writing for the *New Zealand Herald*, is typical: 'The ravishing landscapes of Central Otago are not enough to save this wooden and ill-conceived memoir of childhood, although there are some good teenage performances.'[5]

The film hardly fared better beyond Australasia, but for different reasons. Jeanette Catsoulis, reviewing *50 Ways* for the *New York Times*, concluded that 'the movie's insistently playful tone and cheesy fantasy sequences ultimately work against its ambitions, undermining a story that seethes with abuse and sexual'[6] Similarly, *50 Ways* struck Dennis Harvey, writing for *Variety*, as 'a coming-of-age tale set in rural New Zealand that incongruously mixes a frolicksome tone with disturbing content,' and which was likely to make some viewers find it 'off-key, overfamiliar in gist, or in questionable taste.'[7] In judgments such as these, one sees the consternation overseas critics experience when they encounter the mixing of genres that is, as no less a filmmaker than Peter Jackson has boasted, a markedly distinctive feature of New Zealand films.

Such responses, ranging from consternation to hostility, do not, in my opinion, negate the achievement of either the film or the novel on which it is based. Although both works have been almost completely ignored by scholars to date – *50 Ways of Saying Fabulous* receives only a one sentence acknowledgment in Te Papa's *New Zealand Film: An Illustrated History*, and is not mentioned at all in the surveys by Ian Conrich and Stuart Murray, and by Bruce Babington – it is more than worthy of serious attention, especially considering that it is unique among coming-of-age feature films to date in dealing with adolescent gay male sexuality.[8]

In that regard, however, there is one further preliminary observation to be made before attempting a close analysis of the film. *50 Ways of Saying Fabulous* is anomalous among New Zealand coming-of-age films in that it is not based on an iconic literary work written several decades earlier than the time when it was adapted. This means that there is no significant updating of the action, as usually occurs, and hence no substantial reshaping of the vision that informs the source novel. Moreover, the idea of making a film of this story came from the producer, Michele Fantl, who 'read the novel and loved the book,' subsequently taking it to Stewart Main who was, in effect, hired as a *metteur-en-scène* to bring the project to fruition.[9] This is not to say that Main was not personally invested in the film – he is himself openly gay, having earlier collaborated with his partner Peter Wells on a gay coming-of-age medium-length drama for television, *My First Suit* (1985), and several other gay-themed films: *A Death in the Family* (1986), about Aids, and *One of Them* (1995), a TV drama adapted from a novella by Wells. However, it does mean that *50 Ways* lacks the degree of personal projection found in many other coming-of-age films that are subjected to a substantial rewriting so as to turn them into a vehicle for autobiographical expression on the part of an auteur. In Wells' case, personal expression takes the form of empathic identification with the characters rather than the insertion of objects or incidents that derive from the filmmaker's own biography.

Aitken's Vision of Gay Adolescent Sexuality

Graeme Aitken's representation of the experience of discovering that one is gay is conveyed through a story revolving around a crush that a twelve-year-old boy, Billy, develops for a handsome nineteen-year-old farmhand, Jamie, whom his father hires to help out on a farm in a remote valley in Central Otago. In addition to revealing Billy's inner feelings and desires, this story allows Aitken to develop parallels between Billy and two other adolescents who do not conform to gendered and heteronormative stereotypes: Roy Schulter, another boy in Billy's class who falls hopelessly in love with Billy, only to find his love is unrequited; and Lou, his cousin, who is determined to reject the feminine role to which she is expected to conform. At the same time, these non-conformist characters are contrasted with other characters who represent dominant gender stereotypes: on one hand, Jamie himself, and other farm boys who are hypermasculine in their love of rugby, drinking and smoking, and interest in girls and sex, and, on the other, Belinda, a promiscuous blonde hairdresser who works at a boutique in the nearby town, Glenora, and who is the sexualized female equivalent of Jamie.

Billy's defining characteristics are announced in the prefatory description of *50 Ways of Saying Fabulous*:

> Sweet, fat, theatrical Billy-Boy was never cut out to be a farmer, but as his father's only son he's obliged to try. The cows are wayward and the chores

are gruelling, but Billy finds escape in a fantasy world. A place where the turnip paddock becomes a lunar landscape, a lavender bed jacket a slinky space suit, a cow's tail a head of beautiful blonde hair, and where Billy can become Judy Robinson, heroine of TV's *Lost in Space*.[10]

Aitken has revealed that in many ways Billy is 'my fictional "identical twin" . . . certainly I was fat, theatrical, and a fledgling poofter. I loathed rugby and farmwork, both of which were compulsory, and I did on one occasion use a cow's tail as a hairpiece.' Billy even has 'a two-tone towelling hat exactly like the one I used to wear as a child.'[11] It is probably the closeness of this autobiographical correspondence between the author and his avatar that gives the novel a feeling of authenticity.

By opting for a first-person narrative strategy, Aitken gives us direct access to Billy's thoughts and feelings. What we see is a compelling, rounded, complex psychological portrayal of a gay boy in the process of coming to terms with impulses and emotions that he does not fully understand, and is unable fully to control.

Billy's Relationship with Jamie, the Farmhand

The first impulse to be foregrounded is Billy's erotic attraction to an idealized masculine type, Jamie, who, like other farm boys who have preceded him, embodies everything that Billy feels he lacks. When Jamie arrives at the farm, Billy's nascent sexual feelings are aroused by Jamie's handsome looks and hypermasculinity, which gives him the appearance of the kind of iconic sexualized cowboy that appears on the covers of romance fiction: 'He was dressed casually. Cowboy boots, jeans and a checked cotton shirt, only half-buttoned up. It afforded a glimpse of his chest, which was as tanned as his face.'[12] As their friendship grows, Billy recurrently confesses his fascination with Jamie's naked torso: 'I loved the careless masculine way he tossed his shirt off while we were working, showing off his smooth tanned chest. Sometimes the sight of him shirtless was just too entrancing and I'd find myself leaning on my shovel or a fence, doing nothing but stare.'[13] Billy's fascination with Jamie's shirtless chest relates directly to the shame he feels with his own pudgy body, revealed, for example, when they go for a swim and Billy wonders how he can manoeuver himself into the water without Jamie seeing him, draping his towel round his neck so as to completely hide his own chest.[14]

In order to give expression to the sexual feelings Jamie arouses in him, Billy attempts, without consciously knowing what he is doing, to seduce him. On the occasions when he visits Jamie in his shearer's hut, he steals Jamie's spot on the latter's bed, provoking the young man to wrestle with him, secretly eroticizing this into a disguised form of love-making: 'I loved this tussle. The chance to grip onto him. Feel his skin beneath my fingers. The firmness of the muscles in his arms. I always fought hard, trying to prolong those playful wrestles for as long as possible.'[15]

Predictably, when Jamie reveals his attraction to girls – especially when he takes up with Belinda, the sexually precocious and promiscuous flirt who breaks all the rules in 'a town where a façade of respectability and virtue was expected' – Billy feels acute sexual jealousy when, in his imagination, he feels as if he has been displaced.[16] Billy's sense of betrayal and abandonment is made complete when, on the occasion of a Christmas Eve concert, he dresses up 'to look beautiful. Like Belinda,' but is ridiculed by Jamie, who mocks him: 'I never realised what a perfect little poofter you are.'[17] After this, in an act of vengeful spite, Billy denounces Jamie on account of the marijuana he has been secretly growing in a disused privy, and the latter packs his stuff and drives away soon after.

Roy: Billy's Disavowed Devotee

A major irony in the thematic design of Aitken's novel is the fact that Billy has a double: someone of his own sexual orientation who adores him, just as he adores Jamie. This is Roy Schluter, a classmate with whom he meets up at the abandoned gaol by the river for sessions of masturbation. Billie, however, is so concerned to fit in and be accepted by others, and so unaware of the extent of his own marginalization, that he spurns Roy, acting with great cruelty towards him. The most egregious instance of this cruelty is when Billy and Lou are driving back from the river with Jamie and see Roy walking back home from the gaol, Billy having missed their assignation in order to go swimming with Jamie. Whereas Jamie wants to offer Roy a ride, Billy screams 'No!', to avoid being relegated to the back seat to sit with him, given that Lou is not prepared to share the back seat with 'the Freak.'[18]

Considered in relation to his fixation with Jamie, Billy's physical aversion to, and ultimate repudiation of, Roy suggests that whereas Jamie represents everything that Billy wishes he himself were, Roy represents everything that he fears being, which is why his rejection of Roy is so vehement and cruel. Roy's own reaction is violent and extreme: he sets fire to the tussock grassland of the drought-stricken valley; terrorizes Billy, Lou, and Jamie with gunshots outside their house at night while the parents are away fighting the fire; and shoots Dante, the bull, through the head and cuts its throat, leaving a pool of blood over the driveway. It is only belatedly that Billy realizes his own behavior has been the cause of Roy's emotional breakdown: 'I had to admit to myself that I had begrudged him the basics of a friendship. I'd not only forbidden him to talk to me at school but even out of school, when we were alone together, I hadn't encouraged conversation. Such a secretive, silent friendship couldn't possible satisfy someone who had no other friends.'[19]

Finally, when Billy learns that it was Roy who had started the fire, he realizes that perhaps Roy had done it for love:

> We had done what we knew people in love were supposed to do ... Perhaps Roy assumed that to do such things meant we were in love and that I loved him back. He was so lonely, so reviled. Perhaps he was desperate enough to fall in love with someone as unattractive as myself. Perhaps looks were unimportant to him or perhaps he managed to see me the way I saw myself, through the haze of a childhood fantasy, beautiful like Judy.[20]

Tragically, this realization comes too late for it to furnish Billy with the enhancement of his self-sense that it potentially might have provided, but it nevertheless marks an important stage in the growth of his understanding about who he is.

Defying the Feminine Stereotype: Lou

The other character who plays an important role in Aitken's kaleidoscopic exploration of gendered identities in rural New Zealand is Billy's cousin Lou. Whereas Billy, with his blonde cow's tail, his love of dressing-up, and his fantasized identification with Judy in *Lost in Space*, is a feminized boy, Lou, whose real name is Louise, is a masculinized girl, who identifies herself with Brad in the same TV show. Each of them, therefore, inverts the dominant stereotype of what it is to be masculine and feminine.

Lou wears hobnail boots, and at first Jamie mistakes her for a 'tough little chap.'[21] As Billy starts to realize that Jamie is 'dazzled' by Lou, and that he is, in effect, in competition with her for Jamie's attention, he feels at a disadvantage in comparison because of her competence in all the aspects of country life that leave him feeling inadequate:

> In particular she seemed to be trying to highlight the differences between the two of us and show herself in a more favourable light. Lou could skin a rabbit with a few deft flashes of her pocket knife. I refused to even touch the stiff furry corpse. Lou could whistle to the dogs, guiding them this way and that, rounding up the sheep. I couldn't even whistle. I had to yell at the dogs instead, though they never followed my instructions the way they were supposed to. Lou was faster and more efficient at anything we were doing, whether it was digging a ditch or hammering in staples on a

fence. Lou always finished first and then made a point of having to come and help me finish off. Lou. Lou. Lou.[22]

Lou, nevertheless, is Billy's best friend and ally, perhaps because they each support one another in their unwillingness to conform to expected gender norms. Once Jamie has revealed his true crassness and has packed up and left, meaning that Billy and Lou are no longer rivals for his attention, they revert to their former friendship and resume their inverted roles. When Billy, out of self-pity, retreats to his rocky cave in 'Dragonland,' wanting to die, Lou, as 'chivalric hero,' comes to rescue him in her guise as 'the helpless maiden.'[23] In what will turn out to be their 'final childhood summer,' full of fantasy, Lou affirms both Billy and herself in their respective non-normative gendered identities by cutting off her long red plait to give to Billy as a replacement for the blonde cow's tail he had burnt, saying: 'It looks better on you than it ever did on me.' In return, Billy observes that Lou, with her short hair, looks 'just like Jamie without it.'[24] With this reaffirmation of each other as they fantasize themselves to be, both Billy and Lou are, in effect, accepting as queer the gendered identities that they will inhabit in the adulthood into which they are about to enter.

From Page to Screen: Stewart Main's Adaptation

In adapting this novel for the screen, Stewart Main remains remarkably faithful to Aitken's conception as far as the characterizations of the main protagonists are concerned, and the representation of key elements in the scenes and episodes that he chooses to reproduce. Main's Billy (Andrew Paterson) has the same effeminate traits, the same theatrical flamboyance, the same sensitivity about his weight, and the same desire to be accepted. In one scene, for example, Billy is shown examining his body in a mirror, exclaiming in consternation, 'I'm growing breasts!' Recurrently, he is shown wearing his cow's tail pinned to his two-toned towelling hat to simulate flowing, long blonde hair, and in one touching shot is seen gazing at it with longing, using it as a prop to fantasize about the gendered identity he would like to have, as distinct from the one in which he feels trapped.

Lou (Harriet Beattie), Roy (Jay Collins), and Jamie (Michael Dorman) are similarly characterized exactly as they are in the novel, and there is the same dynamic in the relations that exist between them, and between all of them and Billy. In addition, the location details of the novel are faithfully reproduced in Main's mise-en-scène, including the abandoned hut by the river where the boys meet to masturbate and the Central Otago rocky outcrops that form Dragonland.

Finally, the fantasy world into which Billy and Lou escape is literalized in the film in fantasy sequences that show them in their gender-reversed

Figure 14.1 Billy (Andrew Paterson) fantasizes about wearing his cow's tail in *50 Ways of Saying Fabulous* (dir. Steward Main, 2005).

identifications, with Billy as Lana and Lou as Brad from the TV show *Lost in Space*. Despite preserving this fidelity to the main elements of Aitken's conception, Main nevertheless made certain changes to the source that gave the film a new complexion.

Main's Alterations to the Source

The first major change Main made was to rearrange the episodes he selected from the novel into a new order. Instead of following Aitken by having Jamie arrive at the outset of the action, Main delays his arrival until halfway through the movie. This has the effect of relocating the main focus of the film on to the relationship between Billy and Roy, whose character is accorded a much greater presence in the film. Rather than foregrounding Billy's obsession with Jamie, this reordering focuses on the parallel between Billy and Roy as marginalized outsiders; the depth of Roy's love for Billy and his loyalty, reflected in his intervention when the school bully, Arch (George Mason), attacks his friend; and Billy's unfeeling callousness towards Roy, whose feelings he does not reciprocate, even though he is prepared to use him as a sexual partner.

Main also greatly enhances the role of Lou (Harriet Beattie). He shows her intervening to defend Billy when Arch and his cronies bully him on the school bus; she is turned into the captain of the school's rugby team and is shown tackling Arch to the ground during a rugby game and scoring a try; and in one scene she is shown contemptuously rejecting her mother's attempts to have her

Figure 14.2 Lou (Harriet Beattie) and Billy (Andrew Paterson) in a fantasy sequence from *50 Ways of Saying Fabulous* (dir. Steward Main, 2005).

fitted for a bra, while in another we see her binding her breasts so that she can pass for a boy in the rugby team. The impact of this expansion of Lou's characterization is to emphasize her refusal to conform to normative expectations for her gender, and to strengthen her role in the fiction as the female equivalent to Billy in their inversion of gender stereotypes.

A third modification Main made to the source was to add new episodes and themes to the cinematic version. From the very outset, a rugby theme is introduced that runs throughout the film. It first appears near the beginning in a fantasy sequence when we see Billy as Lana and Lou as Brad fleeing before a gigantic rugby ball that is chasing them. When the ball catches up with them, it traps Billy-as-Lana's ponytail in its seam, requiring Lou-as-Brad to rescue him. Metaphorically speaking, this fantasy episode suggests the attempts of Billy and Lou to escape from the oppressive gender expectations of the rural society in which they find themselves, while the trapping of Billy's ponytail signifies the refusal of that culture to allow him to assume the identity he desires. Similarly, the rescue of Billy-as-Lana by Lou-as-Brad foreshadows, again metaphorically, the role she will play at the end of the film when she salvages his aspirations by cutting off her own ponytail and giving it to him to replace his cow's tail so that he can continue to inhabit his fantasy.

One important new episode that is essential to Main's realization of the story is the birthday party that her mother throws for Lou. Apart from serving to reveal character, as when Billy is prevented from helping himself to a second serving of cake out of Lou's mother's concern for his weight, this sequence

Figure 14.3 Lou (Harriet Beattie) tries to disguise her burgeoning female body in *50 Ways of Saying Fabulous* (dir. Steward Main, 2005).

allows Main to elaborate the theme of betrayal, which has a much stronger presence than it did in the novel. While Billy is taking a bathroom break, Arch exploits his love of sweets by bribing him with chocolate to lure Roy into the bushes of the hedge, where he is ambushed by Arch and his gang, who humiliate Roy by pulling down his pants and pointing out that he has a 'stiffy' (Roy has allowed Billy to touch his erection). This betrayal is merely the first that will occur in the course of the film: when Billy stands Roy up in order to court Jamie; when Billy learns that Lou has told his younger sister Babe (Georgia NcNeill) that he is a 'poofter'; when Lou, who has spied on them through her binoculars, feels that Billy has betrayed their bond as she sees Billy and Roy leaving the hut after one of their assignations; when Billy pretends not to be Roy's friend when Jamie stops to give him a ride; when Jamie discovers that Belinda betrayed him by seeing someone else all the time he was going out with her; and when Jamie himself derides Billy as a 'little poofter,' blaming him for everything that has happened. The theme of betrayal thus runs like a leitmotif through Main's version, serving to underline the cruel consequences that the entry into sexuality and gendered identities, with all its confusions, can have on adolescents during their transition into adulthood.

Generic Consolidation in the Cinematic Version

All of the changes I have outlined in the conversion of the story as told in the novel to the screen are designed to give it the characteristic attributes of a coming-of-age genre film by investing it with greater unity and a firmer three-act structure. To a large extent, this reinforcement of its generic attributes was motivated by a concern that it should be marketable, which in turn required that it should be recognizable in terms of audience expectations.

These concerns led to one further major alteration: the ending. In Aitken's novel, the outcome of Billy's repudiation of Roy in favor of Jamie is transgressive and bloody, with Roy setting fire to the whole district and killing the farm's prize bull. Main, in one of the director's earlier drafts of the screenplay, had continued in this vein, even extending the mayhem by having Billy, Lou, and Roy all wielding and firing shotguns during the climactic scene, in which Roy accidentally shot himself. This scene was followed by a further one that saw Arch killed off as well.[25] Such an ending would have been box office poison, however, given that most spectators watching a coming-of-age film expect that there will be a positive resolution to whatever anguish or uncertainties are involved in the process.

Accordingly, in the final version of the film, the reworked ending is much more anodyne. Instead of setting fire to the district and slaughtering the bull, Main's Roy takes off into the hills because he is falsely accused by Arch of having attempted to murder him. He thus is put in danger from the fire, rather than being the pyromaniac who started it, which prompts Billy to be concerned for his safety. In the film, the most Roy does is to trash Jamie's hut, smash his guitar, take his gun, and fire off three shots to express his grief at the fact that Billy will not requite his love.

The cinematic version of *50 Ways of Saying Fabulous* therefore ends with exactly the uplifting kind of final scene that the producers must have thought would be more palatable at the box office. Billy declares his intention of going to university when he grows up, and reaffirms his bond with Lou, declaring, in response to her observation that 'it's confusing, isn't it,' that this is why 'we've got to stick together – it's the only way to survive.' The very last shots show Babe arriving at the top of the hill that forms Dragonland, meaning that she is now able to join their club. Significantly, though, Billy and Lou now declare that they are not going to play the flying-saucer game – they consider that they are adults now, which attests to the fact that the transition into their nascent gay identities has been successfully accomplished.

Postscript

Just as Stewart Main's adaptation has been virtually ignored by film scholars, so Graeme Aitken, as an author, remains conspicuously neglected by the New Zealand literary establishment. This suggests that the marginalization of the gay characters depicted in both the novel and the film attests to the persistence of a more general phenomenon in New Zealand society at large – a comparable marginalization of gay writers and filmmakers that may be lingering in this country longer than one might have anticipated. Given the remarkable honesty and realism with which Aitken represented his groundbreaking story of a gay boy's coming of age, and the fidelity and skill with which Main turned it into a cinematic adaptation, it would be a great pity if either of these works does not receive the attention they deserve.

Notes

1. An opinion voiced by the New Zealand actress Rima Te Wiata in an interview included as an extra on the DVD release of *50 Ways of Saying Fabulous* (MF Films, 2005).
2. Graeme Aitken, *50 Ways of Saying Fabulous* (Sydney: 20Ten Books, 2015 [1995], Kindle Edition), loc. 1752.
3. Ng Yi-Sheng, Review of *50 Ways of Saying Fabulous*, *fridae*, 21 April 2006.
4. Dean Kiley, 'Un-Queer Anti-Theory,' *Australian Humanities Review* 9 (1998), 1–6.
5. Peter Calder, Review of *50 Ways of Saying Fabulous*, *New Zealand Herald*, 22 August 2006.
6. Jeanette Catsoulis, 'Obstacles Line the Road to Self-Discovery in "50 Ways of Saying Fabulous",' *New York Times*, 2 June 2006.
7. Dennis Harvey, Review of *50 Ways of Saying Fabulous*, *Variety*, 27 September 2005.
8. It should be noted that gay coming-of-age themes feature in a number of New Zealand short films and television films, including *About Face: My First Suit* (Stewart Main, 1985), *One of Them* (Stewart Main, 1997), and *Boy* (Welby Ings, 2004).
9. Director's Commentary, *50 Ways of Saying Fabulous*, DVD.
10. Graeme Aitken, *50 Ways of Saying Fabulous* (Sydney: 20Ten Books, 2015 [1995]), Kindle Edition, blurb.
11. Ibid., loc. 1781.
12. Ibid., loc. 77.
13. Ibid., loc. 101.
14. Ibid., loc. 215.
15. Ibid., loc. 158.
16. Ibid., loc. 418, 502.
17. Ibid., loc. 1300.
18. Ibid., loc. 302, 332.
19. Ibid., loc. 1096.
20. Ibid., loc. 1210.
21. Ibid., loc. 243.
22. Ibid., loc. 502.
23. Ibid., loc. 1505.
24. Ibid., loc. 1535.
25. Graeme Aitken, postscript to *50 Ways of Saying Fabulous*, Kindle Edition.

PART 5

PERSPECTIVES ON MĀORI CULTURE SINCE 2010

15. PARENTAL ABANDONMENT AND THE TRAUMA OF LOSS: *BOY* (TAIKA WAITITI, 2010)

As the new century entered its second decade, the runaway hit *Boy* (Taika Waititi, 2010) announced a noteworthy flourishing of films by Māori filmmakers portraying the experience of Māori children coming of age. There had intermittently been precursors – notably Merata Mita's *Mauri* (1988) and other films with coming-of-age elements, such as Barry Barclay's *Ngati* (1987) and Lee Tamahori's *Once Were Warriors* (1994) – but *Boy*, which was soon to be followed by *Mahana* (Lee Tamahori, 2016) and *Hunt for the Wilderpeople* (Taika Waititi, 2016), attests to an enlarged audience interest in seeing Māori experience depicted on screen.

All of these films have been unusually successful at the New Zealand box office, relative to the size of the population (4.5 million in 2016). *Boy*, when it was released in 2010, garnered $6,750,042, outperforming such international hits as *Harry Potter and the Deathly Hallows (Part One)* ($4,486,256), *The Twilight Saga: Eclipse* ($4,113,338), and *Iron Man 2* ($2,701,225), and breaking all previous New Zealand records. Even this record was shattered by Taika Waititi's next coming-of-age film, *Hunt for the Wilderpeople*, which achieved a staggering $8,703,282, the scale of which can be judged by comparison with the figures for American blockbusters released that year: *Captain America: Civil War* ($3,480,235), *Batman v Superman: Dawn of Justice* ($3,269,068), and *X-Men: Apocalypse* ($1,924,905).[1] Clearly, then, there is something about these New Zealand-made films that has touched a chord with the national audience, which raises questions that this chapter will attempt to address.

The Reception of *Boy* at Home and Abroad

A number of critics and scholars did not share the wildly enthusiastic response of New Zealand spectators to *Boy*, and their negative criticism points to aspects of the film that it is important to explore. When *Boy* had its premiere at the Sundance Film Festival, Peter Debruge, reviewing the film for *Variety*, was highly dismissive, labeling the film 'a let-down' on account of the fact that, in his opinion, 'Waititi has scrubbed away all culturally specific traits from his growing-up Kiwi comedy,' meaning that, 'Without that arthouse-ready anthropological edge . . . "Boy's" prospects look more cult than commercial.'[2] For Debruge, then, the film lacked the cultural exoticism that would give an impression of authenticity.

In New Zealand, certain scholars were equally brutal, especially those who looked at *Boy* through the ideological lens of post-colonial theory. Misha Kavka and Stephen Turner, for example, complained that the film 'works to occlude the attention an audience might otherwise give to the socio-historical conditions of the situation in which the characters in *Boy* find themselves,' thus constituting itself as 'the "postcolonial taniwha" [monster]' that is designed to absolve Pākehā of any responsibility for the 'post'-colonial' condition of Māori, which (implicitly in this view) is abject.[3] On the Māori side, Brendan Hokowhitu complained that *Boy* continued 'the pathologising of Māori masculinities' by presenting Alamein, the adult father of the eleven-year-old hero, as 'another irredeemable representation of Māori masculinity,' and concluded his commentary by lamenting, 'There is nothing in this film that points towards sovereign possibilities for Māori men.'[4] Clearly, the gap between these disparaging views of *Boy* and the enthusiasm it has elicited from a mass audience needs to be explained: the film's appeal obviously springs from something else that both its foreign and its local detractors have either not recognized, or else have not been prepared to acknowledge.

Those who claim that the film is not authentically Māori – a claim usually made by non-Māori – have been judged to be way off the mark by Māori themselves. In the view of Haunui Royal, general manager of programming for Māori TV, Waititi had made an exemplary Māori film: '*Boy* is a Māori story. It's come from the heart of Māoridom and I know it; I can smell it; I can feel it. It's not an intellectual process for me.'[5] Similarly, Leonie Pihama, Director of the Te Kotahi Research Institute at the University of Waikato, affirms a comparable view:

> For me, there is no doubt that *Boy* is a Māori movie by anyone's definition: it is written, directed and produced by Māori. It is a story of a Māori whanau and is located within what is an identifiable Māori community. What *Boy* is *not* is a Kaupapa Māori movie, as in essence it

maintains and reproduces some of the basic stereotypical views of what it means to be Māori, and in particular, what it means to be a Māori man.⁶

By asserting that *Boy* is not 'a Kaupapa Māori movie' while allowing that it is nonetheless a Māori film, Pihama is acknowledging that it is not imbued with the knowledge, skills, beliefs, and values of traditional Māori society in the way that is so strikingly evident in Mita's *Mauri*, which is genuinely a *kaupapa Māori* movie in this sense. The difference between these two films shows how far Māori culture, even in the rural homelands, had changed in the interim between the generation of Merata Mita and Barry Barclay, born in the 1940s, and that of Taika Waititi, who was born in 1975. The big change is that by the mid-1980s, the period in which *Boy* is set, Māori culture had rapidly assimilated aspects of the globalized youth culture emanating from America, resulting in a striking cultural hybridity that is everywhere apparent in the film: in the references to Michael Jackson; allusions to popular TV shows such as *The Dukes of Hazzard*, *Shōgun*, *Dynasty*, *Falcon Crest*, and *Dallas*, and movies such as *E.T. the Extra-Terrestrial*; and especially in the concluding dance routine, which is a mixture of Michael Jackson's *Thriller* dance moves and traditional Māori *haka* moves, to the music of 'Poi E,' a hit song by the group Patea Māori Club that reached number-one in New Zealand in 1984. The cultural hybridity that imbues the film was one obvious reason for its enormous popularity: people recognized a faithful reflection of their own experience. As the Māori actor Tammy Davis, a star in the popular New Zealand TV series *Outrageous Fortune*, wrote in a rebuttal of Peter Debruge's disparaging *Variety* review post on the *Variety* website:

> Peter, growing up Maori on the East Coast of New Zealand is not all riding whales. What culturally specific aspects were you missing? Were young Maori in the early 80s too busy learning to keen and chant and wail to be concerned with schoolyard crushes and the phenomenon that was Michael Jackson?
> Then I am afraid to say I am a let-down of a Maori, because in the 80s this was all there was for me.⁷

Audiences thus responded enthusiastically to *Boy*, in part, because it authentically showed them themselves – a desire that Taika Waititi himself had taken on board:

> I think actually most people want to see themselves or versions of themselves on screen, and I think this film kind of captures New Zealand at a time that had sort of been forgotten, and a lot of people – especially in my generation – never thought they'd see on screen. I think it's about being

able to see yourself at the movies. And all New Zealanders can relate to everything in the film, they don't have to be Maori, they don't have to have grown up in the country.[8]

As much as it affronted post-colonial theorists and those committed to *kaupapa Māori*, *Boy* presented New Zealanders with the reality of what they had become as a result of New Zealand's own coming of age, in which Māori had participated, like everyone else: 'the 80s were like the coming of age decade for us. It was like when we were really finding our way in the world and discovering who we were so it seemed good to make a coming of age film set in a coming of age time.'[9]

There was an even more important reason for the film's popularity, however – one on which the film's detractors have been almost completely silent. *Boy* has a universal appeal for audiences because, at a psychological level, the dynamics of the coming-of-age experience it depicts are recognizable to people in any society, from whatever ethnic group, at any time. The main preoccupation of *Boy* is to show the effects on a child of growing up in a maturational environment marked by the loss of a parent, parental neglect, and emotional deprivation. Waititi addresses these serious issues under the guise of comedy and, in so doing, he created a masterpiece in terms of its revelation of the psychic strategies children adopt in order to survive in the face of trauma.

Genre-Mixing in the Presentation of Boy's World

A number of critics have observed that *Boy*, thematically, has a close relation to an earlier film, *Once Were Warriors* (Lee Tamahori, 1994), which the *New York Times* critic Janet Maslin described as 'social realism with a savage kick' on account of 'its pitiless depiction of these characters' unhappy lives.'[10] *Boy* tells the story of an eleven-year-old Māori child, 'Boy' (James Rolleston), who is living with his grandmother and *whānau*, including his younger brother Rocky (Te Aho Eketone-Whitu), at Waihau Bay on the East Coast of the North Island of New Zealand. The two boys lack both their parents: Joanie, their mother, died giving birth to Rocky, and Alamein (Taika Waititi) has been absent from their lives since that time (we learn that he has been in prison for a bungled burglary). When their Nan (Mavis Paenga) is called away to attend a *tangi* (funeral), Boy is left alone for several days to take care of his brother and young cousins in her absence. While she is away, Alamein returns home with two deadbeat members of his gang, the Crazy Horses, to collect stolen cash he had buried in a field when he was fleeing the police. At first intending to leave with his mates as soon as he can, during the stay at his former home, Alamein is forced to engage in a relationship with his two sons, at the same time setting up his gang headquarters in a garage on the property. Boy, who had previously idolized him in fantasy, eventually sees through Alamein's pretenses at being a hero, and Rocky, who intuits the source of his father's malaise, initiates his spiritual healing by unlocking his father's capacity to grieve, which Alamein had formerly repressed.

Those who have detected parallels between this story and that of *Once Were Warriors* are not wrong. Leonie Pihama, for instance, points to the presence of the same stereotypes:

> Māori children left to fend for themselves; Māori children who are neglected, live in poverty and have to struggle against parties and alcohol for dinner; Māori men who are clearly shown as useless, who lie, bludge, steal, party and smoke dope; Māori fathers who desert their *whānau* and return only to get what they can take; Māori women who are mean spirited and bossy; and Māori boys who supposedly adore their father but at the first opportunity steal from them.

Lamenting the presence of these stereotypes, Pihama exclaimed: 'by the end of the movie I felt like I had sat through a rural based *Once Were Warriors*.'[11] Apart from a difference in the scale of domestic and gang violence – of which there are, indeed, traces in *Boy*, as when Boy sees his friend Dynasty (Moerangi Tihore) sitting in the car next to him with a black eye that her father has given her as a result of Alamein's theft of the marijuana crop she was supposed to be guarding, or when members from a rival gang beat up Alamein and the other members of the Crazy Horses – the only substantive difference between the two films is a comic tone and the presence of fantasy play-acting that overlays events that otherwise would appear tragic. Just as *Once Were Warriors* opens with a shot that juxtaposes an idealized image of New Zealand on a tourist billboard against a contrasting reality of social abjection and family dysfunction, so too does *Boy* open with a shot that at first presents the image of an idealized rural existence of golden cornfields overlooking the sparkling blue waters of an idyllic bay, only to pan right to reveal a pile of derelict, rusty cars at the edge of the field. There is even a parallel to the suicide of the abused teenager Grace (Mamaengaroa Kerr-Bell) in *Once Were Warriors*, when Boy closes his eyes and lets himself fall backwards into the Raukokere River – although in Waititi's more genial vision he is allowed to be saved by the Weirdo (Waihoroi Shortland), in contrast to Grace, who actually dies.

Despite the asseverations of certain critics, the characters and events that constitute these parallels between the two movies do not simply derive from a commercial exploitation of 'lame stereotypes.'[12] Like all New Zealand coming-of-age films, *Boy* is deeply personal, by Waititi's own admission:

> The real personal part of the film is that it's set where I grew up. It's set in the country and we shot in the house that I grew up in which was my

grandmother's house and we grew up like that with a lot of kids. And I went to that school. Some other personal stuff was that a lot of my uncles and my dad included were in gangs.[13]

While Waititi insists that there is no direct autobiographical correlation between real-life people and the characters and events in the film, nevertheless, 'some of the adults are based on adults I've encountered over the years and observed; mixtures of people,'[14] and he emphasizes that 'My point of reference is really what I experienced from being a kid.'[15] In one recent interview, Waititi admitted that in *Boy* he was, in fact, 'playing my dad,'[16] which, given the statement Waititi makes in the person of Alamein in his director's commentary to the effect that 'Boy is "a mirror of me",' suggests that the roles of Boy and Alamein contain elements of both his father and himself.

The presence of this powerful dimension of personal projection in *Boy*, albeit at a displaced, 'invented' fictive remove, brings one back to the comic elements in the film that prevent it from turning into a grim, rural *Once Were Warriors*. Again, Waititi's own comments are illuminating in this regard. In his view, earlier New Zealand movies had been characterized by their grimness: 'Very dark dramas, bad things happening to nice people, very heavy. I didn't want to make a film about child abuse, or child neglect, which was unwatchable.'[17] For the word 'unwatchable,' Waititi might very well have substituted the word 'unbearable'; by mixing comedy and drama, the filmmaker could make watchable and bearable an experience that otherwise potentially could be unbearable, while at the same time blocking any suspicion that he wanted 'to exercise [*sic* for "exorcise"(?)] demons or make it like my kinda spilling my guts out on the screen.'[18] Waititi also points out that his own background is stand-up comedy, recalling that he was, with Jermaine Clement, one half of The Humourbeasts, a comedy duo that they formed while students at Victoria University of Wellington.[19] This combination of potentially traumatic personal experience with a predisposition to act the joker was what motivated the strange blend of comedy and drama that defines the film.

Trauma and its Legacies

At the heart of the film lies trauma, presented both explicitly at a personal level, and implicitly at an environmental and cultural level. At the personal level, the source of the trauma is the death of Boy's mother Joanie, Alamein's young wife. The idea of her is repeatedly evoked in the film: for instance, when Boy attacks another boy in the classroom, and is given a detention, because 'he made fun of my mum'; in recurrent shots of the grieving Rocky, who, believing that he has special 'powers,' has convinced himself that he killed his mother because his powers were 'too strong' at the moment she gave birth to him; in several scenes showing the blood-streaked legs of the mother on her deathbed, with grieving family members looking on; in flashbacks that present Boy's memories of being with his mother in happier times, as when he has a vision of her after being pulled out of the river by Weirdo; in the scenes where the two boys confront their father, with Rocky saying 'Sorry for what I did to Mum,' and Boy upbraiding him for not being there when she died; and finally when the boys find Alamein seated by Joanie's grave, grieving for her at long last. This omnipresence of the mother thus highlights the different ways her death has affected those she has left behind: Boy clings to an idealized fantasy of his father as a hero and tries to deny the reality of his loss by fantasizing about himself as Michael Jackson; Alamein has simply taken flight, abandoning all his responsibilities toward his sons in order to live out his own romantic fantasy of being an outlaw and controlling the world by being a gang leader; while Rocky, locked in a prison of self-generated guilt, suffers in withdrawn silence.

At the level of the external environment, trauma is implicitly present in images of abjection that evoke the traumatic legacy of colonialism. Apart from the rusting chassis of abandoned cars already mentioned, we see another car that is not running properly: the grandmother's Humber, which her grandchildren have to push-start to get it going. We also see a number of other symbolic images, including a derelict house, which provides a site where the children play, and a shot of 'a kid in a boat not going anywhere – a metaphor, for sure.'[20] These images indicate, as Waititi observes in his director's commentary, that the anger and frustration Alamein feels, motivating his ambition to start a gang, is symptomatic of 'a very real phenomenon which is the displacement and disenfranchisement of cultures that have got no other choice but to just start clubs or hang out with people like them because they have nowhere else to go.'[21] The traumatic legacy of colonialism is felt at the individual level as well: '. . . my father was a bit like that, and his father before him . . . it's ingrained in us because of so many years of oppression and frustration, resentment because, you know, the Māori have had a pretty rough time over the last 160 years . . . Not an excuse, but it does come from somewhere.'[22] I have drawn attention to the signs of trauma in *Boy* because recognition of its presence is a precondition for understanding both the pattern and the process of the film and, in particular, its peculiar blend of comedy and drama.

STRUCTURAL PATTERNS AND THE PSYCHODYNAMIC PROCESSES OF THE FILM

Boy has a very carefully designed structure composed of certain patterns that guide the spectator into an affective apprehension of its meaning. The first half of the movie is primarily comic or, in Waititi's terms, 'funny,' while the second half becomes progressively more serious and emotional. The major turning point that signals the change from comedy to drama occurs when Alamein arrives at the store where Boy, who has secretly discovered his father's buried hoard of cash, has bought ice-blocks for his friends. At this moment, Alamein angrily knocks the ice-block that Boy is licking out of his hand (a mild substitute for whacking him), and rips the leather jacket with a gang patch that Boy has donned violently off him. As Waititi observes in his commentary, this reveals the worst side of Alamein, betraying an awareness from which he can no longer hide: that is, that he is 'a useless dad.'[23] From that point on, Boy grows progressively more disillusioned with his father until he attains a clear-eyed view of who and what he really is, untrammeled by any of his earlier romantic illusions.

Along with this shift of tone there occurs another reversal. In the first half of the movie, it is Boy who constructs a romantic fantasy that elevates his father to a heroic, estimable status. When Alamein arrives, the reality he represents is clearly the polar opposite of the ideal in Boy's fantasies. Soon, however, Alamein starts to play to, and encourage, these eulogistic fantasies in order to impress his son and disguise the actual reality. Ironically, as he starts to do this, the pattern inverts itself again, with Boy progressively taking to imitating the loutish gang-behavior of Alamein – swaggering in his leather jacket, drinking beer, and smoking marijuana – in order to impress his father in turn, and thereby gain his acceptance.

Underlying these inversions is the theme of 'potential' that runs through the

Figure 15.1   Boy (James Rolleston) imitating his father in *Boy* (dir. Taika Waititi, 2010).

movie – a notion that Waititi picks up from Alan Duff's *Once Were Warriors*, in which it was elaborated as a major theme, often with considerable tragic irony.[24] Near the beginning of the film, after Boy has delivered a speech about himself before the other members of his school class, his teacher praises the speech and reminisces about how he went to school with Boy's father: 'He was a good student, like you, full of potential.' Having established this parallel between Boy and Alamein in terms of potential, Waititi recurrently shows Boy trying to find out what the word 'potential' means, while all the time ironically juxtaposing this quest against the degenerate image of Alamein in the present, which highlights how the course of action he has adopted represents a betrayal of that potential. A recognition of this betrayal hits home with Alamein at the climactic moment of the film when Boy, who now sees his father with clear-eyed disillusionment, upbraids him: 'I thought I was like you, but I'm not – I don't have any potential!'

The structure of ironic reversals in the film is manifest again in a corresponding shift in the respective attitudes of each of the boys towards each of their parents. Whereas at the beginning of the movie 'Boy is obsessed by the father and doesn't really think about his mother that much,' Rocky, on the other hand, 'is obsessed by the mother and doesn't really want to know the father.'[25] Then, this pattern reverses itself: Boy starts to experience memories of his mother as his disenchantment with his father grows, and Rocky starts to want to get to know his dad, which leads up to the younger boy's attempt to heal his father by touching his forehead, just as E.T. in *E.T. the Extra-Terrestrial* touches the forehead of Elliott, the boy hero in Spielberg's film, with his glowing finger, saying: 'I'll be right here', thus recalling the epigraph from E.T. that Waititi includes at the beginning of his own movie: 'You could be happy here ... We could grow up together. *E.T. the Extra Terrestrial*.'

What all these structural patterns point to, is the presence in the film of a deep underlying source of perturbation, along with the contrasts that exist between the different responses that the main triangle of characters have adopted in response to it, as well as the therapeutic mental operations that are called for if these individuals are ever to have the chance, as E.T. says, to 'be happy here,' and 'grow up together.'

Looking back over the film, one can see, retrospectively, what Waititi has done, which is a testimony to his intuitive genius. In the fantasizing of Boy and the play-acting of his father Alamein, we see in operation the dynamics of the psychic defenses that Sigmund Freud identified in *Jokes and Their Relation to the Unconscious* (1905). In this groundbreaking work, Freud hypothesized, on the basis of his clinical practice, that the functions of jokes is to evade either an external or an internal obstacle that threatens to impede the satisfaction of one's purpose.[26] A developing child, says Freud, 'uses games in order to

COMING-OF-AGE CINEMA IN NEW ZEALAND

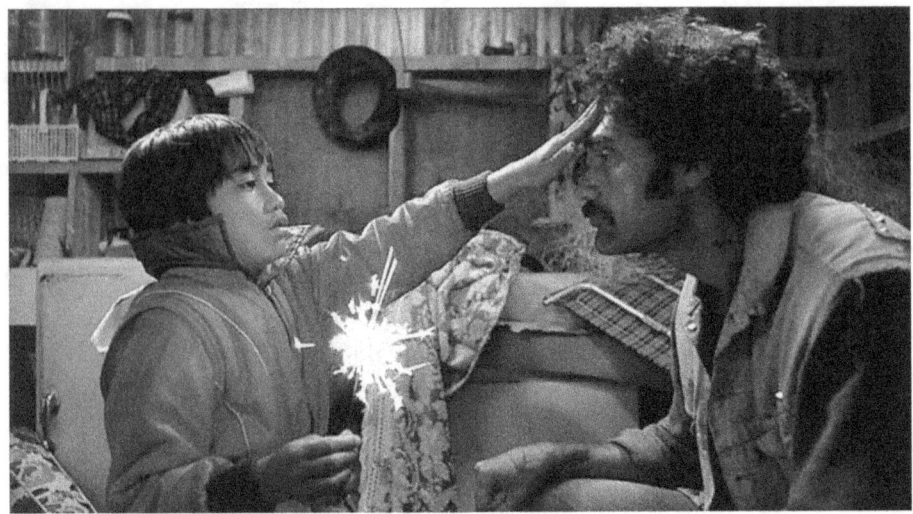

Figure 15.2   Rocky (Te Aho Eketone-Whitu), like E.T., tries to heal his father Alamein (Taika Waititi) in *Boy* (dir. Taika Waititi, 2010).

withdraw from the pressure of critical reason.'[27] This is exactly what we see Boy, and later Alamein, doing in their play-acting and fantasizing.

The actuality that Boy faces is that he is an abandoned child: first, by his mother, involuntarily, and then by his father, who has deserted him out of choice. To counter the emotional devastation that this would inflict on him were he to acknowledge it in consciousness, Boy invents all kinds of fantasies that allow him to deny the fact of his father's desertion: as Waititi says, 'he's always fantasising that his dad is off having adventures around the world and doing these incredible things,' whereas in actual fact Alamein has been in prison as a criminal.[28]

Alamein, too, manifests behavior that is explained by Freud's psychoanalytic theory. Referring to the defensive motives of humor, Freud hypothesizes that 'Defensive processes are the psychical correlative of the flight reflex and perform the task of preventing the generation of unpleasure from internal sources ... Humour can be regarded as the highest of these defensive procedures.'[29] In Waititi's film, Alamein adopts a disguise in the form of play-acting in order to achieve precisely these purposes. Having first sought to evade coming to terms with his grief at the death of his beloved wife, his first impulse was to take literal flight by abandoning his family to seek emotional refuge in a gang which, because he has created it, allows him to feel, unconsciously, that he has some power to control a world that has hurt him so badly. Once he returns – out of less than worthy motives (to retrieve the stolen 'treasure' he has hidden) – and has to confront the reality that he has sons who are growing, one of whom is on the point of entering adulthood, he attempts to take refuge in the same strategy that he sees his son adopting: that is, the elaborating of a fantastical notion of the admirable self he would like to be.

Waititi, however, will not allow this evasion to persist, which is why he converts the comedy into a drama, albeit (because of the generosity of his own vision) not a tragic one. The thing that saves *Boy* from becoming the tragedy depicted in *Once Were Warriors* is the intuitive insight of Alamein's youngest son, Rocky. Although initially it is his mother for whom he grieves, once Alamein has arrived on the scene, Rocky's intuition lets him know the real problem that his father confronts. This is conveyed through his childish drawings (actually, and significantly, done by Taika Waititi in real life), which show Alamein suspended over the dead body of his wife, weeping profusely. This is what Alamein has never allowed himself to do, and which he needs to do in order to be emotionally whole. Everything he has done since the death of his wife has been an attempt to avoid the trauma of that bereavement, which, as Waititi lets us know in his commentary, has been compounded by a sense of the oppression of his people as a result of being colonized. What Boy does in the course of the movie, which attests to his coming of age, is to 'unmask' his father – in other words, to strip him of the defense mechanisms he has adopted to protect himself, emotionally, from acknowledging the depth of his grief.

Rocky thus functions as the redemptive child, a figure who is often encountered in coming-of-age films. He is the one who is able to break through his father's emotional defenses when he approaches him, sparkler in hand, touches him (like E.T.) on the forehead, and says (with a pathos that is unbearable to the audience): 'Sorry for what I did to Mum.' It is this recognition of what his own inability to face his grief has done to his child that jolts Alamein, finally, into going to the grave of his wife, Joanie, in order to release and fully experience his own grief.

When the boys go to the cemetery the next day, they find their father – who earlier had been unable to bring himself to enter it, even though he had hovered around its boundaries once he realized the degenerative effect his presence had been having on his eldest son – in the cemetery, grieving for his dead wife. Boy and Rocky then sit with him and, with characteristic Waititi-esque humor, Rocky exclaims, with the effect of deflating the actual emotional intensity of the situation: 'How was Japan?'

Conclusion

Apart from being profoundly moving as a film in its own right, *Boy* is a significant film in the corpus of New Zealand coming-of-age cinema. Its importance lies in the fact that it marks a new stage of self-confidence on

Figure 15.3 Alamein (Taika Waititi) finally joins his sons in facing up to his grief in *Boy* (dir. Taika Waititi, 2010).

the part of Māori filmmakers as far as the depiction of Māori experience is concerned. Rather than trying to evoke a 'pure' traditional *kaupapa Māori* culture in the way Merata Mita had done in *Mauri*, Waititi is happy to show the hybrid mixture into which Māori culture as he had experienced it as a boy had evolved.

In terms of the symbolic figuration contained in the fiction that constitutes the film, the attempts of the members of Alamein's family to come to terms with the trauma of their past experience within the family represents, at a microcosmic level, the contemporary efforts more generally of Māori to come to terms with the lingering effects of the negative effects of colonization by the Pākehā. Instead of presenting themselves as merely victims of this assault on traditional Māori culture, Waititi's Māori characters display a creative inventiveness in terms of assimilating aspects of global culture into a new form of cultural hybridity that is felt to be sustaining of identity, while at the same time attesting to the fact that Māori were assuming their own rightful place in the modern world.

This new tendency, which *Boy* so powerfully displays, would soon be reinforced and extended in the next two New Zealand coming-of-age films to follow: *Mahana* (2016), marking the return to New Zealand filmmaking of Lee Tamahori, the director of *Once Were Warriors*, and *Hunt for the Wilderpeople* (2016), the second coming-of-age feature by Taika Waititi that surpassed the success even of *Boy*, thus becoming the most successful New Zealand movie of all time.

Notes

1. These box office figures are taken from Box Office Mojo, http://www.boxoffice mojo.com/intl/newzealand/yearly/?yr=2016&p=.htm, accessed 7 August 2016. According to figures released by the New Zealand Film Commission, the box office for *Hunt for the Wilderpeople* has since risen to $11,808,372; see 'Top Twenty New Zealand Films Released At New Zealand Box Office (to 15 July 2016),' NZ Film Commission, http://www.nzfilm.co.nz/sites/nzfc/files/Top%2020%20July%202016.pdf, accessed 12 August 2016.
2. Peter Debruge, 'Review: "Boy",' *Variety*, 23 January 2010.
3. Misha Kavka and Stephen Turner, '*Boy* and the Postcolonial Taniwha,' Special Issue on Taika Waititi's *Boy*, *MediaNZ* 13:1 (2012), 37–46.
4. Brendan Hokowhitu, 'Ta Kapa o Taika: A Commentary on *Boy*,' Special Issue on Taika Waititi's *Boy*, *MediaNZ* 13:1 (2012), 109–19.
5. From an interview of 16 June 2010, reported in Trisha Dunleavy and Hester Joyce, *New Zealand Film and Television: Institution, Industry and Cultural Change* (Bristol: Intellect, 2011), 238.
6. Leonie Pihama, 'A Short Commentary on *Boy*,' Special Issue on Taika Waititi's *Boy*, *MediaNZ* 13:1 (2012), 97–101.
7. Tim Hume, 'Munter Lashes Out over US Film Review,' *Sunday Star Times*, 31 January 2010, posted on *Stuff*, http://www.stuff.co.nz/entertainment/film/3279688/Munter-lashes-out-over-US-film-review, accessed 7 August 2016.
8. Simon Miraudo, 'Interview with Taika Waititi,' *Quicklix*, 25 August 2010, https://www.quickflix.co.nz/News/Article/6919, accessed 7 August 2016.
9. Matt Rodriguez, 'Interview with Taika Waititi,' *Shakefire*, http://www.shakefire.com/interview/taika-waititi-the-interview-boy, accessed 7 August 2016.
10. Janet Maslin, 'For a Family, the War at Home,' *New York Times*, 24 February 1995, http://www.nytimes.com/movie/review?res=990CE0DC1E38F937A15751C0A963958260, accessed 8 August 2016.
11. Pihama, 'A Short Commentary on *Boy*.'
12. Ibid.
13. Waititi, Interview with Matt Rodrguez.
14. Simon Miraudo, 'Interview with Taika Waititi.'
15. Craig Hubert, 'Taika Waititi's Inner Child' [interview], http://www.interviewmagazine.com/film/taika-waititi-boy #, published 29 February 2012, accessed 8 August 2016.
16. Tasha Robinson, 'Making Vampire Comedy: What We Do In the Shadows,' *The Dissolve*, https://thedissolve.com/features/interview/923-jemaine-clement-and-taika-waititi-on-their-years-i/, accessed 8 August 2016.
17. Hubert, 'Taika Waititi's Inner Child.'
18. Interview by Matt Rodriguez.
19. Tasha Robinson, 'Making Vampire Comedy.'
20. Taika Waititi, Director's Commentary, DVD.
21. Ibid.
22. Ibid.
23. Ibid.
24. See, for example, Grace's despair about her unrealized potential just before she hangs herself, or the stream of consciousness during which Nig, who has just joined a gang, bitterly reflects upon how this represents a travesty of his actual potential (Duff, *Once Were Warriors*, 113, 135).
25. Waititi, Director's Commentary.
26. Sigmund Freud, *Jokes and Their Relation to the Unconscious*, trans. and ed. James

Strachey; with a Biographical Introduction by Peter Gay (New York and London: Norton, 1989), Kindle Edition, loc. 156.
27. Ibid., loc. 159.
28. Matthew Toomey, 'Matt's Blog' [Interview with Taika Waititi], *The Film Pie*, http://www.thefilmpie.com/index.php/blog-59/38-blog/1794-my-interview-with-taika-waititi-director-of-boy, created 22 August 2010, accessed 8 August 2016.
29. Freud, *Jokes and Their Relation to the Unconscious*, loc. 300.

16. A MĀORI BOY CONTESTS THE OLD PATRIARCHAL ORDER: *MAHANA* (LEE TAMAHORI, 2016)

When one looks at the sequence of films showing Māori coming-of-age experiences, beginning with Merata Mita's *Mauri* (1988), continuing with Lee Tamahori's *Once Were Warriors* (1994) and Niki Caro's *Whale Rider* (2002), and attaining a spectacular flowering in *Boy* (Taika Waititi, 2010), *Mahana* (released overseas under the title *The Patriarch* [Lee Tamahori, 2016]), and *Hunt for the Wilderpeople* (Taika Waititi, 2016), a distinct pattern becomes apparent. *Mauri*, following the approach advocated by Barry Barclay in his vision for a 'fourth cinema,' adopted a *kaupapa Māori* approach (that is, one that was informed by the attitudes, principles, and values of Māori society) to the telling of a story in which Māori *tikanga* (cultural practices) were observed to the letter. *Once Were Warriors*, also a film about Māori, directed by a Māori, and with Māori actors, depicted, to the contrary, a group of people living in an urban context completely deracinated from their customary culture until one of them, Beth, rediscovered its sustaining values and decided to return to her *marae*. *Boy*, on the other hand, presented that culture as having undergone a transformation even in the rural tribal homelands, with the incursion of popular American culture being embraced enthusiastically by the local youths. *Mahana* continues that trend, revealing a similar kind of cultural hybridity involving the assimilation of American culture, but also trying to match it with a strict observance of *tikanga Māori*, to an extent that was conspicuously absent in *Whale Rider* and, to a lesser extent, in *Boy*. What we see in this pattern are reflections of a culture in the process of change, and, for that reason, it is useful to explore how the forces promoting this change intersect in this very recent film, *Mahana*, which is particularly useful for this purpose because it has been made by a Māori filmmaker whose own personal itinerary reflects a response to those very same forces. Before teasing out the factors involved in that itinerary, however, it is necessary to consider the relationship between Tamahori's film and the novel by Witi Ihimaera from which it was adapted.

Inter-generational Conflict as Presented in Ihimaera's *Bulibasha*

Witi Ihimaera's novel *Bulibasha, King of the Gypsies* (1994) tells the story of Simeon (Himiona in Māori), a teenage Māori boy who challenges the tyranny of his grandfather, Tamihana Mahana, who rules over his extended family with a despotic, oppressive absolutism, in accordance with traditional assumptions of the rights of the pre-eminent male in the patriarchal system enshrined in traditional Māori culture. In order to liberate a space in which Simeon can inhabit his own independent, individual identity, he defies his grandfather's authority by exposing the latter's ignorance, by compelling his father to defend him against the brutality of his own father, and by organizing a vote on a matter of principle that leaves Tamihana defeated and discredited, after which his grandfather, in a state of psychic collapse, dies from a cancer, the existence of which he was too proud to reveal.

In the world of Ihimaera's fiction, Tamihana is merely one in a long line of tyrannical patriarchs that members of the younger generation feel compelled to resist, from Ihaka in *The Matriarch* (1986), through Koro in *The Whale Rider* (1987), to Arapeta in *The Uncle's Story* (2000).[1] These patriarchs are presented as being trapped in a time-warp, arrogant in their presumption of a right to decide every aspect of the lives of those who live under their sway, and committed to an ideal of hyper-masculinity based on physical prowess and brute strength that leaves no room for a male who is sensitive or intellectual, let alone gay (as Ihimaera himself is).

Tamihana in *Bulibasha* is the worst of all of them, his misdeeds being elaborated in more detail than is the case with any of Ihimaera's other patriarchal tyrants. He is a brutal bully, manifest, for example, when he punishes Simeon for not wanting to eat his meal by lifting him up by the scruff of his neck, pulling him into the kitchen, and plunging his head into a pot of *puha* and mashed potatoes, saying 'You're getting too big for your boots, Himiona.'[2] He constantly tries to force Simeon to conform to his conception of masculinity by telling him he needs to get his hair cut, an exhortation that is turned into a violent reality when, as a punishment for Simeon's having gone to see *Twenty Thousand Leagues under the Sea* with a Pākehā friend, Tamihana forces Joshua to cut his son's hair, then seizes the shears to cut it still shorter, drawing blood. The intention of this degrading action is to humiliate his grandson, a humiliation that Simeon feels acutely: 'It was the shame more than anything else. All I had done was allow a Pakeha to befriend me. In so doing I had transgressed some implacable law of Grandfather's. I was being punished.' Tamihana's real motive is revealed shortly after in his words: 'Whakahihi, Simeon, *Whakahihi*. You're getting too big for your boots. Maybe this will teach you where your place is.'[3] Tamihana's violence extends even to his own wife, Ramona, whom he wallops like 'a demented animal,' in a manner reminiscent of Jake in *Once Were Warriors*, just as he kicks Simeon 'in the side of the head, the kidneys and the back,' until his grandmother is moved to defend her grandson by hitting her husband over the head with the butt of a rifle.[4]

Most of all, Ihimaera's characterization of the patriarch is as someone who is deeply ignorant. He disapproves of Simeon reading books altogether: 'The best education is right here ... This is where your world is.'[5] When Simeon gains a prize at his school's prize-giving ceremony, he is viewed as humiliating the *whānau*:

> I was being embarrassing. Becoming more Pakeha and less Maori somehow, because being Maori meant being dumb, always coming last and not caring about it because everybody else was dumb or last too. Or, as my Grandfather would say, becoming whakahihi [i.e. vain, arrogant, proud]. Too big for my boots. Not staying in my place.[6]

Tamihana's attempts to suppress the learning that he fears might give his grandson an advantage over him culminate when Simeon contradicts his grandfather's biblically based view of human evolution, in response to which Tamihana burns his grandson's biology book, an action that exposes to Simeon the elder's secret: 'I had discovered Grandfather Tamihana's weakness. He feared anything that would destroy his world.'[7] Tamihana, in other words, represents an older generation that cannot keep pace with the changes in an evolving world that invites members of the younger generation to entertain a new kind of awareness of themselves, and, along with that, new aspirations. As Ihimaera would have one of his characters say in a later novel, *The Rope of Man* (Auckland: Reed, 2005), 'We wanted to live our own dreams and they were not the dreams of our parents.'[8]

The Relationship between the Source Novel and the Film

Ostensibly, the story presented in *Mahana* is the same as that in *Bulibasha*, but closer inspection reveals that there are very considerable, although not immediately obvious, differences. Many of the differences result from the need to condense the material into a screenplay that could be narrated cinematically within two hours. As the Scottish screenwriter John Collee, chosen by the producer Robin Scholes to write the script for the movie, says, 'In a book like Bulibasha, there was a huge amount of material, and Witi writes in this very free style, often quite unstructured. There's multiple characters and vast sprawling family that takes place over a fair period of time. An adapter needs to pare it down to what they believe is the central story.'[9] And pare it down Collee did – very drastically. In the novel, there are many scenes describing the activities of the members of the Mahana family, especially those in which they compete for pre-eminence over the Poatas, their rivals. These contests mostly take place on the sports field, as when the Mahana women's hockey team plays the Poata women from Hukareka to a draw, or the Mahana men beat the Poata men in a rugby game. There is a description of how, in earlier times, Tamihana and Rupeni Poata broke into 'gladiatorial fights' on the rugby field that were so violent that one of them left Tamihana with a permanently injured leg.[10] In addition, the rivalry between the two families extends even into cultural competitions and local politics, and there are no fewer than three occasions on which cars from the two families race each other to be the first to cross a one-lane bridge. There is even a scene in which Rupeni Poata and Tamihana, their cars having met on the bridge, get out and face each other like the gunslingers in *Gunfight at the OK Corral*.[11] All of these incidents are collapsed into just one car race, while the competitions on the sports field are reduced to just one competition, the Golden Shears shearing contest.

Another episode that is important in the novel, but which Collee omitted, was that in which Tamihana is visited by a blond, blue-eyed Mormon missionary who looks 'like Jesus in a cotton suit,' and succeeds in converting him, which initiates a further conflict with those families in the valley who adhere to the Ringatu religion.[12] Ihimaera uses magical realism to describe this encounter, presenting it as a wrestling match in which Tamihana is supernaturally deprived of his physical strength, which convinces him that the man is an angel. Instead of including this episode, which Collee admitted would have been 'incredibly filmic,' the story they ended up telling 'was much more about the practicalities of life on a farm, sheep shearing, scrub cutting, and so forth.'[13]

This suppression of the element of magic realism and fantasy that is characteristic of Ihimaera's *Bulibasha*, as it had been in *The Whale Rider*, is symptomatic of the movie's approach as a whole. It is seen again in the way that the scriptwriter omits almost all of the references to movies of the 1950s that pepper Ihimaera's narrative, and which indicate the life of the imagination that Simeon inhabits, as well as the parallels he makes between events in his own life and these movies in fantasy. In the novel, for example, Poppy Poata, the girl of Simeon's dreams, is likened to Rhonda Fleming as Cleopatra in *Serpent of the Nile* (William Castle, 1953), while the fights between Tamihana and Rupeni Poata on the rugby field are like the fights in *Hercules Unchained*

(Pietro Francisci, 1959). The Mahana women are compared variously to *Siren of Baghdad* (Richard Quine, 1953) and the army led by the man-hating Amanda Blake in *The Adventures of Hajji Baba* (Don Weis, 1954), while the racing shearers in the Golden Fleece competition (named less fancifully the 'Golden Fleece competition' in the film) are likened to Glenn Ford in *The Fastest Gun Alive* (Russell Rouse, 1956) and Gary Cooper in *High Noon* (Fred Zinnemann, 1952). The range of films that Simeon invokes in his imagination, in fact, is enormous, including *The Dam Busters* (Michael Anderson, 1955), *Rebel without a Cause* (Nicholas Ray, 1955), *The Ten Commandments* (Cecil B. DeMille, 1956), *A Connecticut Yankee in King Arthur's Court* (Tay Garnett, 1949), *River of No Return* (Otto Preminger, 1954), and *West Side Story* (Jerome Robbins/Robert Wise, 1961), among others. In Tamahori's adaptation of *Bulibasha*, the multitude of these references, which in the novel deepen our insight into Simeon's character and emotional life, are replaced by one incident in which the kids go to the cinema to see *3:10 to Yuma* (Delmer Daves, 1957), during which a Māori youth rides his horse down the aisle of the theater, thus setting up the subsequent courtroom scene in which he his tried, together with references to several religious films which Simeon implies Tamihana must have seen (attesting to the old man's hypocrisy in forbidding the young people to attend the Potutahi Cinema), a fleeting reference to a line spoken by John Wayne in *Red River* (Howard Hawks, 1948), and an anticipation at the end of the movie that Simeon and Poppy will go on a date to see Elvis Presley in *Flaming Star* (Don Siegel, 1960). The range of references to movies in the novel is thus greatly reduced to suit the conception (as a western) and more realistic approach of Tamahori's film.

Another aspect of Simeon's character Collee downplays is the very close bond he has with his grandmother, Ramona. In Ihimaera's novel, this closeness is manifest in the way Ramona and Simeon protect each other. On the occasion where Tamihana, having viciously beaten Ramona, begins to beat Simeon, his grandmother intervenes by felling him with a blow to the head, and at the end of the film, Simeon falsifies the result of a vote taken by family members, thus making it possible for Ramona to leave and join her true love, Rupeni Poata. The nature of the bond between grandmother and grandson in this work replicates that between Riripeti and her grandson Tamatea in another of Ihimaera's novels, *The Matriarch*, and in both cases it helps to establish the existence of an empathic feminine dimension in the grandson's personality that helps to explain why he feels discomfort at the expectation he will conform himself to the traditional Māori ideal of masculinity. This dimension in Simeon's character is completely missing from the film.

Finally, apart from narrowing the scope of the movie so that it focuses more exclusively on the coming-of-age story, Collee's scriptwriting changes also allowed him to emphasize another theme he detected in *Bulibasha*:

It's ostensibly a coming-of-age story about a young boy and his struggles with his grandfather, but on a deeper level it's about the contest between male and female power in these big patriarchal societies. And you discover that as the story evolves, but Simeon is really a conduit for the power of women in the two tribes.[14]

In foregrounding this theme, Collee was serving the intentions of Robin Scholes, the producer, who had recruited Lee Tamahori to direct *Mahana*, just as she had brought *Once Were Warriors* to his attention twenty-two years earlier. The theme of women standing up to tyrannical men and discovering their own self-empowerment in the process is the same in each case, being a theme close to Scholes' own heart. As she says: 'Everything that I'm attracted to is about reinvention, redemption – the ability to take something really bad and turn it into something good. This story has it in spades. It's all about the human ability to live with things that have gone wrong.'[15]

Tamahori's Generic Conversion of *Bulibasha* into *Mahana*

The reduction and telescoping of material to which the screenwriter subjected *Bulibasha* so as to give it the unity and focus required of a feature film meshed with the director's formal and stylistic intentions to change the story into something that was rather different from the one represented in the novel. In turn, this had an effect on the nature of the coming-of-age experience that the film depicts.

In Tamahori's view, the film was essentially 'the coming-of-age story of a young man acquiring manhood,' which is signaled by a shot at the end of the movie in which Simeon (Akuhata Keefe) gazes romantically at Poppy (Yvonne Porter), who has just asked him if he would like to go to see a movie with her – an action that foreshadows the formation of the future couple that they will make – to which Simeon answers, 'Sure!'

In addition to this paring down of Ihimaera's broader treatment, Tamahori was also concerned to draw upon the conventions of the American western in order to tell this story, the appeal of which resided in 'its extremely simple moral code and its great landscape structure':

> ... westerns are my favourite genre. Mahana is shot like a western, specifically a 1950s American western. I've always loved the western because it's like a simple morality play, laid out in a way that a child who didn't know the difference between right and wrong could watch it, and see exactly who is right and who is wrong.[16]

The simplicity of this moral vision perfectly matched the type of paring-down of the original for which Collee was aiming in his screenplay. Furthermore, the

Figure 16.1 Simeon (Akuhata Keefe) and Poppy (Yvonne Porter) decide to go on a date together in *Mahana* (dir. Lee Tamahori, 2016).

western genre gave Tamahori a pretext for achieving a long-held ambition, as he confessed to Kim Hill in a radio interview: 'I've always wanted to shoot a film here in New Zealand on an anamorphic widescreen format and put the landscape up large and centre like a lot of westerns I've seen.'[17] In addition, Tamahori felt that the incorporation of elements from the western would be thematically appropriate, given that 'New Zealand Maori in the 1950s loved US westerns. They loved to go and watch them because they were all farmers, and rode horses, and loved to wear western hats and pretend they were cowboys. I wanted to get a touch of that across in this film.'[18]

Accordingly, the director decided to take the generational story as pared down by Collee and 'infuse it with the classic set-pieces from the American western.'[19] Such set-pieces regularly recur in *Mahana*, both in the form of certain types of shot that are characteristic of the western, and also of new scenes that Tamahori added to supplement those he drew from the novel. The episode in which a Māori youth rides his horse into a cinema where *3:10 to Yuma* is screening, for example, has already been mentioned. The director includes this scene not just because Delmer Daves' 1957 film is one of Tamahori's favorite movies, but also because the clips from this western shown on the screen during *Mahana* provide a *mise-en-abyme*, or mirror reflection, of a number of the shots, motifs, and encounters that constitute some of the 'set-pieces' from the genre that Tamahori introduced into his own film: open landscapes with mountainous backdrops, low-angle shots of men in stetson hats, a scene set on a verandah, a conversation with a character sitting on a bed, and men on horseback riding through the town. The event also precipitates the eruption of a brawl of the type that one frequently sees in American westerns.

Similar western tropes are dispersed throughout *Mahana*, including shots of

Figure 16.2 Disruption during a screening at the cinema in *Mahana* (dir. Lee Tamahori, 2016).

solitary riders on horseback silhouetted against the skyline on a hill, as when Simeon takes meat to one of the Mahana crews working on a nearby farm, or when Tamihana (Temuera Morrison) gazes down on Joshua (Regan Taylor) and Simeon as they are working to restore the derelict farm Ramona (Nancy Brunning) has given her son. The shot of the farmhouse itself is a classic one, recalling many such scenes in westerns that show pioneers in the act of building a homestead. And providing the backdrop for all of this, of course, is the feud between two neighboring 'ranchers,' each headed by a patriarch, which is reminiscent of countless such feuds in westerns, the only real difference being that in this case sheep are substituted for cows, as befits the more verdant pastoral context of New Zealand.

The Effects of Generic Simplification on the Coming-of-age Representation

The reduction of Ihimaera's more complex and variegated narrative so as to make it conform to the moral simplicities of the western genre, which Tamahori viewed as being like a 'morality play' revolving around the difference between right and wrong, had the effect of flattening out the character of Simeon. Because Ihimaera's *Bulibasha* is narrated from Simeon's first-person point of view, we see him from the inside, not the outside, and what we see is far more complex than the impression we get of his character from the film. In the novel, we are allowed an insight into Simeon's sense of inferiority: he believes he is 'not handsome,' and through his association with his Pākehā friend Geordie, who also likes books, is made to feel he is a 'sissy': 'in those days you could be a sissy just by liking a picture by a famous artist or classical music or ballet dancing.'[20] This aesthetic, sensitive side to Simeon is almost completely eliminated from the cinematic adaptation, and the omission of the scene where Tamihana burns his biology book also leads to a downplaying of his bookish intellectual curiosity.

One crucial scene in the novel that underlines Simeon's sensitivity – a scene omitted from the film – is the episode in which Tamihana forces Joshua to cut his son's hair, and then seizes the shears to cut it still shorter. This act of violence is also an act of ritual humiliation because it constitutes an indirect form of emasculation, and Simeon experiences it as such: '"Not like this, Dad," I pleaded. "Please. Not in front of everybody." . . . It was the shame more than anything else.'[21] Given his sensibility and his aspirations, Simeon, in Ihimaera's realization, understands that Tamihana's action in forcing his father to cut his hair is a denial of the validity of his very identity as a person, made worse by his own father's unwillingness to stand up for him at that point. Indeed, Simeon in the novel is a prototype of the male protagonists in Ihimaera's later fiction, such as David in *Nights in the Gardens of Spain* (1995), or Michael in *The Uncle's Story* (2000), who would come out as gay, like Ihimaera in real life, but in Tamahori's adaptation there is no allowance for this possibility.

A further aspect of Simeon's character that is occluded in the film is his awareness that other members of his family carry a certain sense of shame at being Māori, revealed in their mockery of him for being 'a brainbox.' Ihimaera's Simeon is determined to refute this assumption, which is why he persists in pursuing his education, to the extent of being willing to sit the School Certificate exams twice in order to gain that qualification. In the film, all of those feelings, and all of that determined effort, are omitted; instead, Tamahori's Simeon is turned into someone who simply attains masculine prowess and competence as he grows up, manifest in the way he stands up to his grandfather, to the extent of physically threatening him, and, most clearly, in the initiative he takes to register a shearing gang in the Golden Shears competition, subsequently playing a crucial role himself as a shearer in the competition in order to make it win by defeating the Poatas, who have already defeated the grandfather's gang. Simeon thus ends up being extolled as superior in terms of the very qualities of shrewdness, determination, and physical prowess that had made his grandfather pre-eminent, which means that he simply displaces and supplants him, rather than representing a new type of man in a new order of things, as he does in Ihimaera's version of the story. In the novel, Simeon's victory is moral and political, rather than literally achieved through physical means.

Cumulatively, these changes to the characterization of Simeon turn him into a different kind of youth altogether. In Ihimaera's novel, what he is standing up for, and why he rebels against his grandfather, is his need to claim a space in which he can be the true self that he is discovering himself to be, and in which he can realize his personal potential and ambitions. In the filmic adaptation,

Figure 16.3 Simeon (Akuhata Keefe) stands up to Tamihana, his grandfather (Temuera Morrison), while his father Joshua (Regan Taylor) stands by in *Mahana* (dir. Lee Tamahori, 2016).

Simeon seems like an adolescent who simply resents being ordered about by a tyrannical authority figure, and he spends much of the movie behaving, and looking, like a sullen, lippy teenager. Both visions – that of the film and that of the novel – have their own validity, but it would be wrong to assume that the film merely replicates that of the novel.

The Question of the Film's Cultural Authenticity

Peter Debruge, the chief film critic for *Variety*, has praised *Mahana* for its 'incredible cultural specificity,' which he sees as being admirably blended with 'Tamahori's internationally accessible storytelling style.'[22] These comments are revealing, as they indicate the aspects of the film that were calculated to elicit a favorable response from the international audience that *Mahana* undoubtedly hoped to reach. Debruge's judgment contrasts radically with his condemnation of Taika Waititi's *Boy*, which he had considered a 'let-down' because, Debruge believed, Waititi had 'scrubbed away all culturally specific traits from his growing-up-Kiwi comedy.'[23] The sharp divergence in Debruge's respective appraisals of these two Māori films raises questions, especially considering that many Māori themselves quickly identified with the experience represented in Waititi's film.

What Debruge's contrasting evaluations point to is the difference between a Māori film that exploits outward markers of cultural difference while proceeding in other respects in accordance with a non-indigenous approach, and a film that does not merely observe *tikanga Māori*, but adopts an approach and ethos that is consistent with *kaupapa Māori* as characterized by Barry Barclay in *Our Own Image*, a treatise in which he expounds his theory of a 'fourth cinema.'[24]

A comparison of *Mahana* with Merata Mita's *Mauri*, for example, brings the difference into stark contrast. Whereas *Mauri* is invested with a pervasive sense of the interconnection between the world of present human reality and the natural world on one hand, and the spiritual world on the other, together with a sense of the past in the present and the present in the future, no deep sense of these interconnections is conveyed in *Mahana*. Instead, as the scriptwriter John Collee says, what is at issue is 'how you graft on new values to an old system of belief and tradition, without destroying the tradition.'[25] The key expression here is 'graft on,' which implies a principle of superimposition, rather than a sense of cultural values that are interfused through the very ways that Māori characters think, feel, and see. Furthermore, Tamahori himself seems to subscribe to this approach, as he revealed in an interview with Helen Barlow: 'Any writer can write for any culture if they understand the story they are telling. In any case Witi's book provided all the frames of reference and he had myself, the actors and Witi to keep him on track with the cultural aspects of the story'[26] – a statement with which one can never imagine earlier Māori filmmakers like Barry Barclay or Merata Mita ever agreeing.

Again, the metaphor of a 'frame of reference,' like that of 'grafting on,' implies a relationship of contiguity rather than of fusion between the cultural ethos of the film and its formal aspects. Indeed, this is exactly what one finds in *Mahana*. The producers were careful to enlist cultural advisers to provide guidance on Māori cultural practices and the Māori language, and these are scrupulously observed and correct. But that does not obviate the fact that the whole generic form and style of the movie is taken from another, alien, culture, resulting in an inescapable kind of hybridity. The effect is to present a coming-of-age story that is universalized, rather than being culturally specific, which is why, it seems, an American critic like Debruge liked the film, whereas he had found *Boy* inauthentic.

Mahana as an Indication of Cultural Change

To conclude, I would suggest that *Mahana* as a film reflects a cultural transition (or perhaps, more accurately, an 'evolution') that is characteristic of a trend in Māori filmmaking generally, and which is mirrored in Tamahori's own personal itinerary. Tamahori was born and raised in Wellington, and thus was formed by urban circumstances in a world dominated by Pākehā values, like many other Māori whose families migrated from their rural homelands into the cities after the Second World War. Following the success of *Once Were Warriors*, Tamahori's first feature film, which reflected the downside of that urban experience, the director relocated to the United States where he made a series of genre films for Hollywood – mainly action movies. *Mahana* marks not only Tamahori's return to New Zealand, but it is also, in his words, 'a nostalgia piece.'[27] In other words, it is a revisiting of a world that is in the past, and the form and procedure of the movie reflects exactly that: in outward appearance, it has the external trappings of Māori life as it was lived in rural settings during the 1950s, but in terms of its generic composition and animating ethos, it represents a new order of things informed by a non-indigenous, globalized culture. As such, it points in the direction that Ihimaera was heading in the fiction he himself would write after Bulibasha, especially in *The Rope of Man* (2005), in which his protagonist, Tama, wishes to escape 'not just from Dad's prohibitions, but also from the overlay of his traditional Maori values . . . I want to make it in the Pakeha World now.'[28]

Both Ihimaera in his novels and Tamahori in this film, then, attest to winds of cultural change that influence the coming-of-age experience of their protagonists. Some indication of where that process might be leading is suggested in the next Māori coming-of-age movie to be released, *The Hunt for the Wilderpeople*, which will be discussed in the next chapter.

Notes

1. For a fuller discussion, see Fox, *The Ship of Dreams*, Chapter 9, 'The Dilemma of the Māori New Man: Inter-generational Conflict in Witi Ihimaera's *The Matriarch*, *Bulibasha*, *The Whale Rider*, and *The Uncle's Story*,' 153–69.
2. Witi Ihimaera, *Bulibasha, King of the Gypsies* (Auckland: Penguin, 1994), 60.
3. Ibid., 126–7.
4. Ibid., 134–5.
5. Ibid., 56.
6. Ibid., 69.
7. Ibid., 157.
8. Witi Ihimaera, *The Rope of Man* (Auckland: Reed, 2005), 222.
9. Liam Maguren, 'Interview: How the Hell Did 'Mahana' get an Oscar-nominated screenwriter?,' *Flicks*, 19 February 2016, http://www.flicks.co.nz/blog/amazing-interviews/interview-how-the-hell-did-mahana-get-an-oscar-nominated-screenwriter/, accessed 9 August 2016.
10. Ihimaera, Bulibasha, 108–9.
11. Ibid., 65.
12. Ibid., 43–5.
13. Maguren, 'Interview.'
14. Ibid.
15. Frances Morton, 'People to Watch this Month: Robin Scholes, Producer,' *Metro*, 1 March 2016, http://www.metromag.co.nz/city-life/people-to-watch-this-month-robin-scholes-producers/, accessed 15 August 2016.
16. Oliver Johnston, 'Mahana (The Patriarch): An Interview with Lee Tamahori and his cast,' *The Upcoming*, 16 February 2016, http://www.theupcoming.co.uk/2016/02/16/berlin-film-festival-2016-mahana-the-patriarch-an-interview-with-lee-tamahori-and-his-cast/, accessed 9 August 2016.
17. Kim Hill, 'Tamahori's back home – to film westerns' [interview], Radio New Zealand, 27 February 2016.
18. Johnston, 'Mahana.'
19. Glen Falkenstein, 'Director Lee Tamahori and Cast Temuera Morrison and

Akuhata Keefe talk Mahana,' *FalkenScreen*, 12 June 2016, https://falkenscreen.com/2016/06/12/director-lee-tamahori-and-cast-temuera-morrison-and-akuhata-keefe-talk-mahana/, accessed 15 August 2016.
20. Ihimaera, *Bulibasha*, 103.
21. Ibid., 126.
22. Peter Debruge, *Variety*, 13 February 2016, http://variety.com/2016/film/reviews/the-patriarch-mahana-film-review-berlin-1201705208/, accessed 15 August 2016.
23. Peter Debruge, 'Review: "Boy",' *Variety*, 23 January 2010.
24. Barry Barclay, *Our Own Image: A Story of a Māori Filmmaker* (Minneapolis and London: University of Minnesota Press, 2015 [1990]).
25. Maguren, 'Interview.'
26. Barlow, 'Mahana.'
27. Ibid.
28. Ihimaera, *The Rope of Man*, 125.

17. DELINQUENCY AND BICULTURAL RELATIONS: *HUNT FOR THE WILDERPEOPLE* (TAIKA WAITITI, 2016)

Shortly after *Mahana*, a second major coming-of-age film was released in the same year, Taika Waititi's *Hunt for the Wilderpeople* (2016), and, like Waititi's earlier exercise in the genre, *Boy* (2010), quickly smashed all previous box office records. Not only has *Hunt for the Wilderpeople* become New Zealand's highest-grossing film to date, but it has also been universally well received by critics, both in New Zealand and abroad, where it has played on the international film festival circuit. Within the context of New Zealand coming-of-age films, it marks a new phase in the evolution of the genre in that a version of the generic model is used as a symbolic paradigm for exploring the dynamics of race-relations between Māori and Pākehā as they advance into the twenty-first century under the influence of biculturalism, which has been sponsored as a state ideology by successive governments since the 1980s.

Hunt for the Wilderpeople tackles much the same theme as *Boy* – the longing of a young teenage Māori boy to find love and acceptance – and adopts the same expressive mode, which is to take material that is intrinsically dark and disturbing and to overlay it with surface humor and a comedic treatment. Waititi also draws heavily on popular youth culture, presenting his adolescent hero as a devotee of hip hop, just as Boy in *Boy* is a fan of Michael Jackson, and includes frequent allusions to popular films, especially New Zealand hits from the late 1970s and 1980s such as *Sleeping Dogs* (1977), *Smash Palace* (Roger Donaldson, 1981), and *Came a Hot Friday* (1985), as well as international hits like *Scarface* (Brian De Palma, 1983), *Thelma and Louise* (Ridley Scott, 1991), and *Lord of the Rings* (Peter Jackson, 2001–3). There is a major difference between *Boy* and *Hunt for the Wilderpeople*, however, in that, unlike *Boy*, the later film is an adaptation. That in itself would not be exceptional were it not for the fact that Waititi treats the source in such a way as fundamentally to change its nature, and in so doing to reshape it in order to make it serve an entirely new purpose. To put it succinctly, whereas the source novel, Barry Crump's *Wild Pork and Watercress* (1986), is a bushman's yarn celebrating the episodic adventures of two odd-couple outsiders who join together to turn their backs on society for the sake of enjoying the freedom that a subsistence life in the bush affords them, Waititi's film converts the basic story into a more conventional coming-of-age narrative involving a rite of passage that exemplifies how an adolescent boy is rescued from delinquency by developing a sense of true values so that he can be reintegrated into society with the prospect of a happy life. The nature of the reshaping of the work is reminiscent of the process in Tamahori's *Mahana* described in the previous chapter, although Waititi's stylistic mode and vision are substantially different. In order to understand the fundamental difference between these two versions of the story, one needs to reconstruct the transformations that occurred in the process of the adaptation.

Barry Crump: A Kiwi Icon

The novel Waititi chose to adapt, *Wild Pork and Watercress*, is inseparable in its subject matter and mode from its author, Barry Crump (1935–96) who, from the 1960s through the 1980s, became a household name in New Zealand on account of his bestselling books, such as *A Good Keen Man* (1960) and *Hang on a Minute Mate* (1961), which sold copies in their hundreds of thousands, and then a series of TV advertisements featuring Crump as a rugged outdoors man driving a Toyota Hilux that turned him into a popular, iconic hero. As a writer, Crump was 'a highly skilled practitioner in the genre of the literary yarn, a mode of male writing with a long history from colonial times,' that 'captured the feel of the idiom of the "ordinary bloke".'[1] His novels revolve around the same basic plot, in which a male narrator finds life in the cities stultifying and, valuing his freedom and independence, takes off into the bush to live a Man Alone existence that shows him to be resourceful, learning to live by his own wits in close harmony with nature, where he encounters a range of colorful types as one episode advances on to the next.

Crump's works always have a strong autobiographical cast. Indeed, his love of the bush and his compulsive need to retreat into it were a reaction to a disturbing childhood. As Crump admitted in a revealing interview, 'It was a real nuisance too, because I'd be working on a farm or something when I was a boy and I'd head for the hills and I wouldn't come back – I'd just have to go up there.' When he was about fourteen or fifteen, he says, he went into the bush and 'didn't come out for the next 12 or 15 years.'² Crump's younger sister tells us why: their father, Wally, was an extremely violent man who would physically abuse his children. When the young Barry knocked over a teapot on the table, which burnt his sister Carol, his father dragged him into the bathroom and held his head under the hot water tap. At times, Barry was beaten within an inch of his life – 'literally flogged until he could no longer move.' After one such occasion, his sister recalls, 'some time during the night Barry dragged himself under the house ... and for three or four days I would just take him food, until he was strong enough to come out.'³

For Crump, therefore, withdrawal into the bush was a means of emotional self-protection, as if the bush functioned for him like the embrace of a protective mother. Hence, in adulthood, he worked as a bush worker in the Kaimanawa forest and South Westland during the 1950s, and from 1952 served as a government deer culler in the Urewera region, where *Wild Pork and Watercress* is set. Predictably, given his disturbed family background, his personal life was a troubled one: he was married five times and involved in numerous liaisons, from which he had many children by different mothers. His relationships were short-lived and violent, and Crump himself confessed that he never stayed anywhere for longer than three months.⁴ By his own admission, he had a loathing of domesticity, preferring the comparative simplicity of life in the outdoors to the complexity of relationships – at least that was the persona he projected, with his trademark bush man's swandri (a woollen tunic-like overgarment popular with hunters and farmhands) and felt musterer's hat, and the colloquial vernacular drawl he affected in his television and public appearances.

Wild Pork and Watercress derives out of, and reflects, his personal experience, the legacy of which inflects the dynamics that drive, and the events that shape, the fable. Crump's son, Martin, who never lived with his father but met him on various occasions, describes an event that attests to the pretext for the novel. Arriving at a rendezvous to meet his father, Martin recounts how he was surprised that 'his [Crump's] sidekick this time was not a woman but a nine-year-old Maori boy called Coonch. They were very relaxed and comfortable with each other, which is more than I can say for the old man and me; we were meeting for the first time in years.' The next day, the three of them traveled to Crump's place at Opotiki, with the nine-year-old driving while Crump sat in the passenger seat, though 'it wasn't legal or ethical.'⁵ Martin was not surprised to find that about a year later Crump had published a new book 'about a grumpy middle-aged white guy and a young Maori boy who have a wonderful adventure.'⁶ The autobiographical roots of this story are reflected in one of the final sequences in Waititi's film that shows Ricky driving a red Hilux during their flight from the special forces in a simulation of Crump's famous TV advertisement, just as the young Māori boy had driven Crump's vehicle in real life.

One further sign of the autobiographical links between Crump and the film occurs during the first shot of Hec (Sam Neill), which shows him carrying an immense pig on his back, imitating an iconic image of Barry Crump similarly carting a boar on his back.[7] By including this visual allusion, Waititi was not merely indulging a joke, but also indicating his sensitivity to the subtext of Crump's storytelling impulse, which is reflected in the story of a Māori boy who feels unwanted and similarly has a craving for a surrogate father and a context that leaves him feeling secure. Indeed, in both the novel and the film, at a climactic moment in the plot of each, the boar becomes a powerful symbol of a menacing and hostile (male) force in the external environment that threatens the two protagonists with what they value most. In the novel, a large boar rips Ricky's dog Willy with his tusks, flings him, and breaks his neck, thus depriving the boy of 'the only thing I ever had of my own.'[8] This episode is recreated in the film, but with a subtle twist: in Waititi's version, it is Hec's dog Zag that is killed, not Ricky's, and it is Ricky who shoots the boar dead, thus saving the life of his uncle, who was about to be gored. In both versions, however, the boar represents a malevolent force associated with masculine brutality that has to be killed before either Hec or Ricky can move on to live a happy life, and behind this emblematic symbol one senses the motivating presence of a violent and abusive father.

Figure 17.1 Barry Crump carrying a pig on his back in the television documentary *Crump* (dir. Michelle Bracey, 1999).

Figure 17.2   Hec (Sam Neill) carrying a pig on his back in *Hunt for the Wilderpeople* (dir. Taika Waititi, 2016).

Wild Pork and Watercress: An Iconoclast's Tale

The nature of the real-life relationship between his father and a Māori boy to which Crump's son attests points to the fundamental difference between the novel and Waititi's film. In *Wild Pork and Watercress*, Ricky, the boy, and Hector, the man in whose household he has been placed by Social Welfare, are never in a hostile relationship with one another; to the contrary, they are in league, because both feel they are misfits.

Ricky, the narrator, tells us that he 'always had trouble fitting in,' being sensitive about the fact that his skin is darker than that of his brother and sister, that he is 'a bit overweight and not much good at sports and stuff like that.'[9] He comes from a broken home. His mother is quarter-Māori, and his parents are divorced, with nobody seeming to know exactly where his father is living. In response to this dysfunctional family life, Ricky slides into increasing delinquency until his mother can no longer handle him and he is placed in a home for delinquent boys. When his mother remarries, his stepfather does not like him being around, and Ricky is again placed in a Social Welfare home for stealing, before joining a bunch of kids who live in a burnt-out bus in Taupo and live off stealing. Finally, he is locked up in a real prison before being given once last chance when his Uncle Hector and Aunt Bella take him into foster-ship on a trial basis. Ricky is warmly received by both of them: Hec does not care about his Māori skin, and Bella shows him affection: 'Being accepted by both of them in that kind of way was so good it got scary at times – almost like fitting in.'[10]

This is a very different situation from that presented in the film, largely because Hec is given a different relationship to the boy. Crump's Hec, while not 'exactly overwhelmed with joy' about having Ricky living in house, does not dislike him to the extent that Hec in Waititi's version does; to the contrary, Crump's Hec feels a common bond with Ricky as an outsider. His past history shows him to have been anti-social, just like Ricky, having been in prison for 'something disgraceful' in his youth, and having received a heavy fine in later life for having cut down an electricity company's power poles with his chainsaw after a dispute.[11] Like Crump himself, in earlier times Hec has also lived a Crocodile Dundee-type of existence in the outback of northern Australia, where he learnt much of his bushcraft from an old aboriginal lady.[12] His reasons, too, for leaving the farm after Bella's death are very different from those in the film: in the novel, his two brothers Wilf and Humphrey and his sister Daphne have decided to sell the farm, which is a family property, in order to split the money, meaning that Hec, like Ricky, will have nowhere to live and is effectually dispossessed. Rather than facing the prospect of living in a single unit in town, Hec prefers to take to the scrub.[13] Reluctantly at first, he eventually agrees to take Ricky with him.

Thereafter, the novel consists of an episodic series of adventures in which the pair exercise their survival skills. These involve using their ingenuity to procure food, as when Hec catches and cooks a trout baked in clay, stuffed with watercress and wineberry, or when Ricky kicks a big eel out of the shallows of a stream, quite apart from their regular diet of wild pigs. They also have to survive natural hazards: for example, an enveloping wave of water that suddenly sweeps down a valley when a dam caused by a slip gives way, or a big earthquake that dislodges rocks from a bluff above them, or when Ricky is swept off his feet while crossing a flooded river. On the bright side of things, they experience the delights of nature, such as the native birds in which Ricky takes a great interest, including a *huia* they see, a native bird thought to be extinct since its last confirmed sighting in the Tararua Ranges in 1907. The rest of their time is spent evading searchers with the assistance of Rob Barton, a farmer in a remote valley who, having come across their base camp, befriends them and buys them supplies and a radio. By the end of the novel, after the pair have spent nineteen months in the bush, Ricky feels that he has had a transformative experience. He is now thin, having shed a lot of his fat, and is fit and healthy. More than that, living in the bush had taught him something other people never could have done:

> It'd taught me how to stick to rules that weren't my rules, just like everything else had to. In fact I was beginning to see how it all works. The rock gives in to the vegetable kingdom. The vegetable world takes from the mineral and gives up itself to the animal world. And then me, human beings, people – the last in the whole arrangement. But I could only take advantage of my place in it by sticking to the rules, and to step out of line could get me killed. It taught you respect, realising a thing like that. It might be the same with everything, for all I know, and just go on forever.[14]

Eventually, having acquired this sum of wisdom, Ricky decides that he wants to quit and, in a reversal of his plea at the beginning of the novel, persuades the reluctant Hec to leave the bush with him. In an Epitaph written by Robby Barton, the farmer who helped them, we are told that this return to society was not a permanent one. After Ricky spent five months in a welfare home until he turned fifteen, and Hec had received a suspended nine-month sentence, paid a $1,000 fine, and been put on a good-behavior bond, the two of them had returned to the bush, to photograph the *huia*, at which point they disappeared. Robby surmises that they are still out there in the Urewera bush, 'two ragged skeletons lying at the bottom of some bluffs, somewhere along the Huiarau Range.'[15]

The fantasy that Crump's novel symbolically figures forth is one of avoidance and escape, in which the outsider-as-outlaw is romanticized, eventuating in a kind of repetition-compulsion enacted by the fictional duo, just as Crump continually did in real life. This is why the ending of the novel is so indeterminate, with the narrator hoping that Ricky and his uncle *are* okay: 'Still sticking it out together and handling their own hassles in their own way.'[16] The possibility that they are simply two skeletons lying at the foot of a bluff, however, generates a tension between a wish-fulfillment fantasy entailed in the escapist dream and a fear that it may actually offer no permanent solution to life's 'hassles' in real life.

Taika Waititi's Changes to the Source

In adapting *Wild Pork and Watercress* for the screen, Waititi radically altered the tone and character of the original work. As he puts it, the novel is not funny: 'At the end of the book, they disappear and it turns out they die out in the bush. You don't want to do that. You don't want this story to go somewhere like that.' His earlier drafts of the film, however, upon which he had been working as early as 2005, were also very dark: 'I guess I had embraced the dark tone of the book.'[17] At some point, Waititi subsequently decided to lighten the tone and give the story a new focus, and to do that he added elements to emphasize the nature of the narrative as a fantasy:

> The script is really fantasy come true. The idea of a kid who just really wants a family. All he wants is people to love him. To get that, he's pushed to do things where the entire country wants him. The police want him. The army wants him. Everyone wants him. Because the idea of that is so dark. The idea of a foster kid who has never really found a home. You don't want to make that too heavy.[18]

Instead of being a fantasy of avoidance and escape, as it had been in Crump's version, Waititi's reworked version transformed it into a fantasy of rehabilitation and acceptance, in which both Ricky (Julian Dennison) and Hec (Sam Neill) end up attaining the love and security within the embrace of a benevolent family for which they have always longed, even though, as the film shows, neither of them had ever consciously acknowledged that fact.

To achieve this transformation, Waititi adopted a number of strategies. First, he streamlined the plot to turn it from a slow-moving episodic structure into 'a short, sharp, exciting journey.'[19] This meant eliminating extraneous episodes, such as Ricky's encounter with an eight-pointer stag, his near-drowning, their discovery of a hot spring in which they take a bath, their attempt to trap possums to pay Robby for the supplies he brings them, and so on. The result is a fast-moving plot with a very marked three-act structure (initial situation – pursuit in the bush – resolution) that is characteristically cinematic rather than literary, just as *Mahana* is in relation to Ihimaera's *Bulibasha*.

Second, it meant changing the backstories of the main characters, adding new characters, motifs, and incidents. Whereas Bella in the novel was Ricky's actual aunt, the sister of his mother, in the film she no longer has any blood relationship to him. This makes her warm acceptance of him all the more striking – 'You can call me auntie, even though I'm not your real auntie' – and sets up a contrast between her and Hec. When Bella (Rima Te Wiata) says to Ricky, 'You can call him uncle if you like,' Hec interjects emphatically 'No, he can't!' indicating his lack of acceptance, which is markedly different from the reaction of Crump's Hec, to whom the color of Ricky's 'Māori skin' doesn't matter.

Bella's family circumstances are also changed. In the novel, she has a clearly demarked family, including a daughter, Judy, who is a nurse living in Africa.[20] In the film, Bella does not know where she comes from or who her family was, which is why she wanted to take care of a homeless kid like Ricky, and why she was prepared to take on someone like Hec knows himself to be. After their relationship has developed as a result of their shared experience in the bush, Hec also tells Ricky that he and Bella could not have children as a result of his infertility, a confession that reflects his growing bond with the boy: 'You're pretty likeable.'

The changes that Waititi makes to Bella's circumstances establish a parallel between her and Ricky, whose backstory is also altered. In the novel, it was his mother's remarriage after a divorce from his father, who was a drunkard, which was the main cause for his removal from his home, given that his stepfather did not want him around. In the film, it is a cause of grief to Ricky that 'I don't know where my dad is,' and that 'my mum got rid of me when I was little.' There is thus a much stronger sense in the film that Ricky feels he has been completely abandoned, which helps to explain the delinquency graphically depicted in a rapid montage sequence at the beginning of the movie in a chapter titled 'A Real Bad Egg.'

It also explains his longing for love, which is symbolized in the repeated motif of a hot-water bottle: Bella places a red hot-water bottle in his bed on his first night in their house; when Bella dies, Ricky observes the absence of a hot-water bottle in his bed and clutches an empty one to his chest; once he has entered the bush, he tries to replicate the comfort he received by trying to warm water in a hot-water bottle over a fire, only to burst it; and at the end of the movie, when the court has placed him to live with Kahu's family, we once again see him with a hot-water bottle in his bed, this time a green one. The hot-water bottle thus serves as an evocative object for Ricky, functioning as a symbolic stand-in for the emotional affection and nurturing of which he has been deprived for much of his life.

All of the other changes Waititi made to the source emphasize Ricky's status as a misfit who is longing for love and to be part of a family. His grief at his own circumstances is reflected in his empathic identification with his friend Amber, who is now dead, having been put in a foster home where her foster father 'did things to her' that she was too scared to report. Briefly, by introducing an allusion to this event, which is not in Crump's novel, Waititi evokes the sexual abuse within the family that was depicted, for example, in *Once Were Warriors* (1994). Ricky's mention of his friend Amber is more than casual, as he recalls her again later when he expresses skepticism about the motives of the Social Welfare Department that is chasing them: 'They don't care about kids like me. They just keep moving us around until something happens like what happened to Amber.' Here, I think, Waititi is intimating that Amber may have committed suicide as a result of sexual molestation – of the sort to which, as the result of a hilarious misunderstanding, the special forces led by the Social Welfare officer, Paula (Rachel House), believe Hec has been subjecting the boy.

Paula, indeed, is an entirely new character that Waititi introduces into the film in order to highlight the perverted motives and mistaken methods of the Social Welfare system in its efforts to tackle the problem of juvenile delinquency, especially among Māori children. Paula herself is Māori, which is Waititi's way of preventing his representation of the Social Welfare Department being construed in racist terms. Notwithstanding this tactful gesture, however, Waititi's portrayal of this character is devastating in its satiric dismemberment. The mantra that she repeatedly cites – 'No child left behind' – takes on an ironic cast when one sees that she means it literally, to the extent that she is prepared to marshal the combined forces of the police and the army to ensure that Ricky does not elude the clutches of the Social Welfare system. For Paula, conformity to the rules of the system is more important than the actual welfare of the child, as is implied in the metaphors she uses in referring to Ricky: 'He is a spanner in the works. I'm the mechanic who is going to make sure he is put back where he belongs, in the toolbox!' Paula thus becomes, as the representative of a state-run system that does not adequately meet the boy's real needs, the agent of his persecution.

The other important new character introduced into Waititi's version of the story is Kahu (Tioreore Ngatai-Melbourne), a Māori girl Ricky meets on his way to seek help for the sick ranger he and Hec meet in a hut. The addition of Kahu to the story introduces a new romantic element that is important to Waititi's conceptualization of the coming-of-age experience Ricky undergoes. When Kahu takes him to her home, the banter between them recalls that between the boy and the girl in Waititi's early short film *Two Cars, One Night* (2004), and an inserted shot displaying Kahu in an idealized mode lets us know that Ricky, for the first time, is romantically smitten by a girl. More than that, however, the normalcy of the life of Kahu's Māori family, in a well-appointed house, well-stocked with food (which Ricky, given his love of food, appreciates), presents to him an image of an alternative to the kind of life he has been living – both before he ran away with Hec into the bush, and that which he has been enduring in the bush. This new kind of possibility is reinforced when Kahu's father returns to the house and treats Ricky like a hero, to the extent of wanting to have a selfie taken with him. His parting words to Ricky are designed to fill him with pride at being Māori, in contrast with the shame that Ricky has previously harbored as a result of his ethnicity: 'Keep striving – stay Māori, bro!'

The effect of all these changes – along with many others, such as the reversal of roles when Ricky fires a rifle to save Hec from the hunters, when Paula catches up with Ricky in the bush and proposes a deal if he testifies against Hec, and when Ricky produces a box with Bella's ashes so that they can be scattered in a waterfall – is to reshape the thematic aims of the film. In essence, the changes signify that, under the superficial comedy, Waititi is exploring, in his view, 'what the story's really about,'[21] which, in his view, concerns social and personal issues that are particularly pertinent to Māori, but not exclusively so.

Figure 17.3 'Shit just got real!' Ricky (Julian Dennison) saves Hec from the hunters in *Hunt for the Wilderpeople* (dir. Taika Waititi, 2016).

The Cinematic Mode of the Film

Despite the underlying seriousness of its thematic intentions, Waititi subjects the film to a mock-heroic treatment that gives it an entertaining, comic tonality. This comedic treatment involves extra-diegetical inserts, such as the fantasy vision of a hamburger Ricky has as he runs out of food in the bush.

There are also countless verbal gags, such as the rivalrous exchange between Ricky and Paula when she momentarily catches up with him during the manhunt:

> Paula: I'll never stop chasing you. I'm relentless, I'm like The Terminator.
> Ricky: I'm more Terminator than you.
> Paula: I said it first. You're more like Sarah Connor in, the first movie too, before she could do chin-ups.

Humor is similarly generated by the hilarious haiku poems Ricky composes and recites during the movie, counting out the syllables on his fingers, such as the first one, which illustrates his anti-social outlook in his delinquent phase:

> Hemi you wanker,
> You arsehole, I hate you heaps
> Please die soon, in pain.

One of the most important methods Waititi uses to achieve a mock-epic effect is to load the film with cinematic references that deliberately invest it with a manifestly over-the-top quality. *Hunt for the Wilderpeople* is replete with allusions to the films of the New Zealand New Wave made by directors like Roger Donaldson and Geoff Murphy, which Waititi confesses he loves: 'I was like, "I'm going to embrace all of that crazy shit from the '80s, these chase films and manhunt films, all those things".'[22] Thus, the pursuit of Ricky and Hec in the bush is presented in terms that are reminiscent of the manhunt in Roger Donaldson's *Sleeping Dogs*, with helicopters and Special Forces hunting the pair. Additional gags are added by having the same actor, Sam Neill, playing one of the two buddies involved, as he did in the earlier film, except this time he is nearly forty years older, and by having an actual television anchor, John Campbell, present a news item on TV, just as an earlier news announcer of the 1970s, Dougal Stevenson, did in *Sleeping Dogs*. The introduction of the character Psycho Sam (Rhys Darby) similarly serves to recall the antics of Billy T. James as the Tainuia Kid in *Came a Hot Friday* (Ian Mune, 1985). There is even a reference to the famous series of advertisements Barry Crump did for television in which he drives a Toyota Hilux recklessly through wild terrain with a terrified companion, Scotty, in the passenger seat; in the film, this is replicated in a sequence in which Ricky, taking the role of Crump in the original advertisements, similarly drives a red Hilux called 'Crumpy,' with Hec taking the place of Scotty, in an effort to escape the Special Forces who have surrounded Psycho Sam's caravan, in which they had taken refuge.

It is at the climax of the film, however, that the allusions to other films reach their peak. Ricky wears a headband that recalls Sylvester Stallone as Rambo in *First Blood* (Ted Kotcheff, 1982), and there is a reference to the final shootout in *Butch Cassidy and the Sundance Kid* (George Roy Hill, 1969), while the car chase across a desert landscape recalls the final moments in *Thelma and Louise* (Ridley Scott, 1991), and evokes the chases in *Goodbye Pork Pie* (Geoff Murphy, 1981). When Ricky and Hec are finally cornered beyond the possibility of escape, their Hilux crashes into a car yard that replicates the yard of wrecked cars in Roger Donaldson's *Smash Palace* (1981). Apart from winking at knowing spectators who might recognize the references to these earlier films, the allusions also emphasize that, in Waititi's own words, this is 'a fantasy tale told in a real world setting,' which means that 'all disbelief is part of the way that you enjoy this film.'[23]

The element of mock-epic that is suffused through *Hunt for the Wilderpeople* is reinforced by a number of cinematographic techniques, including zooms and cross-fades. The sense of time passing is imparted by such devices as images superimposed one on another, and the tail-end of one episode appearing in the left of the frame while a new episode enters from the right. In one memorable sequence, an in-camera, one-shot montage slowly encompasses a 720 degree turn in order to telescope time:

> We hid all the actors beneath the camera and in the bushes. Each time we passed the camera by an actor, either an actor would pop up into frame or would run around the camera to take their place for another pass. We had a fire that was going on in the beginning. Someone would run in and put that out. We had doubles who were in different costumes. I think in the end we had three Hecs and three Rickys in the shot, the real ones and then two doubles each. So it was a real choreography.[24]

Such virtuoso camera work was both instrumental in conveying a sense of the passage of time, and also designed to intensify the sense of fantasy that the film was aiming to generate.

Hunt for the Wilderpeople as a Symbolic Figuration

The function of *Hunt for the Wilderpeople* as a fable emphasizing the need for affection and acceptance as the preconditions for a successful transition into adulthood is obvious, but less obvious is the extent to which Waititi, consciously or unconsciously, turns Crump's original story into one that operates symbolically as well. Read as the fantasy that Waititi insists it is, the story reveals a distinct pattern that moves from initial dispossession, through mutual hostility, to tolerance and mutual acceptance, and, finally, to a shared life as part of the same family. Obviously, this fantasy pertains at the most superficial level to the personal itineraries of Ricky and Hec, but it also operates at a political and historical level as well.

Signs of this deeper level of meaning can be found in a number of changes that Waititi made to the source. The elimination of the blood tie between Ricky and 'Auntie' Bella turns their relationship into one that does not exist as an obligation of consanguinity, but rather as a result of freely willed choice on the part of the receiving foster parents. Generally, the presence of Māori in the story is greatly enlarged, especially by the replacement of the Pākehā farmer, Robby Barton, who helps the pair in Crump's version, with Kahu and her Māori family. Together with the addition of the Māori Welfare Officer Paula (Rachel House), the presence of Kahu and her father helps to reinforce the spectator's awareness of the coexistence of a Māori world as well as a Pākehā one, which, apart from Hec, is represented by the Special Forces and the three white hunters who try to seize the fugitive pair in order to claim the $10,000 reward that is being offered for their capture. The very title of the movie, too, suggests a larger frame of reference in its metaphoric overtones. Ricky gets the idea that he and Hec are 'wilderpeople' when he finds a picture of wildebeests that are 'walking, walking, trying to get somewhere.' His words suggest a journey that is underway, but involving a destination that has not yet been reached. At the most superficial, personal level, it is Ricky and Hec who are undertaking this shared journey as 'wilderpeople,' but at a deeper, political level, it is Māori and Pākehā more generally, whom they represent, who are undertaking a journey that involves a shared and evolving history.

One sure sign that this broader frame of reference was at least latent in Waititi's awareness occurs early in the movie when Ricky imagines himself as a Māori warrior defending 'all his wives,' to which Bella replies: 'Okay, Te Kooti,' referring to the famous Māori guerrilla leader who led a rebellion against the British in the 1860s. This reference to Te Kooti evokes the whole history of race relations between Māori and Pākehā following colonization, often conflicted, and involving injustices such as the seizure of Māori land and cultural dispossession. It is not by chance that the film is set in the Urewera, the rugged hill country from which Te Kooti launched his raids against the British colonists, and by locating the film's action in this region and evoking the history of Te Kooti, Waititi is highlighting the sad plight of Ricky, as a descendant of Te Kooti's people. This is the socio-political situation, the film is implicitly saying, that needs to be remedied, and one of the purposes of the film is to show *how* it can be remedied.

Reconciliation: Waititi's Vision of Bicultural Unity

The dramatically changed ending in the film exemplifies Waititi's hopeful vision for the future. Whereas Ricky and Hec had a relationship of open hostility at the beginning, with Ricky saying 'I hate you!' and Hec replying 'I hate you too!,' Ricky is now able to say 'I'm sorry' and Hec is now willing to let Ricky call him 'Uncle.' This change of attitude on both their parts has been brought about by the development of mutual respect and appreciation through the experience of shared adversity, as a result of which each one of the pair learns from the other. Ricky learns inventive self-sufficiency and respect for the rules, and Hec learns to read, and even to compose a haiku poem, in imitation of two of Ricky's predilections. More than that, Ricky now wants Hec to come and live with him in the home of his Māori foster family, to which Hec agrees. The movie ends with the two of them in happy, bonded unity, signaled in an embrace, before they are seen heading off into the bush once more to find the *huia* – an adventure that Ricky describes as 'majestical,' a word he had earlier chided Hec for using as being incorrect.

Finally, therefore, Waititi's film reshapes Crump's original story into a symbolic embodiment of bicultural unity based on reconciliation, mutual respect, appreciation, and affection. These attitudes, together with the mutual support they sustain, the film is saying, are the true remedies for the destructive personal and social consequences of deprivation and alienation, rather than a Social Welfare system that operates simply as a mechanistic bureaucracy. It is a noble vision that projects the ethos behind the state-sponsored policies of biculturalism that have been pursued by successive governments in New Zealand since the 1980s. Only time will tell whether the ideals of this vision are achieved in actuality.

Notes

1. Terry Sturm, 'Crump, Barry,' in Roger Robinson and Nelson Wattie (eds), *The Oxford Companion to New Zealand Literature* (Melbourne: Oxford University Press, 1998), 120–1.
2. *Crump* (dir. Michelle Bracey, Greenstone TV, 1999), a television documentary feature that may be viewed on NZOnScreen, https://www.nzonscreen.com/title/crump-1999, accessed 25 November 2016.
3. Ibid.
4. Brigid Magner, 'Crump, Barry,' from the *Dictionary of New Zealand Biography. Te Ara – the Encyclopedia of New Zealand*, updated 19 February 2013, http://www.TeAra.govt.nz/en/biographies/6c2/crump-barry/page-3, accessed 30 August 2016.
5. Barry Crump, *Wild Pork and Watercress* (Auckland: Penguin Random House, 2016 [1986]), 5.
6. Ibid., 6.
7. *Crump* (dir. Michelle Bracey, Greenstone TV, 1999). A similar image appeared on the back cover of the hardcover edition of *A Good Keen Ma*n.

8. Crump, *Wild Pork and Watercress*, 172.
9. Ibid., 17.
10. Ibid., 50.
11. Ibid., 21.
12. Ibid., 96; cf. Magner, 'Crump, Barry.'
13. Ibid., 53–4.
14. Ibid., 190.
15. Ibid., 201.
16. Ibid., 202.
17. Silas Lesnick, 'CS Interview: Hunting for the Wilderpeople with Taika Waititi,' ComingSoon.net, 19 July 2016, http://www.comingsoon.net/movies/features/703677-taika-waititi-wilderpeople-ragnarok#/slide/1, accessed 31 August 2016.
18. Ibid.
19. Ibid.
20. Crump, *Wild Pork and Watercress*, 21–2.
21. Andrew Parker, 'On the Hunt: An Interview with Hunt for the Wilderpeople Director Taika Waititi,' *Toronto Film Scene*, 24 June 2016, http://thetfs.ca/2016/06/24/on-the-hunt-an-interview-with-hunt-for-the-wilderpeople-director-taika-waititi/, accessed 30 August 2016.
22. Alex Billington, 'Sundance Interview: "Hunt for the Wilderpeople" Director Taika Waititi,' *Firstshowing.net*, 5 February 2016, http://www.firstshowing.net/2016/sundance-interview-hunt-for-the-wilderpeople-director-taika-waititi/, accessed 30 August 2016.
23. Billington, 'Sundance Interview.'
24. Mekado Murphy, 'Taika Waititi Narrates a Scene From "Hunt for the Wilderpeople",' *New York Times*, 16 June 2016, http://www.nytimes.com/2016/06/17/movies/taika-waititi-narrates-a-scene-from-hunt-for-the-wilderpeople.html?_r=0, accessed 30 August 2016.

CONCLUSION

The coming-of-age films examined in this book could almost serve as a compendium of the most esteemed and successful films to be made in New Zealand, attesting to the vitality and creative inventiveness of what is still a relatively young industry. More importantly, they reveal how films in this genre serve a unique function in the processes of national identity formation because their mass appeal to a national audience turns them into a conduit for a collective experience. Rugby, a national passion, is the only other cultural phenomenon that can lay claim to anywhere near the same status as an experience that is shared by so many people, but the fantasies it elicits are far more limited than those solicited by the imaginative representations of experience presented in coming-of-age films.

One also sees that New Zealand coming-of-age films have this draw-card appeal because they hold up a mirror in which New Zealanders can recognize who they are in relation to who they have been in the past, and who they might wish to become in the future. Films in this genre serve this function more effectively than those of any other genre because it is intrinsic to their very nature that they show young people in a process of becoming as these individuals respond to cultural, socio-economic, and political circumstances that produce effects threatening their happiness. Given the personal investments and projection on the part of the filmmaker that almost invariably shape the films, they are always anchored in a reality that is recognizable, and one that is always shared by members of the audience because of its closeness in chronological time to the circumstances that produced the impulse to make the film in the first place.

The very fact that these films identify and address threats to the happiness of young people in the process of becoming, usually with at least an implicit suggestion of how these threats might be overcome, makes coming-of-age films an invaluable indicator of how a society is evolving over time. In the case of New Zealand cinema, a number of significant shifts can be observed that reflect social changes since the post-Second World War period. An early preoccupation with the repressive aspects of the puritanical value system and paternalistic, authoritarian social system that prevailed through most of the twentieth century and still defined New Zealand into the 1970s, becomes replaced by the 1990s by a concern with individuals and groups who are marginalized on account of their personality type, their gender, their ethnic background, or their sexual orientation. This shift in focus reflects the liberalization in all domains of life that occurred during the 1980s under the influence of the neoliberal/postmodern ideologies that flooded the western world during this period. As the new millennium proceeds, those preoccupations appear in turn to be in the process of being superseded by a concern with the reform of traditional cultural practices, particularly as they involve relations between the two historically dominant races in New Zealand – Māori and Pākehā.

In terms of how they relate to coming-of-age films from other countries, New Zealand films in this genre tend to be differentiated not only in terms of their specific thematic concerns, but also by their willingness to mingle components drawn from different genres. There is no New Zealand coming-of-age film, for example, that reproduces the transition into manhood of the boy protagonist in the Jordanian film *Theeb* (Naji Abu Nowar, 2014), who simply learns the need to embrace the honor codes and fortitude of adult males in his Bedouin culture. Conversely, there is no New Zealand film that is the equivalent to the American film *Little Men* (Ira Sachs, 2016), which presents a relationship between two boys that is threatened by class and ethnic barriers, only to have the relationship ended by a reaffirmation of those same barriers. By way of contrast, New Zealand coming-of-age films never accept the status quo, but instead actually depict, or at the very least intimate, a utopian future world in which such problems are resolved. This optimism, one suspects, derives from the liberal values upon which New Zealand as a society was founded, including those of Fabian socialism that was strongly represented in the country at the turn of the twentieth century.

Despite the fact that the coming-of-age genre has played an important role in the development of New Zealand's cultural identity, however, the corpus of films discussed in this book also contains signs of a trend that poses a danger for the future: a trend towards generic standardization motivated by a concern to make the film marketable to an international audience. This tendency was evident as early as *The Scarecrow* (1982), resurfaces in *Whale Rider* (2002), and is alarmingly apparent in *Mahana* (2016). The problem with the reductiveness that this generic standardization entails is that the true nature of culturally specific issues of concern tend to become obscured, leading to a flattening and universalization in the representation that deprives it of its potent meaningfulness for New Zealanders: their ability to recognize a version of their own experience becomes obscured by the barrier of inauthenticity that an excessively uniform application of a particular cinema genre interposes between the spectator and the representation at hand.

As Peter Jackson has observed, New Zealand films, for the most part, characteristically end up 'muddying the genres': 'We do a bit of this and a bit of that and throw it together.'[1] This is what gives New Zealand national films their cultural distinctiveness, because it allows them to capture the shades of emotion, self-protective defense, and displaced investments that are typical of people from a culture that inculcates into them a need to disguise their true feelings. When a filmmaker abandons this generic eclecticism by applying a standardized genre too consistently, he or she loses the quirky complexity that characteristically makes New Zealand coming-of-age film pertinent and interesting. In the process, such a filmmaker risks converting himself or herself from an *auteur* (in the French sense) into a *metteur-en-scène*, given that his or her film will no longer present a story that seems imbued with the ethos of its national cultural context, but rather with the values of a standardized, universalized international culture – one that is dominated by the preoccupations of Hollywood.

In the case of many filmmakers who have made the move to Hollywood, this produces a sharp contrast between their national films and their international films. This is as true of filmmakers from other countries as it is of filmmakers from New Zealand. Compare, for example, Mathieu Kassovitz's *Babylon A.D.* (2008), a bland, conventional, science-fiction action film, with his searing coming-of-age film *Hate* (1995), which portrays the discrimination against, and disadvantages suffered by, three youths trying to make their way in the socio-economically deprived suburbs of Paris. Or, to take a New Zealand example, the difference between Roger Donaldson's American genre potboilers, like *The Bank Job* (2008), and his personal New Zealand films like *Sleeping Dogs* and *Smash Palace* (1981). As far as their value for a local audience is concerned, Hollywood needs to be kept at a distance in the making of New Zealand coming-of-age films, unless – as is the case with Taika Waititi's remarkable diptych of coming-of-age films, *Boy* and *Hunt for the Wilderpeople* – the tropes of Hollywood are woven into an idiosyncratic blend of elements in which the authentically local interfuses with the international so as to illuminate the psychic and emotional reality of people living in this country.

While there is no sign that the making of coming-of-age films in New Zealand is waning, if those which are made are to continue to provide their most important functions for New Zealanders, funding policies for filmmaking need to ensure the survival of low-budget, auteur films that are able to capture the idiosyncratic specificities of New Zealand experience as its culture continues to evolve in a changing world. Only time will tell whether the need to provide for the making of such films – that present images in which New Zealanders can recognize themselves in terms of the deepest, most often disguised and hidden, needs – will be recognized, and supported.

Note

1. Barr and Barr, 'NZFX: The Films of Peter Jackson and Fran Walsh,' 156.

BIBLIOGRAPHY

Aitken, Graeme, *50 Ways of Saying Fabulous* (Sydney: 20Ten Books, 2015 [1995], Kindle Edition).
Aitken, Matthew, 'Sightlines on the Usurper: Narrative Technique and Narrative Structure in *Vigil*,' *Illusions* 4 (Summer 1987), 4–9.
Anon., 'The Making of Sam Pillsbury,' *Auckland Metro* 10 (April 1982), 88–9.
Babington, Bruce, 'Boom Times: The Early 1980s,' in Diane Pivac (ed.) with Frank Stark and Lawrence McDonald, *New Zealand Film: An Illustrated History* (Wellington: Te Papa Press, 2011), 181–205.
Bakhtin, M. M., 'The *Bildungsroman* and Its Significance in the History of Realism (Toward a Historical Typology of the Novel),' in M. M. Bakhtin, *Speech Genres and Other Late Essays*, trans. Vern W. McGee, ed. Caryl Emerson and Michael Holquist (Austin: University of Texas Press, 1981).
Barclay, Barry, *Our Own Image: A Story of a Māori Filmmaker*, Foreword by Jeff Bear (Minneapolis and London: University of Minnesota Press, 2015 [1990]).
Barr, Jim, and Mary Barr, 'NZFX: The Films of Peter Jackson and Fran Walsh,' in Jonathan Dennis and Jan Bieringa (eds), *Film in Aotearoa New Zealand* (Wellington: Victoria University Press, 1996), 150–60.
Benjamin, Julie, and Helen Todd with Merata Mita, 'Meshes of an Afternoon: An Interview with Merata Mita,' *Alternative Cinema* 11:4 (1983/4), 40.
Bollas, Christopher, *Being a Character: Psychoanalysis and Self Experience* (London and New York: Routledge, 1992).
Boyle, Karen, '"Not All Angels Are Innocent" – Violence, Sexuality, and the Teen Psychodyke,' in A.H. Karriker (ed.), *Film Studies: Women in Contemporary Cinema* (New York: Peter Lang, 2002), 35–50.
Brown, Ruth, 'Closing the Gaps: "Once Were Warriors" from Book to Film and Beyond,' *JNZL: Journal of New Zealand Literature* 17 (Summer 1999), 141–55.
Calder, Peter, 'Small Print Marks Director's Big Step,' *New Zealand Herald* (24 August 1989): s.1, 18.

——, 'The Peacemaker; An Innocent Abroad,' *New Zealand Herald* (11 August 2001): F1, 3, 5.
Chapman, Robert, 'Fiction and the Social Pattern: Some Implications of Recent N.Z. Writing,' *Landfall* 7:1 (1953), 26–58.
Ciment, Michel, 'The Red Wigs of Autobiography: Interview with Jane Campion,' *Positif*, April 1991. Reprinted in Virginia Wright Wexman, *Jane Campion: Interviews* (Jackson: University Press of Mississippi, 1999), 62–70.
Coney, S., Review of *Vigil*, *Broadsheet* 127 (March 1985), 42–3.
Conrich, Ian and Stuart Murray (eds), *New Zealand Filmmakers* (Detroit: Wayne State University Press, 2007).
Considine, David M., 'The Cinema of Adolescence,' *Journal of Popular Film & Television* 9:3 (Fall 1981), 123–36.
——, *The Cinema of Adolescence* (Jefferson, NC: McFarland, 1985).
Cook, David A., 'Auteur Cinema and the "Film Generation" in 1970s Hollywood,' in Jon Lewis (ed.), *The New American Cinema* (Durham and London: Duke University Press, 1998), 12–37.
Cross, Ian, *The God Boy* (Christchurch: Whitcombe & Tombs), 1972.
——, 'The God Boy (A lecture delivered to Stage 1 English students at the University of Otago on 20 September 1962),' *Journal of New Zealand Literature: JNZL* 8 (1990), 3–14.
D'Cruz, Doreen, and John C. Ross, *The Lonely and the Alone: The Poetics of Isolation in New Zealand Fiction* (Amsterdam and New York: Rodopi), 2011.
Dart, William, 'Kiwi Rural Gothic,' *Art New Zealand* (Online) 24 (Winter 1982).
De Souza, Pascale, 'Maoritanga in *Whale Rider* and *Once Were Warriors*: A Problematic Rebirth through Female Leaders,' *Studies in Australasian Cinema* 1:1 (2007), 15–27.
Denham, Carl, 'Profile: Heaven's Above! A Religious Film-maker,' *New Zealandia* 2 (June 1989), 38–41.
Dennis, Jonathan, 'Perimeters: Vincent Ward, an Interview,' in Jonathan Dennis and Jan Bieringa, *Film in Aotearoa New Zealand* (Wellington: Victoria University Press, 1992), 89–91.
Doherty, Thomas, *Teenagers and Teenpics: The Juvenilization of American Movies in the 1950s*, 2nd edn (Philadelphia: Temple University Press, 2002).
Driscoll, Catherine, *Teen Film: A Critical Introduction* (Oxford: Berg, 2011).
Duff, Alan, *Once Were Warriors* (New York: Vintage, 1995 [1990]).
——, *Out of the Mist and Steam: A Memoir* (Auckland: Tandem Press, 1999).
Dunleavy, Trisha, and Hester Joyce, *New Zealand Film and Television: Institution, Industry and Cultural Change* (Bristol: Intellect, 2011).
Evans, Patrick, 'The Provincial Dilemma: After *The God Boy*,' *Landfall* 117 (March 1976), 25–36.
Fox, Alistair, *Jane Campion: Authorship and Personal Cinema* (Bloomington and Indianapolis: Indiana University Press, 2011).
——, *Speaking Pictures: Neuropsychoanalysis and Authorship in Film and Literature* (Bloomington and Indianapolis: Indiana University Press, 2016).
——, *The Ship of Dreams: Masculinity in Contemporary New Zealand Fiction* (Dunedin: Otago University Press, 2008).
——, Hilary Radner, and Barry Keith Grant (eds), *New Zealand Cinema: Interpreting the Past* (Bristol: Intellect/Chicago: Chicago University Press, 2011).
—— and Gabrielle Hine (eds), *Cinematic Adaptation and the Articulation of New Zealand Identity* (Dunedin: Centre for the Research on National Identity, 2011).
Frame, Janet, *An Autobiography* (Auckland: Vintage, 2004).
——, 'My Say' (Interview with Elizabeth Alley), in Elizabeth Alley and Mark Williams

(eds), *In the Same Room: Conversations with New Zealand Writers* (Auckland: Auckland University Press, 1992).
Freud, Sigmund, *Jokes and Their Relation to the Unconscious*, trans. and ed. James Strachey, with a Biographical Introduction by Peter Gay (New York and London: Norton, 1989 [Kindle edition]).
Grant, Barry Keith, 'The Films of Peter Jackson,' in Ian Conrich and Stuart Murray (eds), *New Zealand Filmmakers* (Detroit: Wayne State University Press, 2007), 320–35.
Gunn, Kirsty, *Rain* (London: Faber & Faber, 1994).
Halbwachs, Maurice, *On Collective Memory*, ed. and trans. Lewis A. Coser (Chicago: University of Chicago Press, 1992).
Harding, Bruce, '"The Donations of History": Mauri and the Transfigured "Māori Gaze",' in Alistair Fox, Hilary Radner, and Barry Keith Grant (eds), *New Zealand Cinema: Interpreting the Past* (Bristol: Intellect/Chicago: Chicago University Press, 2011), 217–37.
Herman, David, 'Beyond Voice and Vision: Cognitive Grammar and Focalization Theory,' in Peter Hühn, Wolf Schmid, and Jörg Schönert (eds), *Point of View, Perspective, and Focalization: Modeling Mediation in Narrative* (Berlin and New York: Walter de Gruyter, 2009), 119–42.
Higson, Andrew, 'The Concept of National Cinema,' *Screen* 30:4 (1989), 36–47.
Hühn, Peter, Wolf Schmid, and Jörg Schönert (eds), *Point of View, Perspective, and Focalization: Modeling Mediation in Narrative* (Berlin and New York: Walter de Gruyter, 2009).
Ihimaera, Witi, *Bulibasha, King of the Gypsies* (Auckland: Penguin, 1994).
——, *The Rope of Man* (Auckland: Reed, 2005).
——, *The Whale Rider* (Auckland: Heinemann, 1987).
Jeffers, Thomas L., *Apprenticeships* (London: Palgrave, 2005).
Jones, Lawrence, '" . . . Essentially It's the Same Story": Maurice Gee, Brad McGann and the Creative Adaptation of *In My Father's Den* (2004),' in Alistair Fox and Gabrielle Hine (eds), *Cinematic Adaptation and the Articulation of New Zealand Identity* (Dunedin: Centre for the Research on National Identity, 2011), 43–53.
——, '"I can really see myself in her story": Jane Campion's Adaptation of Janet Frame's *Autobiography*,' in Hilary Radner, Alistair Fox, and Irène Bessière (eds), *Jane Campion: Cinema, Nation, Identity* (Detroit: Wayne State University Press, 2009), 77–100.
——, 'Man Alone,' in Roger Robinson and Nelson Wattie (eds), *The Oxford Companion to New Zealand Literature* (Melbourne: Oxford University Press, 1998), 331–2.
——, 'The Novel,' in Terry Sturm (ed.), *The Oxford History of New Zealand Literature in English*, 2nd edn (Auckland: Oxford University Press, 1998), 119–244.
——, 'Ronald Hugh Morrieson and Post-Provincial Fiction,' *Landfall* 144 (December 1982): 461–71.
Kiley, Dean, 'Un-Queer Anti-Theory,' *Australian Humanities Review* 9 (1998), 1–6.
King, Michael, *Wrestling with the Angel: A Life of Janet Frame* (Auckland: Viking, 2000).
Kovács, András Bálint, *Screening Modernism: European Art Cinema, 1950–1980* (Chicago and London: University of Chicago Press, 2007).
Legat, Nicola, 'Atareta Poananga and Te Ahi Kaa: Their Message for Pakeha,' *Metro* 5:57 (March 1986), 44–58.
Lewis, Brent, 'Sam Pillsbury,' *Pacific Way* 50 (April 1992), 45.
Lewis, Jon, *The Road to Romance & Ruin: Teen Films and Youth Culture* (New York: Routledge, 1992).

Lippy, Tod, 'Writing and Directing *Heavenly Creatures*: A Talk with Frances Walsh and Peter Jackson,' *Scenario* 1 (1995), 217–24.
Matthews, Philip, 'Local Infections: New Zealand Horror,' *Landfall* 201 (May 2001), 183–7.
McDonnell, Brian, 'Once Were Warriors: Controversial Novel Becomes Blockbuster Film,' *Metro Magazine: Media & Education Magazine* 101 (1995), 7–9.
——, '*The God Boy*: Adaptation from Novel to TV Film. Part 1: Ian Cross's Novel,' *New Zealand Journal of Media Studies* 6:1 (1999), 61–9.
——, '*The God Boy*: Adaptation from Novel to TV Film. Part 2,' *New Zealand Journal of Media Studies* 7:1 (2000), 3–18.
——, 'The Making of *The Scarecrow*,' *Auckland* 10 (April 1982), 84–6.
——, 'The Physician Who Assumed His Patient's Fever: Peter Jackson's Narrative Strategy in *Heavenly Creatures*,' *Studies in Australasian Cinema* 1:2 (2007), 161–73.
——, *The Scarecrow: A Film Study Guide* (Auckland: Longman Paul, 1982).
Martens, Emiel, 'Maori on the Silver Screen: The Evolution of Indigenous Feature Filmmaking in Aotearoa/New Zealand,' *International Journal of Critical Indigenous Studies* 5:1 (2012), 2–30.
——, *Once were Warriors: The Aftermath: The Controversy of OWW in Aotearoa New Zealand* (Amsterdam: Aksant, 2007).
Martin, Adrian, 'Teen Movies: The Forgetting of Wisdom,' in Adrian Martin, *Phantasms* (Ringwood, Victoria: McPhee Gribble Publishers, 1994), 63–9).
Martin, Helen, 'Through a Maori Lens' (Interview), *The Listener* (14 October 1989).
Martin, Helen, and Sam Edwards, *New Zealand Film 1912–1996* (Auckland: Oxford University Press, 1997).
Mauron, Charles, *Des Métaphores obsédantes au mythe personnel: Introduction à la psychocritique* (Paris: J. Corti, 1995 [1963]).
Millen, Julia, *Ronald Hugh Morrieson: A Biography* (Auckland: David Ling Pub., 1996).
Milton, John, *Complete Poems and Major Prose*, ed. Merritt Y. Hughes (Indianapolis and New York: The Odyssey Press, 1957).
Mitchell, Tony, [Interview with Vincent Ward on *Vigil*] *Art New Zealand* 30 (Autumn 1984), 36–9.
Molloy, Maureen, 'Death and the Maiden: The Feminine and the Nation in Recent New Zealand Films,' *Signs* 25:1 (1999), 153–70.
Morrieson, Ronald Hugh, *Predicament* (Auckland: Penguin, 1986 [1974]).
——, *The Scarecrow* (Auckland: Penguin, 2010).
Petrie, Duncan, 'From the Cinema of Poetry to the Cinema of Unease: Brad McGann's *In My Father's Den*,' *Illusions* 37 (Winter 2005), 2–8.
Pivac, Diane, and others, *New Zealand Film: An Illustrated History* (Wellington: Te Papa Press, 2011).
Prendergast, Stephen, 'Interviews with Vincent Ward,' *Wellington City Magazine* (August 1985), 46–7.
Pryor, Ian, *Peter Jackson: From Prince of Splatter to Lord of the Rings* (Auckland: Random House, 2003).
Radner, Hilary, Alistair Fox, and Irène Bessière (eds), *Jane Campion: Cinema, Nation, Identity* (Detroit: Wayne State University Press, 2009).
Rains, Stephanie, 'Making Strange: Journeys through the Unfamiliar Films of Vincent Ward,' in Ian Conrich and Stuart Murray (eds), *New Zealand Filmmakers* (Detroit: Wayne State University Press, 2007), 273–88.
Reid, Nicholas, *A Decade of New Zealand Film*: Sleeping Dogs *to* Came a Hot Friday (Dunedin: John McIndoe, 1986).
Robinson, Roger, and Nelson Wattie (eds), *The Oxford Companion to New Zealand Literature* (Melbourne: Oxford University Press, 1998).

Rueschmann, Eva, *Sisters on Screen: Siblings in Contemporary Cinema* (Philadelphia: Temple University Press, 2000).
Sargeson, Frank, 'Two Novels by Ronald Hugh Morrieson: An Appreciation,' *Landfall* 98 (June 1971), 133–7.
Schlickers, Sabine, 'Focalization, Ocularization and Auricularization in Film and Literature,' in Peter Hühn, Wolf Schmid, and Jörg Schönert (eds), *Point of View, Perspective, and Focalization: Modeling Mediation in Narrative* (Berlin and New York: Walter de Gruyter, 2009), 243–58.
Scott, Jill, *Electra after Freud: Myth and Culture* (Ithaca, NY: Cornell University Press, 2005).
Selbo, Julie, *Film Genre for the Screenwriter* (New York and London: Routledge, 2015).
Shary, Timothy, and Alexandra Seibel (eds), *Youth Culture in Global Cinema* (Austin: University of Texas Press, 2007).
Thompson, Kirsten Moana, 'Once Were Warriors: New Zealand's First Indigenous Blockbuster,' in Julian Stringer (ed.), *Movie Blockbusters* (London: Routledge, 2003).
Thornley, Davinia, 'Executing the Commoners: Examining Class in *Heavenly Creatures*,' in A. H. Karr (ed.), *Film Studies: Women in Contemporary World Cinema* (New York: Peter Lang, 2002), 51–68.
Truffaut, François, *The Films in My Life* (New York: Da Capo Press, 1994).
Walker-Morrison, Deborah, 'A Place to Stand: Land and Water in Māori Film,' *Imaginations: Revue d'études interculturelles de l'image/Journal of Cross-Cultural Image Studies* 5:1 (6 April 2014), http://imaginations.csj.ualberta.ca/?p=5221, accessed 18 July 2016.
Ward, Vincent, *Edge of the Earth: Stories and Images from the Antipodes* (Auckland: Heinemann Reed, 1990).
——, *The Past Awaits: People, Images, Film* (Nelson: Craig Potton Publishing, 2010).
Weinert, Friedel, *The Scientist as Philosopher: Philosophical Consequences of Great Scientific Discoveries* (Berlin and New York: Springer, 2004).
Wexman, Virginia Wright, *Jane Campion: Interviews* (Jackson, MS: University Press of Mississippi, 1999).
Wikse, Maria, *Materialisations of a Woman Writer: Investigating Janet Frame's Biographical Legend* (Oxford: Peter Lang, 2006).
Wild, Harriet, 'Primal Curiosity, Primal Anxiety: The Child Settler in *Vigil* and *The Piano*,' *New Zealand Journal of Media Studies* 12:2 (2011), 67–86.
Wiles, Mary M., 'Narrating the Feminine Nation: The Coming-of-age Girl in Contemporary New Zealand Cinema,' in Timothy Shary and Alexandra Seibel (eds), *Youth Culture in Global Cinema* (Austin: University of Texas Press, 2007), 175–88.
Williams, Sue, 'A Light on the Dark Secrets of Depression,' *Australian*, 2 May 1995. Reprinted in Wexman, *Jane Campion*, 175–6.
Winnicott, D. W., *The Maturational Process and the Facilitating Environment: Studies in the Theory of Emotional Development* (New York: International Universities Press, 1965).

INDEX

1984 (George Orwell), 47
3:10 to Yuma (Delmer Daves), 207, 209
50 Ways of Saying Fabulous, 5, 6, 18, 21, 25, 175, 176, 177, 185
400 Blows, The (François Truffaut), 3, 5, 7, 8, 36

adaptations, 18, 19, 27, 138, 148
Adventures of Hajji Baba, The (Don Weis), 207
Aitken, Graeme
  autobiographical projection of, 179
  gay sexuality, vision of, 177–8
  mentioned, 25, 175, 180, 181, 182, 185
  neglected author, as, 186
Aldrich, Robert, 127
American Graffiti (George Lucas), 9
American New Wave, 43, 46, 48, 49
American western, 19, 208, 209
American youth culture, 43
Among the Cinders (Rolf Hädrich), 17
Angel at My Table, An (Jane Campion)
  adaptation, as, 95
  autobiographical elements in, 20, 101–4
  marginalized heroine in, 25
  mentioned, 5, 18, 96, 109, 164
  Mita's view of, 105
  setting of, 21–2
  style of, 10
  and *Jake's Long Shadow* (Alan Duff), 133
Apron Strings (Sima Urale), 26
art-cinema, 10, 68, 69, 78, 113, 171
art-house style, 172
auteur film, 7
Autobiography, An (Janet Frame)
  Faces in the Water and, 102
  Frame's purpose in, 96
  mirror for Campion, as, 100
  narrative technique of, 95
  mentioned, 25, 98, 99, 104, 109

Babington, Bruce, 158, 176
Babylon A.D. (Mathieu Kassovitz), 233
Baker, Heretaunga Pat, 86
Bakhtin, Mikhail, 5
Balzac, Honoré de, 9
Bank Job, The (Roger Donaldson), 233
Barclay, Barry, 'Fourth Cinema'
  theory of, 25, 80, 212
  Mauri, view of, 81
  Whale Rider, view of, 159
  mentioned, 189, 191, 203, 213
Barlow, Helen, 213
Barnett, John, 149
Batman v Superman: Dawn of Justice (Zack Snyder), 189
Baysting, Arthur, 44, 45, 48

Bergman, Ingmar, 11, 37, 43, 69, 70
Bertolucci, Bernardo, 6, 171
biculturalism, 90, 119, 159, 216, 229
Bildungsroman, 5, 13, 232
Bollas, Christopher, 8
Bonnie and Clyde (Arthur Penn), 49
Born to Dance (Tammy Davis), 18
Boy (Taika Waititi)
   Alamein, characterization of, 196
   autobiographical elements in, 194
   bicultural perspective of, 26
   box office success of, 189
   cultural hybridity in, 54, 91, 200
   fantasy, role of, in, 197–8
   generic elements in, 159, 233
   Hunt for the Wilderpeople, compared with, 216–17
   mentioned, 6, 18, 24, 121, 133, 203
   Once Were Warriors, relation to, 192–3
   parental neglect in, 23
   reception of, 190–1, 212, 213
   Rocky as redemptive child in, 199
   setting of, 21, 22
   style of, 8
   trauma in, 195
Braindead (Peter Jackson), 6, 17, 23, 111, 112
Breaking Away (Peter Yates), 9
Bresson, Robert, 10, 69, 171
Bright Star (Jane Campion), 10
Brown, Riwia, 125, 126
Bulibasha: King of the Gypsies (Witi Ihimaera)
   film version, compared with, 205–6, 208–10
   Hollywood movies in, 207
   intergenerational conflict in, 204
   Māori culture, challenged in, 159
   mentioned, 148, 214, 223
Butch Cassidy and the Sundance Kid (George Roy Hill), 48, 49, 227

Calder, Peter, 176
Came a Hot Friday (Ian Mune), 216, 226
Campbell, Gordon, 163
Campion, Anna, 99
Campion, Edith, 100, 101, 102, 104
Campion, Jane
   Bresson's influence on, 10
   evocative objects, use of, 9, 104
   mentioned, 11, 109
   personal elements in films of, 20, 95, 99–101, 102, 105

Cannes Film Festival, 65, 78, 79, 137; *see also* Angel at My Table, An (Jane Campion)
Captain America: Civil War (Anthony Russo, Joe Russo), 189
Caro, Niki
   adaptation, approach to, 152–4
   feminist vision of, 149, 154, 155–6, 158, 162
   Māori criticism of, 156–7
   mentioned, 159
   see also Whale Rider (Niki Caro)
Cassavetes, John, 171
Catsoulis, Jeanette, 176
Clement, Jermaine, 194
Cloud of Unknowing, The (Anon.), 172
Coeur fidèle (Jean Epstein), 10
Collee, John, 205, 206, 207, 208, 209, 213
Colmant, Marie, 104
Come as You Are (Brad McGann), 170
coming-of-age films
   adaptations, as, 40, 56
   art cinema style and, 9–11
   bicultural perspectives in, 26
   childhood as theme in
   colonial legacy in, 24
   cultural value systems, and, 22
   evolution in New Zealand of, 24–6
   family dysfunction in, 23
   French New Wave and, 6–9, 36
   functions of, 11
   generic attributes of, 4–6, 43
   genre-mixing in, 126–7
   literature, dialogue with, 18–20
   national cinemas and, 11–13, 161–2, 231–2
   patriarchal authoritarianism in, 23
   personal cinema, as, 20–1, 104
   rural settings of, 21–2
   sexuality, preoccupation with, 23
   themes in, 22–4
Connecticut Yankee in King Arthur's Court, A (Tay Garnett), 207
Conrich, Ian, 176
Considine, David, 6
Contempt (Jean-Luc Godard), 8
Cross, Ian
   mentioned, 36, 37, 38, 40, 56, 61
   The God Boy and, 32–5

Crump, Barry
  biography of, 217–18
  Hunt for the Wilderpeople, referenced in, 219, 226–7
  as Kiwi icon, 217
  Wild Pork and Watercress, and, 220–2, 224, 228
Crump, Carol, 218
Crump, Martin, 218

Dallas (TV series), 191
Dam Busters, The (Michael Anderson), 207
Davis, Tammy, 191
Death in the Family, A (Stewart Main, Peter Wells), 177
Debruge, Peter, 190, 191, 212, 213
Donaldson, Roger
  adaptation, approach to, 42–3
  autobiographical motivations of, 50–3
  Five Easy Pieces and, 49–50
  mentioned, 9, 17, 226, 233
  Smith's Dream and, 44–5
  see also *Sleeping Dogs* (Roger Donaldson)
Dowling, Jonathan, 42
Dreamers, The (Bernardo Bertolucci), 6
Dreyer, Carl, 69
Driscoll, Catherine, 4
Duff, Alan
  autobiography of, 123–4, 130–1
  mentioned, 22
  Once Were Warriors, and, 122–4, 126, 127, 197
  sequels to *Once Were Warriors*, and, 132–3
Dukes of Hazzard, The (TV series), 191
Dynasty (TV series), 191

E.T.: The Extra-Terrestrial (Steven Spielberg), 191, 197
East of Eden (Elia Kazan, 7
Easy Rider (Dennis Hopper), 46, 49
Electra complex, 145
European art cinema, 9, 68
evocative objects, 8
expressionism, 10, 11, 60

Faces in the Water (Janet Frame), 102
Falcon Crest (TV series), 191
Fantl, Michele, 177
Fastest Gun Alive, The (Russell Rouse), 207

First Blood (ted Kotcheff), 227
Five Easy Pieces (Bob Rafelson), 46, 49, 50, 51
Flaming Star (Don Siegel), 207
Flight of the Albatross (Werner Meyer), 18
Fourth Cinema, 25, 80, 81, 159, 203, 212
Frame, Janet, *An Autobiography*, and, 95, 96–8, 99, 100–1, 102, 104, 109
Frame, Lottie, 101
Freud, Sigmund, 197

Gance, Abel, 10
Gee, Maurice
  In My Father's Den, and, 163–7, 170
  mentioned, 66, 109, 161, 162
  puritanism, view of, 32, 35
Gerrard, Lisa, 153
God Boy, The (Murray Reece)
  400 Blows, influence of, 36
  adaptation, as, 18, 27, 38
  delinquency in, 23
  family dysfunction in, 32–5
  film style of, 35–8, 68
  mentioned, 5, 17, 25, 40, 58, 65, 105
  puritanism, portrayal of, 22, 31–2, 61, 109
  repression in, 38–9
Good Keen Man, A (Barry Crump), 217
Goodbye Pork Pie (Geoff Murphy), 227
Grace, Patricia, 84
Graduate, The (Mike Nichols), 9
Grant, Barry Keith, 113
Gunfight at the OK Corral (John Sturges), 206
Gunn, Kirsty, 138–40, 141, 142, 145, 146, 149

Halbwachs, Maurice, 12
Hamlet (Shakespeare), 74
Hang on a Minute Mate (Barry Crump), 217
Harry Potter and the Deathly Hallows (Part One) (David Yates), 189
Harvey, Bob, 44
Harvey, Dennis, 176
Hate (Mathieu Kassovitz), 233
Haysom, Trevor, 167
Heavenly Creatures (Peter Jackson)
  mentioned, 18, 20, 118
  mode of, 112–15
  Oedipal theme in, 111–12

personal investments in, 110–11
puritan repression in, 22–3, 108–9
Hei Tiki (Alexander Markey), 81
Hercules Unchained (Pietro Francisci), 206
High Noon (Fred Zinnemann), 207
Hill, Kim, 209
Hinemoa (Gaston Méliès), 17
Hokowhitu, Brendan, 148, 149, 158, 190
Holroyd, Michael, 96
Holy Smoke (Jane Campion), 102
Home Away from Here, A (Brad McGann), 170
How Chief Te Ponga Won His Bride (Gaston Méliès), 17
Hulme, Juliet, 108, 109
Humourbeasts, The, 194
Hunt for the Wilderpeople (Taika Waititi)
  bicultural perspective of, 26, 228–9
  box office success of, 121, 189
  genre cinema, as, 159
  Māori film, as, 203
  mentioned, 18, 43, 200, 233
  New Zealand New Wave, references to, 226–7
  personal film, as, 20
  rural setting of, 21–2
  theme of, 216
hybridity, 91, 113,159, 172, 200, 203, 213

I Saw in My Dream (Frank Sargeson), 32
Ihimaera, Witi
  Bulibasha, and, 204–5
  Caro, contrasted with, 158
  challenger of traditional Māori culture, as, 159, 204–5, 211–12
  magic realism, use of, 153, 206
  mentioned, 25, 148, 207, 214
  narrative technique of, 210
  tikanga, respect for, 156
  Whale Rider, and, 150–2, 154
impressionism, 10, 69, 171
In My Father's Den (Brad McGann)
  family secrets in, 23
  adaptation, as, 27
  changes to source in, 167
  coming-of-age film, as, 161–2
  genre of, 173
  mentioned, 22, 66, 109
  personal elements in, 167–70
  setting of, 20, 21
  style of, 171–2

In My Father's Den (Maurice Gee), 32, 35, 66, 163–5
In the Cut (Jane Campion), 102
indigenous cinema, 80, 81, 159

Jackson, Michael, 191, 216
Jackson, Peter
  Braindead, and, 6, 111
  film style of, 8, 113–14
  generic hybridity, use of, 113
  mentioned, 20, 137
  national filmmaker, as, 110
  personal element in films of, 110–12
  see also Heavenly Creatures
James, Billy T., 226
Jeffs, Christine, 137–8, 140–6, 149; *see also Rain* (Christine Jeffs)
Jokes and Their Relation to the Unconscious (Sigmund Freud), 197
Jones, Lawrence, 31, 32, 58, 59, 101
Jules and Jim (François Truffaut), 8
Jurassic Park (Steven Spielberg), 121

Ka'ai, Tania, 148, 157
kaupapa Māori, 191, 192, 200, 203, 212
Kavka, Misha, 190
Kieslowski, Krzysztof, 171
Kiley, Dean, 176

La Bohème (Giacomo Puccini), 114
Lagoon, The (Janet Frame), 98
Lanza, Mario, 114
Leone, Sergio, 127
Life of Pi, The (Ang Lee), 6
Little Men (Ira Sachs), 232
Loach, Ken, 126
Lord of the Rings: The Fellowship of the Ring (Peter Jackson), 216
Love Finds Andy Hardy (George B. Seitz), 6
Loved by a Maori Chieftess (Gaston Méliès), 17, 80

Madama Butterfly (Giacomo Puccini), 114
Mahana (Lee Tamahori)
  adaptation, as, 205–8
  American western, and, 19, 208–10
  cultural hybridity in, 200, 203, 213
  generic standardization of, 232
  mentioned, 23, 24, 25, 159, 217, 223
  reception of, 212
  setting of, 21
  traditional Māori culture, and, 91

Main, Stewart
  adaptation, approach to, 181–4, 185, 186
  gay films of, 177
  genre-mixing, use of, 6
  see also 50 Ways of Saying Fabulous
Malick, Terrence, 171
Man Alone theme, 6, 31, 39, 44, 47, 217
Man Alone (John Mulgan), 32
Māori nationalism, 90
Markey, Alexander, 80
Martin, Helen, 70, 111
Maslin, Janet, 192
Matriarch, The (Witi Ihimaera), 148, 204, 207
Matthews, Philip, 142
Mauri (Merata Mita)
  aroha, theme of, 86–7
  kaupapa Māori film, as, 84, 191, 200, 203, 213
  mentioned, 5, 17, 25, 105, 189
  music in, 153
  personal film, as, 81–2
  setting of, 21
  traditional Māori culture, view of, 24, 86–9, 150
  uniqueness of, 90
  see also Mauri (Merata Mita)
Mauron, Charles, 112, 170
McDonnell, Brian, 117, 127, 131
McGann, Brad
  adaptation, approach to, 165–7
  film style of, 171, 173
  generic hybridity, use of, 172
  mentioned, 66, 109, 161, 163
  personal references in films of, 20, 167–9
  short films of, 170
  vision of, 162
  see also In My Father's Den (Brad McGann)
Méliès, Gaston, 17, 80
Millen, Julia, 57
Milton, John, 105
minimalism, 10, 11, 69, 171
Mita, Merata, An Angel at My Table
  indigenous woman filmmaker, as, 25, 80–1, 84, 90
  Māori musical instruments, use of, 153–4
  mentioned, 95, 150, 189, 191, 200, 213
  personal references in Mauri, 81–3

view of, 105
see also Mauri
Moravia, Alberto, 8
Morrieson, Ronald Hugh
  autobiographical projection of, 57–8, 63, 64
  cultural milieu of, 61
  mentioned, 19, 109
  narrative technique of, 62
  personality of, 57
  puritanism, exposé of, 66
Muldoon, Robert, 17
Mulgan, John, 32
Mune, Ian, 35, 36, 44, 45, 48, 49, 143
Murphy, Geoff, 48, 54, 82, 83, 143, 226
Murray, Stuart, 176
My First Suit (Stewart Main), 177
My Little Loves (Jean Eustache), 8
My Wedding and Other Secrets (Roseanne Liang), 26

Nana (Jean Renoir), 10
Napoléon (Abel Gance), 10
Narbey, Leon, 153
national cinema
  attributes of, 12
  mentioned, 24, 27, 65, 161, 162
  national literature, relationship with, 18, 105
Neill, Sam, 47, 50, 219, 223, 226
New Hollywood, 9, 19, 43
New Wave
  influence of, 6–8, 36, 40
  mentioned, 3
  personal cinema and, 20
  shooting style of, 8–9
New Zealand Film Commission, 17, 42, 65, 125, 147
New Zealand New Wave, 24, 29, 42, 68, 226
Ngati (Barry Barclay), 25, 81, 189
Nicholson, Jack, 50
Nights in the Gardens of Spain (Witi Ihimaera), 211
Nights in the Gardens of Spain (Katie Wolfe), 22, 26, 148

Once Were Warriors (Lee Tamahori)
  box office success of, 121–2
  Boy, compared with, 192–4, 197, 199
  generic elements in, 126–7
  mentioned, 18, 22, 24, 200, 203, 205, 224

INDEX

parental neglect in, 23, 25
personal elements in, 21, 126
source novel, compared with, 122–6, 133
Once Were Warriors (Alan Duff), 122, 124, 131, 197, 208
One of Them (Stewart Main, Peter Wells), 177
Oracles and Miracles (Stevan Eldred-Grigg), 66
Our Own Image (Barry Barclay), 80, 212
Out of the Mists and Steam (Alan Duff), 123
Outrageous Fortune (TV series), 191
Owen, Rena, 122
Owls Do Cry (Janet Frame), 98, 100, 172

Parker, Honorah (a.k.a. Honorah Rieper), 108
Parker, Pauline, 18, 108, 109
Passion of Anna, The (Ingmar Bergman), 11
Peckinpah, Sam, 127
Persona (Ingmar Bergman), 11
personal films, 7
Phillips, Jock, 31
Piano, The (Jane Campion), 102
Pihama, Leonie, 190, 191, 193
Pillsbury, Sam
  adaptation, approach to, 40, 55, 57, 60–6
  mentioned, 19, 20, 109
  see also *Scarecrow, The* (Sam Pillsbury)
Plumb Trilogy (Maurice Gee), 35, 66
Possum (Brad McGann), 170
Potiki (Patricia Grace), 84
Predicament (Ronald Hugh Morrieson), 58
puritanism, 22–3, 32–5, 58, 61, 65, 66, 119, 137, 167

Rafelson, Bob, 50
Rain (Christine Jeffs), 21, 22, 23, 137, 146, 147, 149
Rain (Kirsty Gunn), 137, 138
Rebel Without a Cause (Nicholas Ray), 6, 7, 207
Red River (Howard Hawks), 207
Reece, Murray
  adaptation, approach to, 35–8, 40, 61
  mentioned, 32, 42, 43, 56
  see also *God Boy, The* (Murray Reece)

Reid, Nicholas, 70, 71
Reilly, Patrick, 96
River of No Return (Otto Preminger), 207
Roché, Henri-Pierre, 8
Rooney, Mickey, 6
Rope of Man, The (Witi Ihimaera), 205, 214
Runaway (John O'Shea), 17

Sargeson, Frank, 32
Scarecrow, The (Ronald Hugh Morrieson), 19, 58
Scarecrow, The (Sam Pillsbury), 17, 20, 40, 55, 57, 58, 60, 61, 63, 65, 68, 109, 232
  genre film, as, 61
  themes of, 61
Scarface (Brian De Palma), 216
Scholes, Robin, 125, 206, 208
Scott, A. O., 142
Selbo, Julie, 5, 43, 232
Serpent of the Nile (William Castle), 206
Shadbolt, Maurice, 57
Shōgun (TV mini-series), 191
Siegel, Don, 127
Siren of Baghdad (Richard Quine), 207
Sleeping Dogs (Roger Donaldson)
  autobiographical elements in, 48, 50–2
  generic hybridity of, 43
  Hunt for the Wilderpeople, and, 226
  intertextual allusions in, 48
  mentioned, 9, 216, 233
  New Hollywood, influence of, 19, 43
  self-projection in, 53
  setting of, 21–2
  source, relation to, 44–7
  style of, 68
  success of, 17, 42
  tropes from American cinema in, 45
Smash Palace (Roger Donaldson), 48, 227, 233
Smith, Patti, 169
Smith's Dream (C. K. Stead), 42, 44, 45, 47, 56
Sons for the Return Home (Paul Maunder) 17
Stead, C. K., 42, 45–7, 50, 51, 53, 56
Stephens, Mark, 125
Stevenson, Dougal, 226
Strength of Water, The (Armagan Ballantyne), 18
Strongest God, The (Heretaunga Pat Baker), 86

245

Summer of '42 (Robert Mulligan), 9
surrealism, 10, 113
Suzanne's Career (Éric Rohmer), 8
symbolic landscape, 70

Tamahori, Lee
  adaptation, approach to, 124–5, 126–7, 204, 208–10
  mentioned, 200
  Māori life, depiction of, 25, 91, 210–11, 213, 214
  Once Were Warriors, view of, 122
  style of, 212
  see also Once Were Warriors (Lee Tamahori); *Mahana* (Lee Tamahori)
Tarkovsky, Andrei, 171
Te Māori exhibition, 90
teen film, 4, 5, 18, 24, 232
teen films, 5
Television One (New Zealand), 31
Ten Commandments, The (Cecil B. DeMille), 207
Theeb (Naji Abu Nowar), 232
Thelma and Louise (Ridley Scott), 216, 227
Third Man, The (Orson Welles), 117
tikanga Māori, 86, 203, 212
To The Is-Land (Janet Frame), 100, 101
Toon, John, 142
Top of the Lake (Jane Campion), 139
Treaty of Waitangi, 90
Truffaut, François 3, 5, 7, 8, 9, 20, 36, 43, 232
Turner, Stephen, 190
Twilight Saga: Eclipse, The (David Slade), 189
Two Cars, One Night (Taika Waititi), 225

Ulzana's Raid (Robert Aldrich), 127
Uncle's Story, The (Witi Ihimaera), 151, 152, 159, 204, 211
Under the Mountain (Jonathan King), 18
Utu (Geoff Murphy), 82

Vigil (Vincent Ward)
  art-film style of, 69–71
  attachment relationships in, 76
  cultural hybridity in, 76
  Elektra complex represented in, 23
  mentioned, 16, 109

  personal film, as, 20–1, 71–3
  reversal in, 77
  setting of 22
  symbolism in, 74, 76–8

Waitai, Rana, 125
Waitangi, Treaty of, 24
Waitangi Tribunal, 90, 158
Waititi, Taika
  adaptation, approach to, 20, 217, 219–20, 222–5
  bicultural perspective of, 26, 229
  comedic approach of, 192, 195–6, 199, 226–7
  cultural hybridity, use of, 54
  global culture, responsiveness to, 159
  Māori culture, attitude towards, 91, 190, 212
  mentioned, 43, 189, 191, 197, 200, 233
  personal elements in films of, 193–4
  symbolism, use of, 228
  Truffaut, influence of, 8
  youth culture, use of, 216
  see also Boy (Taika Waititi); *Hunt for the Wilderpeople* (Taika Waititi)
Walker, Ranginui, 133
Walsh, Fran, 20, 109, 110, 111, 137;
  see also Heavenly Creatures (Peter Jackson)
Ward, Vincent
  film style of, 68–70
  mentioned, 11, 23, 73, 95, 145
  New Zealand culture, view of, 16
  personal allusions in *Vigil* of, 20, 71–2, 74, 77
  see also Vigil (Vincent Ward)
Welles, Orson, 10, 117
Wells, Peter, 177
Wendt, Albert, 17
West Side Story (Jerome Robbins, Robert Wise), 207
western, 54, 80, 86, 90, 154, 207, 208, 209, 210, 232
Whale Rider (Niki Caro)
  adaptation, approach to, 152–4
  feminist vision of 154–8
  genre cinema, as, 147, 159, 232
  mentioned, 23, 161, 203
  reception of, 148–9, 156
  setting of, 21
  transcultural perspective of, 162, 232
Whale Rider, The (Witi Ihimaera), 150, 151

What Becomes of the Broken Hearted (Alan Duff), 132
Wild One, The (László Benedek), 7
Wild Pork and Watercress (Barry Crump), 20, 43, 217, 218, 220–2
Wild Reeds (André Téchiné), 8

Winnicott, D. W., 39, 117, 137
Woman Is a Woman, A (Jean-Luc Godard), 8

X-Men: Apocalypse (Bryan Singer), 189

EU representative:
Easy Access System Europe
Mustamäe tee 50, 10621 Tallinn, Estonia
Gpsr.requests@easproject.com

www.ingramcontent.com/pod-product-compliance
Lightning Source LLC
Chambersburg PA
CBHW050846230426
43667CB00012B/2175